"Hard to believe but even harder to forget."
—SAM LEVENSON

"I loved it. Mr. Goldberg has put together an
excellent book of history, drama, and humor."
—HARRY GOLDEN

A Jew helped invent the airplane.

•

Mohammed, the founder of Islam, called himself
a "Jewish prophet"!

•

What do Alexander the Great, Rembrandt, Stalin,
and Elizabeth Taylor have in common?
(Don't ask!)

The
Jewish
Connection

The incredible ... ironic ... bizarre ...
funny ... and provocative
in the story of the Jews

M. Hirsh Goldberg

BANTAM BOOKS
TORONTO · LONDON
NEW YORK

THE JEWISH CONNECTION

*A Bantam Book / published by arrangement with
Stein and Day, Publishers*

PRINTING HISTORY
*Stein and Day edition published November 1976
Bantam edition / December 1977*

ISBN 0-553-10870-0

Published simultaneously in the United States and Canada

*Bantam Books are published by Bantam Books, Inc. Its trade-
mark, consisting of the words "Bantam Books" and the por-
trayal of a bantam, is registered in the United States Patent
Office and in other countries. Marca Registrada. Bantam
Books, Inc., 666 Fifth Avenue, New York, New York 10019.*

PRINTED IN THE UNITED STATES OF AMERICA

To the memory
of our son
Jonathan
our very special gift
for three years

AUTHOR'S NOTE

All of the facts and incidents in this book can be documented. Over the course of three years of research, hundreds of sources were consulted and checked for accuracy. In short, everything between these covers is the truth, the whole truth, and nothing but the truth, so help me . . . well, you know Who. After all, isn't He the Ultimate Jewish Connection?

We must study in greater detail than their neighbors, these numerically and geographically insignificant Jews, who gave to the world one of its greatest literatures, two of its most influential religions and so many of its profoundest men.

WILL DURANT, *The Story of Civilization*, Volume I

Contents

I

Hidden
Places

*A new view of the Jew—
and the world*

FACT: Theodor Herzl, founder of the State of Israel, once wanted to convert Jews to Christianity.

FACT: Herzl predicted the date on which modern Israel would be created—and was correct within two months.

FACT: The Balfour Declaration favoring Palestine as a homeland for the Jews was weakened by the only Jew present when its wording was discussed.

FACT: Israel's birth can be traced to a chemical discovery based on horsechestnuts.

FACT: The Dead Sea Scrolls were first deciphered on the night the United Nations voted to create Israel.

ALTHOUGH THE HIGHLIGHTS of Jewish history are generally well known—from the story of the Patriarchs to the struggle for the modern State of Israel—the ironies and oddities, the gallery of incredible individuals, the events of amazing coincidence are largely undiscovered. Indeed, the nooks and crannies of Jewish existence have been little explored, but it is precisely in these hidden-away corners that much of the rich, varied, and strange workings of the Jewish experience—and the world at large—can best be seen.

A journey through the Jewish Connection reveals many things—the unusual, mostly overlooked contributions of the Jews to the world, the unseen influence of Judaism on the culture of mankind, the surprising number of major events in which Jews have played a part—events as diverse as the spread of monotheism and the invention of the telephone.

In addition, by turning away from the usual narratives of the past, by searching out and studying the small diamonds of fact that have been hidden by the passage of time or overwhelmed by the accumulation of events, we can gain a clearer picture of the world—Jewish and otherwise—and how it has been shaped.

I first realized several years ago that the real story of the Jews—the ironic side at least—was often overlooked. While scanning a book on Israel, I came across an astonishing statement: Zionist leader Theodor Herzl once wanted to convert Jews to Christianity.

Fortunately, the brief reference to Herzl's interest in conversion noted that he had dealt with the subject in his diaries. Intrigued, I went to the library and found the passage in the first section of his extensive diaries, which he began shortly after deciding to devote himself to Zionism. Wrote Herzl on a spring day in 1895 as he looked back on his life:

About two years ago I wanted to solve the Jewish Question, at least in Austria, with the help of the Catholic Church. I wished to gain access to the Pope (not without first assuring myself of the support of the Austrian church dignitaries) and say to him: Help us against the anti-Semites and I will start a great movement for the free and honorable conversion of Jews to Christianity.

Free and honorable, by virtue of the fact that the leaders of this movement—myself in particular—would remain Jews and as such would propagate conversion to the faith of the majority. The conversion was to take place in broad daylight, Sundays at noon, in St. Stephen's Cathedral, with festive processions and amidst the pealing of bells. Not in shame, as individuals have converted up to now, but with proud gestures. And because the Jewish leaders would remain Jews, escorting the people only to the threshold of the church and themselves staying outside, the whole performance was to be elevated by a touch of great candor.

We, the steadfast men, would have constituted the last generation. We would still have adhered to the faith of our fathers. But we would have made Christians of our young sons before they reached the age of independent decision, after which conversion looks like an act of cowardice or careerism. As is my custom, I had thought out the entire plan to all its minute detail. I could see myself dealing with the Archbishop of Vienna; in imagination I stood before the Pope—both of them were very sorry that I wished to do no more than remain part of the last generation of Jews—and sent this slogan of mingling of the races flying across the world.

Ironically, it was Herzl's editor and publisher, Moritz Benedikt, an anti-Zionist, who convinced Herzl of the impracticality of his plan. Wrote Herzl:

But one thing in Benedikt's response struck me as being true. He said: For a hundred generations your line has preserved itself within the fold of Judaism. Now you are proposing to set yourself up as the terminal point in this process. This you cannot do and have no right to do. Besides, the Pope would never receive you.

Herzl admits in his diary that he later came to realize his idea was "a feeble, foolish gesture." Says Herzl, "Anti-Semitism has grown and continues to grow—and so do I." But only after he gave up the idea of converting Jews to Christianity did Herzl turn to Zionism and the writing of what became entitled *The Jewish State*, the document that gave the impetus to the movement to provide a land for the Jewish people.

Amazed by my discovery, I began to wonder. Were there other such ironies nestled in Jewish history, especially—as this one had been—significant facts about important people and events? For I was not interested in uncovering just exotic tidbits about minor figures. No, I was seized by the possibility that there might be a whole new way of looking at the Jews, who, in the Bible, probably have the longest continuously recorded history of any people, whose thoughts and movements for thousands of years have been in full view of the world, and yet—as demonstrated by Herzl—whose story may well have a side that has never been told. The Jewish people may indeed be like the moon—small in the firmament, always there, but with a side hidden from view.

I began to look. As I looked, I found. And, as I found, a pattern emerged. The substance of Jewish experience took on a new coloration, for I was finding that much that was revealing about the big picture could be found in the small picture; that what took place on the stage of world events could be amplified by what went on behind the stage. I had discovered what I call "the nook and cranny" concept of history.

The first pattern that emerges from such a study is

the coincidence that can be found in even the most momentous events. This can nowhere be better seen than in the efforts this past century to found the State of Israel—and Theodor Herzl stands at the center of the irony.

Herzl, born in 1860 and dead by 1904, is one of the most improbable figures in history, for he was ignorant of the people he led and the movement he launched. He was so uneducated about the Jewish religion that, in addition to advocating conversion to Christianity as a possible solution to the Jewish problem, he also insisted on having a Christmas tree in his home, decided not to circumcise his son (to whom he gave a German, not a Hebrew name), and knew so little Hebrew that when he wanted to recite a sentence in the language it had to be written out for him in Latin characters. He understood so little about the nature of Jewish yearnings that in his first edition of *The Jewish State* in 1895 he did not call specifically for Palestine as the site for the Jewish homeland or Hebrew as its language. Later, he would agree for a time to founding a Jewish homeland in Argentina or Africa. He was oblivious of the fact that Zionism was a concept that others before him had discussed, written books about, and sought in various ways to organize. Indeed, to label the growing discussions about a return to Zion, the word "Zionism" had been coined by a Viennese student, Nathan Birnbaum, in 1882—a full decade before Herzl became involved in the Jewish Question.

And yet, once Herzl had become intrigued with the idea, he encountered a startling array of unusual happenings throughout the rest of his life.

His first encounter was probably the most significant of all. On January 5, 1895, while serving as a foreign correspondent for the Viennese newspaper *Neue Freie Presse*, Herzl was in Paris covering the celebrated court-martial of Captain Alfred Dreyfus, a Jew who was found guilty of selling military secrets to the Germans on trumped-up charges heavily laced with anti-Semitism.

For a number of years Herzl had thought about combatting the rise of anti-Semitism, but he had felt little urgency and had no particular plans. He stood with other journalists that cold, gray January day— ever the imposing figure with his black eyes and luxurious beard—watching the military ceremony in which Dreyfus was stripped of his position in the French army, his saber broken and his face slapped in symbolic gesture to denote the beginning of his punishment—life-long banishment to hard labor on Devil's Island. And then, as he watched Dreyfus being led away, Herzl heard a roar rising from spectators: "Death to the Jews!"

The mob was not yelling for the death of traitors, nor for the death of *a* Jew. It was condemning *all* Jews.

Herzl was shaken by the experience. Prior to this, he had personally been the target of only a few anti-Semitic slurs, but now he was exposed to the naked ugliness of a mob in anti-Semitic frenzy. Dreyfus's degradation was a catalyst in Herzl's life. Soon afterward he began feverishly writing *The Jewish State*, as both a need and a plan for a Jewish homeland took shape in his mind.

Little did Dreyfus know what a central role his agony would play in the eventual creation of Israel. Ironically, Dreyfus was himself an assimilated Jew who knew little of his religion. Preoccupied with his career in the French army, he was oddly unaware of the anti-Semitic aspects of the charges made against him at his trial. When he was publicly humiliated and the crowds raged against him, his response was a shout not in defense of his Jewishness, but for his beloved country: "I am innocent! Long live France!"

Thus, one of the most meaningful scenes in modern Jewish history involved two assimilated Jews, ignorant of their backgrounds, nonpracticing, and until then noninvolved as Jews.

As Herzl began his Zionist activities in earnest, he was almost immediately helped by an odd coincidence. He moved to Vienna and, according to one of his biographers, found himself aided by a book that had been published there five years earlier by another Viennese Jewish journalist. The book, entitled *Freiland*, a popular economic work on Utopia set in Africa, paralleled on a secular level Herzl's ideas for creating a homeland for the Jews. Because they were familiar with the book, Dr. Heinrich Meyer-Cohn, a banker and philanthropic Jew known as a lover of Zion, and Dr. Moritz Gudemann, Chief Rabbi of Vienna, were receptive to Herzl and his ideas. They may also have been influenced by the fact that Herzl's name was similar to that of the author of *Freiland*: Theodor Hertzka. However, the similarity proved to be a point of possible confusion, and later, in the preface to *The Jewish State*, Herzl drew a distinction between his work and Hertzka's, saying his own ideas were more realistic.

The high point of Herzl's efforts was his convening of the First Zionist Congress in Basle, Switzerland, on August 29, 1897. (Actually, the First Zionist Congress was not the first Zionist Congress, but the second. A World Congress of all Zionist groups had been held twelve years before—the Kattowitz Conference in 1885—but it did not create the dynamic organization that grew out of Herzl's First Zionist Congress.)

In connection with this important development, Herzl came to make a most uncannily accurate prediction. Writing in his diary on September 3, 1897, following the conclusion of the congress, he said: "At Basle, I founded the Jewish State. If I said this out loud today I would be greeted by universal laughter. In five years perhaps and certainly in fifty years, everyone will perceive it." Herzl's prophecy of fifty years was incorrect—by two months! On November 29, 1947, when the United Nations voted to create a Jewish State, the world did indeed "perceive it."

When Herzl died he considered himself a failure because he had been unable to achieve the one realistic goal he had set for himself—a charter to Palestine. But within twenty years the Balfour Declaration advocated Palestine as a homeland for the Jews. As another odd twist of Jewish history, the famed document, now preserved in the British Museum, was never read in the House of Commons, was never officially published, and was never announced by Britain's Prime Minister.

In addition, while the Balfour Declaration was the object of much internal debate and bickering among British officials, the wording of the key passage in the eventual document—a watered-down reference to "a national home for the Jewish people" in Palestine rather than the stronger reference to "the national home"—was determined as the result of the urging of the only Jew present during the deliberations! Sir Edwin Montagu, then Secretary of State for India, was strongly anti-Zionist. An assimilated Jew, he was afraid of an anti-Semitic reaction to a too-strong document. That one-word difference—*a* national home instead of *the* national home—came to haunt Zionists.

Sitting outside the door during the final debate over the Balfour Declaration was Chaim Weizmann, whose role in promoting Zionism is another fascinating chapter in Jewish history.

A brilliant chemist, Weizmann was asked by a desperate British government to develop a synthetic for the acetone used in the production of explosives during World War I. Weizmann soon developed a synthetic acetone made from, among other things, horsechestnuts. His discovery led the British leader David Lloyd George to offer Weizmann a high honor. Weizmann, a fervent Zionist, is reported, in a legendary account cited by John Gunther in *Inside Asia*, to have asked instead for a "national home for my people." Although Weizmann downplays the story in his own memoirs, Lloyd George wrote that his meetings with Weizmann led him to support the Zionist thesis, to bring Weizmann into contact with Foreign Minister Balfour, and to help push for what came to be the Balfour Declaration. Said Lloyd George in 1925, "Acetone converted me to Zionism." In other words, Israel may well owe its birth to a chemical discovery.

The founding of the State of Israel, then, is a product of numerous ironies, coincidences, and strange occurrences. While history concerns itself with the grand sweep of wars, power intrigues, and high-level political decisions, some of the most significant events are hidden in the unexplored nooks and crannies. For, just as wars are still won or lost by the lowly foot soldier, so too history—especially Jewish history—is shaped not only by what happens on the world stage, but also by what happens beneath, behind, and to the sides.

Such ironies may well constitute a message. Is there not a guiding hand orchestrating people and events in ways and for reasons we cannot fathom?

Consider one final "coincidence" in connection with the founding of modern Israel—a dramatic joining together of the creation of the State of Israel with one of the world's great historic cultural events, the discovery of the Dead Sea Scrolls.

One day in 1947, while tensions were mounting between Arabs and Jews in Palestine, Elazar L. Sukenik, professor of archeology at the Hebrew University, received a call from a friend, an Armenian who dealt in antiquities. The Armenian asked Sukenik to look at a piece of leather parchment with writing, and determine its age.

Sukenik recognized the writing as dating back two thousand years to a period in which he was an expert—the period leading up to the destruction of the Second Temple in the year 70. Trying to contain his excitement, he asked if there were more such pieces of parchment. He was told that an Arab antiquities dealer in Bethlehem had entire scrolls.

On the morning of November 29, after a perilous bus trip into Arab territory with his friend, Sukenik was taken to the attic of the Arab dealer's house and shown three scrolls that had been found in a cave by Bedouins. After reading a few sentences of what Sukenik found to be "beautiful Biblical Hebrew" in a text that was new to him, he agreed to buy the scrolls, for the university, along with the jars in which they had been hidden, if he could have time to examine them closely and assess their value. The Arab dealer agreed to let him take them home for several days. With the ancient documents wrapped in paper and tucked under his arm, Sukenik hurried back to his small house in Rehavia, a section of Jerusalem.

That night, as Sukenik deciphered the first of the Dead Sea Scrolls, in Flushing Meadow, New York, the United Nations was voting on partitioning Palestine and creating a Jewish state.

While Sukenik worked in his study, his youngest son, Mati, in the next room listened to a radio broadcast of the progress at the United Nations. As the speeches began, Sukenik was working painstakingly on a scroll not previously known to exist. The UN meeting extended through a long, historic evening in New York; in Jerusalem, Sukenik's labor was interrupted from time to time by his son's calling out the votes. As the two-thirds majority in favor of partition was finally reached, Sukenik was absorbed in an engrossing passage. Written in an age when the Jewish people still resided in their homeland, it was part of a prophetic hymn foretelling both their exile and their eventual return.

"I was driven from my home like a bird from its nest. . . . I was cast down, but raised up again." And at the beginning of this and other hymns found throughout the scroll was the declaration: "I give thanks to Thee, O Lord." Because of this refrain, the scroll became known as *The Thanksgiving Hymns*.

The irony is not only that a scroll of thanksgiving

was read for the first time in the modern era on an historic night on which Jews had good reason to give thanks. The Dead Sea Scrolls themselves, termed the "greatest manuscript discovery of modern times," serve as a dramatic link between Jewish life two thousand years ago in the Land of Israel and the return of the Jews to Israel today. For Sukenik soon found that among the Dead Sea Scrolls lying in his home that night was a scroll that held added significance for Jews—it foretold the triumph of the Sons of Light (seen to symbolize the new Israel) over the Sons of Darkness (viewed as representing the surrounding enemy nations).

It is as though the scrolls lay dormant as long as Jewish sovereignty over the land was in abeyance. The question must then be asked—was the discovery of the Dead Sea Scrolls at the time of Israel's rebirth a mere coincidence, or a special piece of irony with a message?

II

Is Nothing Sacred?

*The first step in understanding the
Jewish Connection is the Law of Irony*

FACT: The Star of David is not of Jewish origin—and the ancient Israelites never used it as their religious symbol.

FACT: The word "Jew" is not used in the five books of Moses.

FACT: The Wailing Wall—Judaism's holiest site—was built by a king of non-Jewish descent.

FACT: Titus, the Roman general who destroyed the Temple, was in love with a Jewish woman and considered making her Empress of Rome.

FACT: The original pizza had a surprising Jewish ingredient.

FACT: Adolf Hitler's family doctor was a Jew to whom Hitler gave gifts and wrote of his gratitude.

FACT: The discovery of petroleum (wait till the Arabs hear this) was made by a Jew.

IN OUR EXPLORATION of the Jewish Connection, we must first understand one of life's most often overlooked rules—the Law of Irony. It holds that, more often than not, what we think is true proves not to be and that the facts, diligently pursued, reveal a different and often more intriguing reality. The Law of Irony declares that we must discover the incongruities, seek out the contradictions, learn that history may be the direct opposite of what it has seemed. To see clearly we must open not only our eyes but our minds.

The Law of Irony is based upon the realization that in the long course of history truth gets lost in both translation and transition. That the eras of history come and go, but the errors in history books invariably remain. That nations, like people, tend to remember the comfortable myth and forget the uncomfortable facts. In making our way through life, many of us embrace stereotypes that more often than not steer us wrong.

The Law of Irony calls upon each of us to probe and pull and poke accepted truths to see if they deflate. If they remain firm, fine; but if a long-cherished notion wobbles under the assault, then we are dutybound to discover the truth.

The Jewish experience is a case in point.

Indeed, use the Law of Irony for even a quick look at the Jews and a long list of accepted truths explode. Would you believe, for instance, that the most widely recognized Jewish ceremony, the most widely honored Jewish contribution, and the most widely accepted Jewish symbol are incorrectly understood?

Let us take a close look at the Bar Mitzvah ceremony, the Ten Commandments, and the Star of David.

The Bar Mitzvah is one of the most widely observed Jewish ceremonies, important for its social, cultural, as well as religious implications. Comedians and novelists variously celebrate or castigate it. Others have theorized it is but a pale reflection of the rites of passage for young men in primitive tribes, from which it probably evolved.

There is only one difficulty with such emphasis on the Bar Mitzvah: not once is it mentioned in the Bible.

The ceremony of Bar Mitzvah, which is Hebrew for "son of the commandment," is simply a reminder that Jewish law assumes a child to become a religiously responsible adult at the age of thirteen plus one day. Since one of the requirements and privileges of the Jewish adult is being called to the reading of the Torah, the first Torah-reading service after a boy reaches thirteen is an important occasion. This is also the first time a Jewish youth can publicly declare his allegiance to the Torah. Only in relatively modern Jewish history, however, has the occasion been celebrated with festivities and a special ceremony.

Various Jewish historians trace the formal Bar Mitzvah ceremony back only 400 to 600 years. Writes Chaim Bermant in *The Walled Garden: The Saga of Jewish Family Life and Tradition,* "As Jewish ceremonies go, the Bar Mitzvah is something of an innovation, for it only goes back some 500 years."

Thus, a Jewish boy can technically be considered an adult without such a ceremony. Indeed, one of modern Israel's heroes never had a formal Bar Mitzvah for either of his two sons. His name: Moshe Dayan.

Also misunderstood, the Ten Commandments are never called that in the Bible or in Hebrew! In fact, there aren't and never were ten commandments. In the Jewish tradition, the first of this group of laws is not stated as a command, but as an assertion of fact: "I am the Lord thy God." What follows is a series of positive and negative moral precepts. As a result, in rabbinic literature the entire group is called *Asereth Hadibroth*, which means "ten sayings." The Bible itself, in Deuteronomy 4:13 and 10:4, refers to them not as Ten Commandments but as *Asereth Hadevarim* or "ten words."

Perhaps most ironic, the very sign of the Jew in today's world—the six-pointed Star of David—is not really the historic symbol of Jewry, nor was it used as a religious sign by the Israelites. It became the emblem of the Jewish people in 1897, when the Zionist conference convened by Theodor Herzl chose it as the insignia of their movement. But even though each of the Twelve Tribes in the Land of Israel had its own symbol, not one tribe used the Star of David.

The six-pointed star was used as an ornament, possibly as a magical sign, in civilizations as different as Mesopotamia and Britain. Iron Age examples have been found in India and the Iberian Peninsula. The *Encyclopaedia Judaica* traces it to the Bronze Age, 4,000 years ago.

The oldest known use of the star in a Jewish context is on a seal from 2,600 years ago, found in Sidon, Lebanon. Another star was discovered on a frieze in a synagogue built more than 900 years later on the shores of the Sea of Galilee. Today tourists looking at these preserved ruins can also see a swastika— another demonstration of how symbols change, since the swastika was once a sign of peace.

In the summer of 1973 construction workers in the town of Ramle near Tel Aviv discovered the Star of David worked into a 1,200-year-old mosaic floor. The floor, however, was not Jewish, but Moslem.

Yet the six-pointed star is associated as a personal symbol with the two most important rulers of Jewish history, King David and King Solomon. In London and Leningrad copies of 1,400-year-old amulets show the Star of David on one side and on the other the words "Seal of Solomon."

The seven-branched candelabrum or menorah used in the Temple services has a much longer history as a solely Jewish symbol used for traditional purposes. In *The Jews of Ancient Rome* by Professor Harry J. Leon we learn that Jewish catacombs dating back more than 2,000 years show the seven-branched candelabrum to be the "most frequent by far" of symbols displayed on the burial inscriptions. Other symbols found there include the lulav and esrog from the Succoth or Tabernacles holiday, the shofar blown on Yom Kippur and the New Year, and the Temple Ark containing the Law. There are inscriptions decorated with birds, chickens, cows, rams, trees, and scrolls. There is even one example of a swastika. But in contrast to a modern Jewish cemetery, where the Star of David is virtually the only symbol, those twenty-century-old catacombs have no Star of David.

The Jews seem to be a people unusually touched by irony. Indeed, irony is probably the main element in what is considered the Jewish sense of humor. We see this in the naming of Isaac, the child born to Abraham and Sarah to begin the Jewish nation.

The Bible tells us that Abraham and Sarah were still childless in their old age. God's promise to Abraham that he would father a great nation seemed to be in danger. But God finally sent three angels to tell the couple they would have a child. Sarah, ninety years old at the time, had a very natural reaction to the prediction. She laughed.

When the prophecy came true and she gave birth to a boy, Sarah called him a most unusual name: "Isaac," which in Hebrew means "he laughed." A look at the Jewish Connection makes the name seem entirely appropriate.

Who else but Someone Who likes a good laugh would create a world in which:

• The name of the Jews' greatest leader—Moses— is not Hebraic, but derived from the language of the

Jews' ancient enemy, Egypt. "Moses" is Egyptian for "Child of the Lake," and this was the name given by Pharoah's daughter to the baby she spotted in a cradle floating in the bulrushes of the Nile.

• The word "Jew" never appears in the five books of Moses and is used for the first time rather late in the canon of Jewish books—in the Book of Esther, which tells of the persecution of the Jews in Persia around 2,300 years ago. Actually, the word "Jew" evolved from the name of Jacob's son Judah, which means "to praise God." But the patriarchs Abraham, Isaac, and Jacob, as well as Moses, were never referred to as Jews.*

• The most distinctively Jewish dress style of the past few centuries—the long black coats and large furry hats worn by Hasidic Jews—originated among non-Jews. High-ranking Polish gentiles wore such clothing hundreds of years ago, but it was forbidden to the Jews.

• "Kike," the derogatory word applied to the Jews in the nineteenth and twentieth centuries, was quite possibly the creation of Jews.** Although the word has vague origins, many authorities believed it was first used by German Jews of New York, who looked down on the more religious, but less affluent, East European Jews flooding into America. Perhaps these newcomers were referred to as "kikes" because so

---

* Just as the word "Jew" doesn't appear until the Book of Esther, the term "anti-Semite" wasn't used until the late nineteenth century. It was coined in 1879 in a pamphlet entitled "The Victory of Judaism Over Germany," a violent attack on the Jews. The author was a German named William Marr, himself a half-Jew.

** That a Jew would employ the term "kike" against another Jew can be seen in a passage in *Here at The New Yorker*. Brendan Gill, a writer for over forty years with the celebrated magazine, reveals that its publisher, Raoul Fleischmann, was a Jew "who would speak of Jews he disliked as 'kikes.'" Fleischmann's father, by the way, was from Vienna, which made him figuratively a borderline German Jew, one of those said to have originated the word. Raoul Fleischmann's father did give one term to the language. To dramatize the freshness of the Fleischmann bread (the Fleischmann family was famous for its yeast) and as an act of generosity, his father would give away at 11 P.M. that day's unsold bread. According to Gill, the line of poor people at the bakery door gave rise to the expression "breadline."

many of their names ended in "ky" or "ki." Leo Rosten in *The Joys of Yiddish* acknowledges such a possibility but feels that a stronger case is made for a non-Jewish origin for the term. Yet no less an authority than H. L. Mencken, in his comprehensive work *The American Language*, cites a source that offers a Jewish origin for it.

• The most famous American company dealing in Kosher wine sells more to non-Jews than to Jews. Manischewitz Wine Company sells only 10 percent of its product to Jews—and actually sells more wine at Christmastime than at Passover.

• Jerusalem, whose name means "City of Peace," has been ruled by fifteen different peoples: the Canaanites, Israelites, Egyptians, Assyrians, Babylonians, Persians, Greeks, Romans, Byzantines, Saracens, Arabs, the Crusaders, Ottoman Turks, the British, and today once again the Jews. Remarkably, through all these conquests, from the time the Jews entered the Promised Land, Jerusalem has never lost its Jewish associations.

Judaism's holiest site today is the Wailing or Western Wall, a reminder of the Second Temple. Israel's most symbolic place is Massada, the fortress near the Dead Sea that witnessed the three-year struggle of the Jewish zealots against the Romans.* Ironically, both were built by a king of non-Jewish, Arab descent.

The rebuilding of the Second Temple and the construction of Massada were just two of the many projects of King Herod the Great, King of Judea from 37 to 4 B.C.E.

The Romans appointed Herod as king and imposed him on the populace because of his family's allegiance to Rome. His mother, Cypros, was the daughter of an Arabian chief of the Nabateans and is said to have converted to Judaism. History is not clear about her

---

* Israeli soldiers entering the armored corps today are sworn in at a ceremony held atop Massada.

conversion, and one biographer of Herod, in fact, says she did not convert and flatly terms Herod a non-Jew. Herod's father, Antipater, was not descended from a Jewish family either, but was an Idumean, a member of a tribe whose ancestry has been traced by some historians to Esau's marriage to a daughter of Ishmael, the father of the Arabs. The writer of a book on the Dome of the Rock, which now sits on the Temple mount area, calls Herod's father "a fiery Idumean Arab." Antipater's family became Jewish when the Idumeans were forcibly converted to Judaism, one of the rare instances in Jewish history of forced conversion, since the Jewish religion has always insisted that proselytes be sincere.

King Herod was hated by the Jews during his reign (he was called "the Edomite slave"). He built Massada as a refuge in case of a revolt, and the eight-year task of rebuilding the Temple was really his attempt to gain the allegiance of the people. The rebuilt Temple was of such splendor that the Talmud exclaimed, "He who hath not seen the Temple of Herod hath not seen the most beautiful building in the world."

But Herod seems to have had the worst sense of public relations since the builder of the Tower of Babel. He alienated the Jews by trying to place a golden eagle, honoring Rome, over the Temple entrance and by conducting a reign of butchery to solidify his control (he killed all the members of the Jewish high court, the Sanhedrin, and murdered three of the twelve children born during his nine marriages). Near the end of his life he seriously contemplated a most novel way to insure that his death would bring the nation into mourning: he planned to order that all the notables he had imprisoned be executed at the time he died. And yet, if it had not been for this descendant of non-Jews and Arabs, Israel would not have today two of its most significant sites.

Another impetus for irony is our world's impulse for change. Consider the fact that today Jews do not actively seek converts. This has been true since Christianity first flowered, but it has not always been so. For centuries, Judaism competed against paganism and idol worship. With only the worship of animals and stone idols as alternatives, Judaism appealed to many. Indeed, if it had not been for the requirement of circumcision and a set of rules that could seem long to a prospective convert, Judaism might have become the only religion in a vast region of the world.

When the early Christian fathers dropped circumcision and lowered other barriers to conversion, Christianity easily overtook Judaism. Then, as Christianity acquired not only individual converts, but whole nations, Judaism kept a low profile so as not to alienate the authorities. At the same time another irony developed. Christianity, and later Islam, enthusiastically undertook the task of eradicating idol worship and spreading the message of monotheism, so Judaism no longer needed to seek converts so aggressively. The Jewish concept then took hold that "salvation is for the righteous of all peoples."*

However, in the days before Christianity, the Jews had such a force of Billy Grahams that the Roman satirist Horace alluded to their proselytizing in one of his works. In fact, the zeal of Jews in the Roman empire was so intense—and the number of converts so large—that in 139 B.C.E and again in 19 B.C.E., Jewish missionaries were exiled from Rome. Women struggling for new status today will be interested to know that among those who converted to Judaism were many women, including some of royalty. One such convert was no less than the Roman Empress

---

* Jewish missionary work flourished in the East until the advent of Mohammed in the 600s. In Arabia, whole tribes converted to Judaism, including two kings of the Himyarites. French Bible critic Ernest Renan remarked that "only a hair's breadth prevented all Arabia from becoming Jewish."

Poppaea—the wife of Nero. Which probably meant that Nero burned while his wife fiddled with Judaism.

Converts to Judaism enriched even the religious leadership of the Jews two thousand years ago. Of the two hundred Tannaim, the rabbis of the century before and after the destruction of Jerusalem, seven were of non-Jewish origin. Of the Amoraim, the rabbis of the generations following the Tannaim, at least three were of Gentile extraction. My favorite example, though, as reported by the eminent Jewish historian Cecil Roth, is that the grandson of a proselyte once became High Priest of the Temple.

The many ways in which Jews have contributed to the world have been obscured either by ignorance (sources often do not list a person's Jewish origin, presumably so as not to categorize people) or prejudice (reference books may not list a person's Jewish background so as not to promote a Jewish achievement.) Thus, when the Jewish Connection in an invention, discovery, or creation is unveiled, the ironies fly.

Petroleum, that lovely product the Arabs find themselves sitting on, was discovered not by an Arab or even a Texan, but by a Jew, Abraham Schreiner (1820-1900). Schreiner was an amateur scientist who discovered the use of petroleum for lighting purposes at Boryslaw, Galicia (then a province of northern Austria) in 1853, where he later built a distillation plant. The American discovery of petroleum did not occur until a year later, in 1854.

Furthermore, Italians should realize that their beloved pizza is derived from a very Jewish ingredient—matzoh, the unleavened bread of Passover. According to *The Illustrated Book of World Records* and *The People's Almanac*, pizzas were first made more than 2,000 years ago "when Roman soldiers added olive oil and cheese to matzohs." Mamma mia!

Christians have for years now been singing "White

Christmas," the top-selling song of all time, and "Easter Parade," the most popular Easter song. Who do you think wrote these two songs? The answer: a Jewish composer from New York City, Irving Berlin.

Berlin was born in Russia in 1888 as Israel Baline. His first successful song was "Alexander's Ragtime Band" in 1911, and since then he has written thirty Broadway shows, seventeen Hollywood musicals, and three thousand songs. He never had formal musical training and has to use a special piano when he composes because he can't read music and never learned to play the instrument properly.

Then there are the ironies that arise when we question popular myths. There is the theory, for instance, that history's most notorious anti-Semites became haters of Jews because of distasteful personal experiences with Jews. Actually, the opposite is true. There is evidence that the most virulent enemies of the Jew have at times been helped by Jews or have had Jewish friends.

Titus, the Roman general (and later emperor) who conducted the massive destruction of Jerusalem in the year 70, was in love with a Jewish woman and kept her as his mistress for thirteen years. She was Berenice, a sister of the Jewish King Agrippa II (which made her a real Jewish princess). Titus met her before the Roman war with the Jews and continued the relationship during and after it.

In Rome, he set her up in a palace on the Palatine and court gossips said that he wanted to marry her. They must have seemed an odd couple, though. She was twelve years older than he, had been married three times, and had two children. As if that wasn't enough, there were persistent rumors that she and her brother Agrippa had had an incestuous relationship. But she was noted for her beauty, even in middle age, and Titus was so infatuated that he is reputed to have killed one of his officers because of her.

Public pressure from Romans kept Titus and Berenice from marrying, since it was unthinkable that the Empress of Rome would be a Jew as well as a native of a country that had rebelled against Rome. Titus eventually sent her away to Gaul, but when he became emperor on the death of his father she returned, only to encounter renewed resistance to the marriage. Born in the year 28, she died in Gaul sometime after the year 100.

Benito Mussolini had not one, but two Jewish mistresses! These two women are credited with being more than mere playmates for the Italian dictator. Drew Pearson, the political columnist, noted that it was a Jewish woman, Margherita Sarfatti,* who as one of Mussolini's mistresses "taught Mussolini most of his original social reforms." A socialist, she left Mussolini when he "took up with Hitler," but not before she had completed a biography of Mussolini entitled *Dux*.

Pearson does not mention an even more important Mussolini mistress: Angelica Balabanoff,** a blond, Russian-born Jewish socialist whom Mussolini had met in 1902, when she was thirty-three and he was a nineteen-year-old socialist in exile in Switzerland. Balabanoff befriended him and, at a time when he was living on meager wages as a bricklayer, helped him get work as a translator. They shared many a night at her place, chain-smoking cigarettes and discussing socialism and other ways to reshape the world. A decade later, when he was elected to the Socialist Party's national executive committee and made editor of its daily newspaper *Avanti!*, he requested that Angelica Balabanoff be deputy editor.

---

* The Pearson statement is made on page 552 of *Drew Pearson Diaries, 1949-59*, edited by Tyler Abell. But either Pearson or Abell made an error. The Pearson book lists her name as "Scarfati," but the spelling "Sarfatti" is used in a biography of Mussolini (*Ducel* by Richard Collier) and in his wife's memoirs (*Mussolini: An Intimate Biography by His Widow*). Mrs. Mussolini devotes a chapter to her husband's mistresses and, as part of her attempt to show that the Duce wasn't anti-Semitic, points out that two of them were Jewish.

** Later she was known as "the Grandmother of Socialism" and became close to Lenin and Trotsky.

Once in power, Mussolini appointed several Jews to his government. Aldo Finzi was a member of Mussolini's first government, and Guido Jung for several years served as Minister of Finance (mainly because Mussolini assumed that "a Jew should be at the head of finance"). If we are to listen to Mussolini's wife, though, the height of the Duce's "benign feelings toward the Jews" was that Mussolini had a Jewish dentist. "He was called Piperno and was an orthodox Jew," wrote Mrs. Mussolini. "The Duce could have had his teeth attended to by a dentist of another faith, but he never considered the possibility and continued going to Dr. Piperno."

The anti-Jewish feelings spouted by the Nazis were promulgated in Germany nearly a century earlier by, among others, the composer Richard Wagner. Indeed, Adolf Hitler looked to Wagner, an early advocate of Teutonic supremacy, for both philosophic and musical inspiration, and during the twelve years of the thousand-year Reich, Wagnerian music emboldened the Nazis while it sounded the death knell for Jews. And yet Richard Wagner too was helped by a Jew.

While escaping his creditors in East Prussia, the still-struggling composer made his way to England and then back to the Continent, where he met the successful German-born Jewish composer Giacomo Meyerbeer. Meyerbeer, who had made his debut as a pianist at the age of seven, was at the height of his career. He praised Wagner's *Rienzi*, even though it departed from the then popular style, and gave him letters of introduction. Six years later, Wagner wrote to Meyerbeer, "it is a great happiness to be indebted to you" and signed his letter, "Your everlastingly indebted Richard Wagner." Five years later, however, Wagner lashed out at Meyerbeer and his fellow Jews in *Das Judenthum in der Musik* (*Judaism in Music*).

The most incredible case of an anti-Semite being helped by Jews—and showing friendliness to Jews—involves the biggest anti-Semite of them all. That's right: some of Adolf Hitler's best friends were Jewish!

Politics aside, Hitler had more reasons to like Jews than to hate them. The shopworn story that Jewish art dealers spurned Hitler's paintings when he was a poor, struggling artist (as well as just a poor artist) is not true, according to an Afterword by Robert G. L. Waite in a wartime psychological report on Hitler written for the U.S. Office of Strategic Services by Walter C. Langer and later published as *The Mind of Adolf Hitler*. Waite states that Gestapo files clearly show Jewish art dealers befriended the youthful Hitler in Vienna when he was destitute and "paid generously for his mediocre water colors." Indeed, most of the paintings Hitler did sell were bought by Jewish dealers.

During this period in his life, Hitler was also shown compassion by his landlady, a Jewish woman, who charged him only a small rent because of his situation. Once, to provide more space for Hitler and a friend, she even moved out of her own apartment.

Another Jew who befriended Hitler at that time was a Hungarian old-clothes dealer who gave him a long black overcoat. In *The Rise and Fall of the Third Reich*, William Shirer relates that Hitler wore it so much that the shabby black coat hanging down to his ankles was still remembered by those who knew him then. Interestingly, Shirer says the coat "resembled a caftan"—which, together with its dark color, must have made Hitler look like a Hasidic Jew of that era. A friend of Hitler's in those bleak days, Reinhold Hanisch, wrote that "Hitler at that time looked very Jewish."

As Führer, Hitler hired a Jew to cook for him. One Fräulein Kunde was sent to Hitler by the head of Rumania, who, like Hitler, had stomach problems. And, when Himmler questioned the suitability of der Führer's having a Jewish cook and suggested that she be removed, Hitler became furious.

A Jew even figured in Hitler's rise to power. As a lance corporal during World War I, Hitler was awarded the Iron Cross First and Second Class. This was an important military honor, and Hitler wielded it as a vital political tool. He wore the medal wherever he went, to buttress his claim of being a hero in the World War I fight for Germany's honor. But, as Langer points out, Hitler would not have been awarded such an honor "without the persistent efforts of the regimental adjutant, Hugo Gutmann, a Jew."*

The Hitler family, too, showed friendliness toward Jews. Hitler's older half-sister Angela, following World War I, managed the Mensa Academica Judaica in Vienna, and when non-Jewish students rioted in the city, she protected the Jewish students, even wielding a club against the rioters. Yet Angela was the only member of his family with whom he kept in touch as he climbed in power politics (he stayed at her house and fell in love with her daughter, who later committed suicide).

Perhaps most fascinating of all is Hitler's relationship with the Jewish physician Dr. Eduard Bloch.** Dr. Bloch was the Hitler family doctor for a number of years when Adolf was young. It was Dr. Bloch who treated Hitler's mother when she was dying of cancer, and after the funeral Hitler accompanied his sisters to thank him. According to Bloch's remembrance of the occasion, Hitler told him, "I shall be grateful to you forever." Hitler felt so warmly toward the doctor that, when he was struggling in Vienna as a young artist, he sent him two postcards, one of which Hitler hand-painted. Both carried Hitler's messages of appreciation and were signed, according to Walter Langer, "From your ever grateful patient,

---

* Lucy Dawidowicz in *The War Against the Jews, 1933-1945* makes note of Hitler's being awarded the Iron Cross, First Class. But obviously unaware of Gutmann's role, she emphasizes that Hitler must have been greatly helped because this decoration was "seldom given to a soldier of his low rank" and that Hitler had not done anything outstanding to deserve it: "no one knows for what act of bravery it was presented."

** Dr. Bloch's remarkable relationship with Adolf Hitler is spelled out in two articles he wrote for *Collier's Magazine* on March 15 and 22, 1941. The title: "My Patient, Hitler."

Adolf Hitler."* Langer comments that "one of the very few cases of which we have any record where Hitler showed any lasting gratitude" was in this correspondence to a Jew.

How could the Jews' worst enemy have been so warm to Jews on a personal level? The answer is partly a truth we all have experienced—it is easier to hate the nameless and faceless, to forget what is distant and care only about what is close. Interestingly, in all my research on the Holocaust, I have yet to encounter a reference to Adolf Hitler's visiting a concentration camp. It seems he did, on one occasion, view films and photographs taken of the victims of his Final Solution—but films and photographs provide the distance that enables a person to observe, but not to see.

It is on one hand ironic that Hitler never seems to have once gone to witness in person the procedure he so passionately sponsored. But on the other hand the irony is revealing, as an extreme example of man's refusal to confront unpleasant truths or overturn comfortable myths.

If we really want to understand not only the world of the Jews, but the world in general, we must be ready to throw off the cozy blanket of easy thinking and plunge ourselves under the cold shower of brisk facts. If we do so, we will be rewarded with the recognition that our world is a far more varied, rich, exciting, and meaningful place than we thought.

This is why the Law of Irony is so important to the Jewish Connection.

---

* There seems to be some discrepancy about the exact wording on the postcards, with Langer and Waite, in another book, giving slight variations (Waite says it read: "Your eternally grateful patient . . ."). But Dr. Bloch in his *Collier's Magazine* article of March 22, 1941, says it read: "The Hitler family sends you the best wishes for a Happy New Year. In everlasting thankfulness, Adolf Hitler." In any case, Hitler rewarded his doctor by letting him leave for America at the age of sixty-nine with sixteen marks, instead of the customary ten. After thirty-seven years of practice, Dr. Bloch reported, he was plunged into "material poverty." But he had gotten out with his life.

III

Become a Jew
and See the World!

*How the Diaspora made
the Jewish Connection possible*

FACT: All the victims of the bombings of Hiroshima, Nagasaki, Tokyo, Rotterdam, Coventry, and London together do not equal the number of Jews killed by the Romans in the siege of Jerusalem in the year 70.

FACT: Jews lived in Germany before the Germans.

FACT: Jews have served as the leaders of nine non-Jewish nations.

FACT: A Jew once owned one-fourth of Russia's railroads.

FACT: The oldest stone house in England was originally used as a synagogue.

FACT: Many calamities for the Jews have occurred on the same day of the year.

The enemy trapped the Jews in the city by building a wall around it. Foodstuffs could not be brought in; starvation and crowded conditions gave rise to disease, and epidemics spread among the city's populace. But, surprisingly, the Jews held on.

Then the enemy massed troops outside the wall and brought up the latest in weaponry. They attacked, using fire to spread destruction. The Jews repelled the enemy a number of times. So savage was the resistance that the campaign to destroy the Jewish population took much longer and cost more troops than anticipated. Street by street the fighting raged, with hand-to-hand combat between the heavily armed troops and the emaciated defenders. Some Jews tried to escape through the sewers, but they were flushed out by fire.

At the end, the Jews had taken a heavy toll of their enemy, but the city lay in smoking ruins. The remaining Jewish survivors were rounded up to be used as slave laborers or to be killed.

What episode in Jewish history is depicted in this scenario?

Most people would say this was the Warsaw Ghetto uprising against the Nazis in 1943. But, in fact, the scene just described was the Roman destruction of Jerusalem and the Second Temple in the year 70.

A closer examination of these two events, undeniably tragic in themselves, will lead us to a new appreciation of the long exile of the Jews from the Promised Land. It is one of the more ironic touches in Jewish history that, without the Diaspora, the

Jews would never have survived the onslaughts of their enemies.

The destruction of the Second Temple and the attack on the Warsaw Ghetto, although separated by nearly two thousand years, have an eerie sameness. The Germans sealed off Warsaw's Jewish population with an eight-foot brick and concrete wall. The Romans built a high earthen barricade around Jerusalem to make certain the Jews could not escape. Germans shot, on the spot, Jews discovered outside the Warsaw Ghetto. The Romans crucified the Jews they found, placing crosses atop the hill to terrorize those watching from inside the city; as many as five hundred were crucified in one day. The Germans tried to starve the Polish Jews into submission, reducing their rations at first to eight hundred calories a day and later cutting off all food to the ghetto. The Romans used the tactic of siege to bring about starvation in Jerusalem. Wrote Josephus, a Jew who surrendered to the Romans, collaborated with them, and later recorded the times vividly in his authoritative *The Jewish War*, "In the city famine raged, its victims dropping dead in countless numbers, and the horrors were unspeakable."

In both episodes the actual fighting was in some ways similar. "Since the ghetto was impenetrable in a frontal attack, General Stroop's forces set fire to the buildings with incendiary bombs and flame throwers," is how Nora Levin describes the Nazi assault on the Warsaw Ghetto in *The Holocaust*. Titus's Roman legions used flaming torches of wood to set fire to the Temple and other buildings in the final battle. As Josephus wrote, "Through the roar of the flames as they [the Romans] swept relentlessly on could be heard the groans of the falling . . . the entire city seemed to be on fire. The Temple Hill, enveloped in flames from top to bottom, appeared to be boiling up from its very roots."

The Nazis not only killed, but plundered Jews of their possessions; the Romans "were so avaricious that they pushed on, climbing over the piles of corpses; for many valuables were found in the passages and all scruples were silenced by the prospect of gain." The Romans took so much gold from the Jews that its price fell by half in Syria.

The Nazis used Jews for slave labor; the Romans sent thousands of Jewish captives to work on projects in Egypt. The Nazis made grisly sport with their victims and conducted fiendish medical experiments before killing the Jews; Titus had thousands of Jewish captives killed in gladiatorial contests and staged fights between them and wild beasts to celebrate his victory and, on one occasion, his brother's birthday; and Vespasian, the Roman Emperor, had nonswimmers shackled with their hands behind them and thrown into the deepest parts of the Dead Sea to test the theory that no one could sink in the heavily salted water.

There was one difference between the two events. Three years after destroying Jerusalem, the Romans put down the final Jewish revolt of the war by capturing Massada. Three years after the Holocaust ended, the State of Israel was reborn.

The destruction of the Second Temple serves, with the Holocaust, as a frame for the Jewish experience in the world. For instance, just as no other people in the modern era has suffered a devastation comparable to that of the Jews during the Holocaust, the attack on Jerusalem was unparalleled in the ancient world. "No destruction ever wrought by God or man approached the wholesale carnage of this war," said Josephus.

How many people were killed by the first atom bomb? The Hiroshima municipal government lists 86,528. How many died in the A-bomb blast at Nagasaki? Forty thousand. How many fatalities resulted from the B-29 incendiary raid on Tokyo on March 9, 1945? One hundred thousand. The Germans leveled Rotterdam, assaulted Coventry and London. These cities, devastated during World War II, are now synonyms for extremes of destructive force unleashed on cities. But all the victims of Hiroshima, Nagasaki, Tokyo, Rotterdam, Coventry, and London together do not equal the number of Jews killed by the Romans in the siege of Jerusalem.*

According to Josephus, Jerusalem's fatalities numbered 1,100,000. Throughout his otherwise accurate history Josephus tends to inflate figures, so over a million dead may be an exaggeration, although quite possibly not. Jerusalem normally had a population of about 120,000, but the city and its surrounding area could accommodate 2,500,000, the number Josephus reported to have been trapped by the Roman siege during that year's Passover pilgrimage.

Tacitus, the Roman historian, listed the number killed at 600,000—still an appallingly high figure, and still more than died at Hiroshima, Nagasaki, Tokyo, Rotterdam, Coventry, and London combined. An additional 114,000 Jews were taken captive, of whom 17,000 were slaughtered in bloody shows as the Romans brought them to Rome by way of Syria.

The siege of Jerusalem dealt a blow to the Jewish state from which recovery would take nearly two thousand years, but even this unparalleled destruction could not wipe out the Jewish people. To explain their miraculous survival, we must discard the common misconception that the dispersion of the Jews was a result of the Roman destruction of Jerusalem, and realize that for several hundred years more Jews had been living outside the Land of Israel than in it. In fact, by the year 70 more Jews were living in Alexandria, Egypt, than in Jerusalem.

Two thousand years ago there were eight million

---

* The only comparable experience of a city is the siege of Leningrad during World War II. Harrison Salisbury in The 900 Days says that at the Nuremberg Trials in 1946 the number who died in Leningrad from all war causes was placed at 671,635. Some now consider this figure low. But Leningrad was never taken, and so the vast majority of its fatalities were from starvation and not directly from the fighting (less than 10 percent of the figures represent death by bombs, shells, or other military means). Also, Leningrad was not destroyed physically, as Hiroshima, Nagasaki, and Jerusalem were.

Jews throughout the world—more, proportionately, than there are today. Within the Roman empire, Jews represented 6 to 9 percent of the population. In the eastern half of the empire, Jews represented as much as 20 percent. Josephus wrote, "Men of Jewish blood in great numbers are diffused among the native populations all over the world, especially in Syria, where the two nations are neighbors."

When Titus returned to Rome, triumphantly leading a procession of Jewish slaves, the city had a Jewish population of fifty thousand—with eleven synagogues.

The exile of the Jews from the Promised Land had begun six centuries earlier, in 586 B.C.E., with the destruction of the First Temple by the Babylonians. Most of the Jewish population at that time was carried off to Babylonia (now called Iraq). Only seventy years later, after the victory of the Persians over the Babylonians, were Jews allowed to return to Israel and rebuild their homeland and their Temple.

However, many Jews, while vowing never to forget their allegiance to the Land of Israel, decided to remain in Babylonia because of the climate of religious freedom fostered by King Cyrus. The large Jewish community in Babylon was able to build colleges and conduct world-wide trade. Great prophets arose, and most of the Talmud was assembled there. It is, in fact, the Babylonian Talmud—not the offshoot known as the Palestinian Talmud—that over the centuries has been referred to as *the* Talmud.

While large numbers of Jews remained in Babylonia and others returned to the Land of Israel, another body of Jews responded to the opening world of the time by moving to other countries. Alexander the Great, then building his empire, proved friendly to the Jews, and they in turn accorded him an honor rarely given a non-Jew—they named their children after him. The name Alexander is still recognized as one of the few non-Biblical names that have been accepted by the Jews.

There is some evidence to support the legend that Alexander first colonized Alexandria, Egypt, with Jews from Palestine. Whether this is true or not, the dispersion of the Jews is unmistakable. At the time of the Roman destruction of the Second Temple, 250,000 Jews were living in Alexandria and one million in Babylonia—in contrast to Jerusalem's all-Jewish population of 120,000.

It was as though the Jews had sensed that it was best not to put all their people into one land's "basket." For, if all Jews had been living in Palestine at the time of Rome's conquest, there would have been no exile, no Diaspora, and most likely, no Jews at all within a few generations. Thus the Diaspora, long considered a threat to the Jewish people, was, in fact, their salvation.*

The Roman conquest of Jerusalem represents one of several curious occurrences in Jewish history: while one Jewish community has been threatened, another of almost equal size has existed in safety. During the Holocaust, when 6 million European Jews perished, an American Jewry numbering close to that figure was protected. Today, while 2,500,000 Russian Jews are persecuted in Russia, slightly more than that number live in Israel.

The Diaspora, like so many other elements of the Jewish Connection, is steeped in paradox. Consider the fates of those countries responsible for destruction of the Temples. Babylon is no more, even as a place on a map; it is real only to archeologists and historians. The mighty Roman empire is gone, its only remnant a city with mighty traffic jams. The victors have perished, while the Jews have survived

---

* While the Diaspora ironically insured the physical survival of the Jews, another irony came to insure their religious survival. At the time of the fall of the Temple, the Romans inexplicably allowed Rabbi Jochanan Ben Zakkai to maintain an academy on Palestinian soil at Yavneh, where over the next sixty years the sages were able to resolve religious problems for Jewry with guidance for the changed conditions of Jewish life—guidance that has lasted to the present day.

with their religious and cultural heritage intact. As English historian Michael Grant says in the opening sentence of *The Jews in the Roman World*, "To study the Jews in the Roman world is one of the best ways of making close contact with that world, because although the ancient Romans and the Greeks have gone forever, the Jews are still with us; in them, continuity between ancient and modern life exists for everyone to see."

The dispersal of the Jews throughout the world seems to have been foreordained in the Bible. Adam and Eve are exiled from the Garden of Eden. Abraham is told by God to leave his parents and start a new life in Canaan. Isaac must find a wife in another country. Jacob and his children have to leave their home and travel to Egypt to avoid a famine. Joseph is sold into exile by his brothers. Moses is forced to flee Pharaoh's house and wanders in the desert before returning to free the Children of Israel. The flight of the Israelites from slavery in Egypt into freedom is yet another chapter in the Bible's tale of exiles.

The very name "Hebrew" can be traced to this theme. In Joshua 24:3, we find God's statement that He took Abraham "from the other side of the River [Euphrates]." The word *Evri*, or *Hebrew*, first used in Genesis 14:13 as a designation for Abraham, means "one from the other side." The origin of the Jews dates from Abraham's willingness to travel to a new land—a Promised Land—and devote himself, his family, and the nation they would found to the service of God. But note that such a nation could only come into being once Abraham had exiled himself from his home.

For more than 2,500 years the Jewish people have felt the pull of the Diaspora (Greek for "scattering"), so that as of today they have existed longer without a homeland than with one, and have moved from one state of exile into another. Israel now has immigrants from more than a hundred countries. Seventy countries have Jewish populations of five hundred or more.

Jews can be found in all fifty states of the United States, and in all parts of the world. There are black Jews and Oriental Jews. China, India, Ethiopia, Mexico, Chile, Cuba, Afghanistan, Japan—Jewish communities have existed in each. When Bolivia was colonized in the sixteenth century, there were Jews among those first settlers. When Australia was founded by England with a group of eleven convicts, Jews were among that contingent. Marranos, the secret Jews of Spain, were among the first Europeans to settle in the Philippines after the Spanish conquest of the islands in the sixteenth century. New Zealand had Jews among its pioneers. A Jewish community has existed in America for more than three hundred years and in Italy for close to three thousand.

Clearly, the exile is central to the Jewish place in the world—and to the Jewish Connection.

Another pattern in Jewish history can be found in the date of the destruction of the Second Temple. The ninth day of the Hebrew month of Av (the fifth month of the Jewish calendar, usually corresponding with the middle part of July through early August) is traditionally a day of tragedy for the Jewish people.* It was on this day that spies sent out by Moses to explore Canaan returned with a false report, pessimistic about the Israelites' chances of conquering the land. Because the Jews too readily believed the report and wanted to turn back instead of trusting in God, the group that had fled Egypt was made to spend the next thirty-eight years wandering in the desert so that a new generation, untainted by such rebellion, would be prepared to enter the Promised Land. The rabbis predicted in the Talmud that for crying over the report that night the Jewish people would cry on that day "for generations to come."

Since then, the ninth day of Av (referred to in

---

* The Jewish calendar is so accurate that, unlike the Julian and Gregorian calendars, it has never had to be adjusted.

Hebrew as "Tisha b'Av") has been a day of dread. On that date in 586 B.C.E. the First Temple was destroyed by the Babylonians, and on the very same day more than six hundred years later the Romans under Titus destroyed the Second Temple. Josephus remarked on this coincidence: "We may wonder too at the exactness of the cycle of Fate: she kept, as I said, to the very month and day which centuries before had seen the Sanctuary burnt by the Babylonians."

The ninth of Av is mentioned in Zechariah 8:19 as the "fast of the fifth month." In commemoration of this—and in mourning for the destruction of the Temples—the rabbis decreed the ninth of Av to be a strict fast day. Known also as the "Black Fast," Tisha b'Av is even today treated by Orthodox Jews as a fast day with special prayers and readings.

The first major calamity to befall the Jews following the destruction of the Second Temple was the fall of the fortress of Bethar on Tisha b'Av in 135, ending the Bar Kochba war of rebellion against the Romans. (It is interesting to note the survival power of the Jews, for this revolt occurred just sixty-five years after the great devastation loosed on them by Titus.)

Another major calamity occurred on Tisha b'Av in 1290 (corresponding then to July 18), when the official decree expelling the Jews from England was signed. This date marked the first nation-wide rejection of the Jews. The proclamation outlawing the Jews from Spain in 1492—one of the greatest upheavals in Jewish history, since it uprooted one of the largest and most successful Diaspora communities ever to exist—had as its original deadline for departure July 31. Near that date, however, the deadline was extended to August 2—the ninth of Av.

Various additional tragedies have occurred on Tisha b'Av, including the slaughter of Bar Kochba's followers in 138, Hadrian's leveling of Jerusalem, the execution of Rabbi Akiba and nine of his followers, and others involving the Crusades, pogroms, and assaults on Jewish communities.

Even the day on which Jews were first forced into a ghetto coincided with the ninth of Av—July 26, 1555—when the Jews of Rome were ordered to live in a district near the Tiber.

In our time, the ninth of Av continues to be ominous, not just for Jews but for mankind. There are numerous dates in 1914 that could be considered the beginning of World War I, starting with July 28, when Austria declared war on Serbia. But the date that propelled the world into its first global-scale war was August 1, 1914, when Germany declared war on Russia. That day was Tisha b'Av. In World War II, the Holocaust can be tied into many dates, but the day Reinhard Heydrich was ordered to carry out the Final Solution was July 31, 1941. The next night, as his first orders were going into effect, began Tisha b'Av.

Jewish history is not so neat that all calamities can be said to occur on Tisha b'Av (there are too many calamities in Jewish history for even a month of Tisha b'Avs), but enough have happened on that day to link the present and past of Jewish experience with a dotted line formed by the dates. Surely this is a more orderly pattern than the chaos we usually associate with history.

Although the image of the Wandering Jew has been for centuries a sort of mark of Cain on the Jewish people, the dispersal of the Jews has in itself been one of the great forces of world history. Lewis Mumford noted the implications of the Jews' migration: "This people became the catalytic agent of the new transformation of society: their presence was necessary but they were unaffected by the change that took place. Without them, nothing so significant might have happened on the world stage."

The Jew has been present at some of mankind's most unusual events. For instance, Charlemagne (742-814) appointed a Jew named Isaac as interpreter and guide for an embassy to be set up in Baghdad. In 802,

Isaac returned to Charlemagne's court and created a great stir with a gift sent by the Caliph to the Christian emperor: an elephant, the first ever seen in the West.

A Jew also crops up in the story of the Colossus of Rhodes, which was one of the Seven Wonders of the world until it was destroyed by an earthquake. Years later a Jew purchased the debris and, according to several historical sources, used nine hundred camels to cart it away.

Dispersion through many nations has caused Jews to compete against people of many nationalities. It is, then, significant that Jews have held national chess titles in the United States, Russia, Canada, Hungary, Argentina, Poland, Rumania, France, Austria, Belgium, Australia, and Czechoslovakia—all just since World War II.

Jews have even served as leaders of non-Jews. In modern times, Catholic Rome elected a Jew, Ernesto Nathan, as mayor. Dublin did the same on several occasions, electing and reelecting as mayor Robert Briscoe, an Irish Jew.

In fact, Jews have served as the heads of governments in the Diaspora in nine different countries: England (Benjamin Disraeli*), France (Léon Blum, Pierre Mendès-France, and René Mayer), Italy (Luigi Luzzatti and Sidney Sonnino), Austria (Bruno Kreisky), Australia (Sir Isaac Isaacs), Bavaria (Kurt Eisner), Hungary (Béla Kun), India (Marquis of Reading), and Palestine (Sir Herbert Samuel). Jews have headed countries located on three continents—Europe, Asia, and Australia—and would have had a national leader in Africa, but Saul Solomon (1816–1892), known as the "Disraeli of South Africa" and

---

* Born Jewish and reared as a Jew until the age of twelve, when he was baptized into the Church of England, Disraeli was Prime Minister twice, even though when he first was elected to Parliament he had trouble because of his Jewish ancestry. He never denied his heritage, but boasted about it in political speeches.

head of the Liberal Party in the Cape Parliament, declined several offers to serve as Prime Minister.*

Italy provides a fascinating example of the involvement of Jews in high places. This Catholic nation has had Jews on three different occasions as Prime Minister and a Jewish president of its Supreme Court. Luigi Luzzatti, founder of the People's Bank in Italy, was Minister of Finance seven times and in 1910 became Prime Minister. Sidney Sonnino, a half-Jew, was Prime Minister of Italy twice. Ludovico Mortara, who systematized Italian civil law procedure, was president of the Italian Supreme Court and served as Minister of Justice.

Involvement of the Jews in high places was actually greater centuries ago than it is today. Before the Crusades, it was not unusual for a European ruler to appoint a Jew to help run the government—especially in the sphere of finance, where many Jews were given the responsibility of minting money and collecting taxes. The Spanish kings did this until the expulsion of the Jews in 1492. In fact, Spain's Finance Minister at the time of the expulsion was a Jew, Don Isaac Abarbanel, and King Ferdinand and Queen Isabella thought so highly of him that they offered to make an exception and let him stay, but he refused. The rulers of Provence, in southeastern France on the Mediterranean, relied on the assistance of Jews until the region lost its independence in 1210. The rulers of Austria and Hungary followed this practice throughout the thirteenth century. In sixteenth- and seventeenth-century Poland, Jews even ran the estates and held the keys to the churches.

The popes too, until the thirteenth century, appointed Jews as aides. In fact, a Jew who was the private financial adviser of the Pope in 1179 was able to persuade the Catholic leader to stop a church council that year from passing a law requiring Jews to wear a special mark on their clothing. The regulations

---

* Jews, however, have been mayors of South Africa's leading cities.

were adopted in 1215 at the Lateran Council, but only under another Pope—Innocent III.*

Sultans too relied on Jewish advisers. Under Suleiman the Magnificent, Jews became so prominent as diplomats that Christian ambassadors had to solicit Jewish support before being permitted to approach the Arab leader.

This is not to say that Jewish existence in the Diaspora has been free of sorrow. Persecution, after all, was part of the engine driving Jews around the world. Scores of countries and cities expelled Jewish populations. Russia banned its Jewish population twice, and France outlawed Jews on four separate occasions within the same century.

But there were periods of coexistence in which the Jews could participate fully in their adopted countries. Some enlightened leaders not only welcomed but sought the Jewish Connection. The Bishop of Speyer, Germany, observing that wherever there was a Jewish population there was a prosperous community, in 1804 issued an edict whose opening sentence read: "Desiring to make a town out of the village of Speyer, I thought to raise its dignity many times by getting Jews to settle there."

Wherever leaders realized Jews could help the economy, the Jews were welcomed. Louis the Pious, the son of Charlemagne, changed the market day of Lyons from Saturday to a weekday to accommodate Jewish merchants. And England's King William II, successor to William the Conqueror, decreed that Jews in his realm could not convert to Christianity because such a conversion would deny him "a valuable property" and give him "only a subject."

There is no doubt that countries that welcomed the Jews profited from their Jewish Connection. Says the multi-volume *The Story of Civilization* in *The Reformation:* "So prominent was the Jewish role in the

---

* Hitler's Nuremberg Laws required Jews to wear a special symbol (a Star of David) and to abide by other restrictions first outlined by the Lateran Council.

foreign commerce of Europe that those that received the Jews gained and those countries that excluded them lost in the volume of their international trade."

The Diaspora has enabled the Jew to leave his mark in many countries. For instance, the oldest private stone dwellings in England are associated with Jews. Sitting at the foot of Steep Hill in Lincoln is a group of three buildings that date from about the thirteenth century. One of them, the House of Bellasez the Jewess, is said to be the oldest inhabited house in England. *Jewish Historical Treasures* says the second building, called Jews' Court, was used as a synagogue before England's Jews were expelled in 1290. The third, known as Aaron's house, a two-story cottage, was the home of the wealthiest Jew of England in his day. Aaron of Lincoln loaned money for the construction of abbeys and was owed $750,000 at his death; his loans to barons of $2.5 million were confiscated by the crown. Many authorities consider Aaron's house the oldest stone house in England.

Some of the earliest examples of the French language are found in the writings of the great Jewish commentator Rashi and his school, the Tosafists. Rashi, who was born in Troyes, France, in 1040, and died there in 1105, would paraphrase many Aramaic words and expressions found in the Bible and the Talmud either in a clear Hebrew or in the vernacular French.*

But the most ironic example of the Jewish Connection in Europe involves Germany.

Jews lived in what is now Western Germany before the destruction of the Second Temple. As early as the beginning of the fourth century, they had an organized community in Cologne, with a synagogue, lay leaders, and rabbis. The rights of this Jewish enclave were laid down in an edict by the Emperor Constan-

---

* Because students came from other countries to study with Rashi, the commentaries also include Russian, Slavonic, and German words—another indication of the extent of the Diaspora.

tine in the year 321. Not until later did the Teutons cross the Rhine and settle in the old Roman province. Until then, a person could be better understood in Cologne if he spoke Hebrew than German!

Jews became an integral part of German history and, by the twentieth century, had developed such a strong allegiance to their adopted home that they may have overlooked signs of the upcoming campaign against them and all of European Jewry. Richard Grunberger in *The 12-Year Reich* talks of the "pathetic fallacy of patriotism to which German-born Jews were extraordinarily prone." The Jew had so flourished in Germany that, on the eve of the Holocaust, Jews, although just under 1 percent of the population of Germany, constituted 16 percent of its practicing lawyers, 10 percent of its doctors and dentists, and 17 percent of its bankers. In the commercial community, Jews accounted for 11 percent of the personnel in real-estate brokerage, 25 percent in retailing, 30 percent in the clothing trade, and 70 percent in department stores. And yet the German Jews were not as prosperous as believed. In 1933, one-third of Jewish taxpayers had an annual income of less than 2,400 marks, and 25 percent of Berlin's Jewish population of 170,000 were on charity.

Ironically, the great Jewish community that developed in Berlin over the centuries was there by invitation—and its taxes had helped unify Germany!

When Frederick William von Hohenzollern (1620-1688), called the Great Elector, became Margrave of Brandenburg, he found no permanent Jewish settlements in the state or its capital, Berlin. Jews had once lived there, but had been expelled the preceding century. Eager to increase population, stimulate commerce, and create wealth, Frederick William in 1650 invited Polish Jews to conduct trade in his lands. In 1671 he welcomed fifty wealthy Jews who had been expelled from Vienna. So began the Berlin Jewish community—and so began the Jewish participation in the growth of Germany, for the taxes that the Jews paid to Frederick William, according to historian Jacob R. Marcus in *The Jew in the Medieval World*, "gave him the means, in part, which enabled him to free himself from the control of the privileged estates and thus to build up a modern, centralized, bureaucratic state."

The German-Jewish Connection doesn't stop here. During the Thirty Years' War the German emperors introduced what came to be known as "Court Jews," and throughout the seventeeth and eighteenth centuries, wrote historian Heinrich Graetz, "every state in Germany had its Court Jew or Jews, upon whose support the finances of the land depended."

In this period Jewish financiers were also important to other countries in Europe. In 1688, the son of Isaac Lopez Suasso of the Hague loaned William III 2 million crowns—an enormous amount—for his expedition to England in 1688, free of interest and even refusing a receipt.

But the Jews helped Germany in many other ways. The Berlin Stock Exchange was a Jewish institution from its inception. Of its first four presidents, two were Jews. Out of 23 members on the Exchange, 10 were Jews. The German navy was built up for World War I in large part through the efforts of a distant relative of pianist Artur Rubinstein. He was Albert Ballin (1857-1918), a German-Jewish industrialist in the shipping field who headed the largest shipping company in Germany, with four hundred vessels, and who was responsible for the American-German shipping agreement of 1912 and other measures to eliminate unnecessary competition. Ballin was adviser to William II in economic matters and could have risen in German government but refused to convert to do so. In 1957, on the hundredth anniversary of his birth, West Germany issued a postage stamp to honor him.

During World War I, nearly a fifth of Germany's Jews served in the German armed forces (92,000, with 78 percent at the front and 12,000 killed in action).

Eleven thousand five hundred were awarded Germany's Iron Cross.

After the war, Jews participated in the attempt to rebuild the nation. Six of the 423 delegates at Weimar who drafted the new constitution were Jews—and the actual author of the constitution was Hugo Preuss, a Jewish professor of law.

From 1905 to 1931, ten German Jews won Nobel Prizes in science.

But, under the Nazis, Germany didn't care to acknowledge its Jewish Connection. The Nazi party's official rallying cry was "Germany awake! Let Judah perish!"—an uncanny echo of the legend that appeared on Roman coins after the war against the Jews: "Judah is destroyed."

Nothing can better demonstrate the irony inherent in the Diaspora than a look at precisely how the Nazis engineered the Holocaust. For central to the operation of the Final Solution—the extermination camps, the gas chambers, the crematoria—were the railroads. And the railroads were there because of the Jewish Connection.

In their deadly campaign, the Nazis first used roving bands of firing squads, but even though they could kill 33,000 Jews in two days at Babi Yar—the ravine in Russia where on Yom Kippur the Nazis herded and shot the Jewish population of the surrounding area—the leaders of the Reich found their operation too unwieldy, public, and inefficient. So they created a new science of genocide with the elaborate system of concentration camps and gas chambers, where thousands could be killed and cremated in hours. But how could the Jewish populations spread throughout Europe by the Diaspora be brought to the extermination centers? Airplanes, trucks, buses, ships—these could transport only small numbers of Jews at a time. Only the railroads could accommodate the large numbers that would allow for speedy extermination. Carrying thousands of people at a time, with a minimum expenditure per person of fuel and manpower, the railroads offered an ideal solution.

Hence the Warsaw Ghetto was built around the Poznan-Berlin railway line. The Auschwitz death camp was built near a small town of Upper Silesia in an area west of Cracow; the train from Prague to Cracow passed the village, and a railroad spur led to a siding close by its gas chambers. Once the Final Solution was determined, the freight trains ran night after night with human cargoes so tightly packed into twenty, thirty, or forty locked cattle cars that people had to stand without food or water for as long as a week, en route to the extermination camps. This ruthless efficiency explains how the Nazis were able, for instance, to kill 437,000 Hungarian Jews at Auschwitz in less than two months near the end of the war.

On September 21, 1939, at a meeting with S.S. officers and Adolf Eichmann, Reinhard Heydrich spelled out the plan for Polish Jews: they were to be concentrated at a few places and, so that "subsequent measures" could be facilitated, reports Lucy Dawidowicz in *The War Against the Jews*, Heydrich emphasized "these concentration points should be at rail junctions or places located along railroad lines."

On January 20, 1943, Heinrich Himmler, concerned because the battle at Stalingrad had diverted much of the available rail transport from the Final Solution, wrote to the State Secretary for Transportation that "I must have more trains for transports. I know very well how taxing the situation is for the railroads. . . . I must make this request of you: Help me get more trains."

Even as Germany's defeat seemed imminent, the use of trains to transport Jews to their death was considered as important as their use to transport military personnel and supplies.

The irony, of course, lies in the Jewish Connection: much of Europe's railroad system was originally developed by Jews.

In the 1830s, the new and struggling railroad industry was severely undercapitalized; money was sorely needed to launch construction. Jewish financiers were the only private bankers—except for the British—who were ready to risk their funds in this fledgling enterprise. By the time the railway industry was under way, Jews were involved in the building of railroads in France, Austria, Belgium, Italy, Spain, Hungary, Switzerland, Prussia, Sweden, Russia and Germany.*

In 1825 Nathan Meyer Rothschild, seeing the opening of the first successful railroad in England, called on the rest of his family to begin investing in railroad construction on the continent. Salomon Rothschild in Austria sent a professor from the Vienna Institute of Technology to study England's newfangled means of transport. By 1829, the Rothschilds were ready to propose a railroad that would run from Vienna to Galicia and Trieste—right through the Hapsburg Empire. The July Revolution, the rivalry of other Jewish banking houses, and other obstacles kept the Rothschilds from breaking ground until 1836; and only part of their proposed route, a northern railroad line from Vienna to Bochina in Galicia, opened in the 1850s.

The founder of the Paris house of Rothschild was more successful in shorter time. James (Jacob) Meyer de Rothschild, fifth son of Meyer Amschel Rothschild, was influential in French finance for over fifty years. By 1830, his firm was the dominant factor in the Rothschild family fortune; by 1848 he had created a banking house said to be twice as rich as all the others in Paris combined. He entered the railroad business by constructing a local line between Paris and St. Germain. Then, in 1837, with this line operating successfully, he sought the government concession for the Paris-Versailles railway, competing with the Fould brothers (Jews who had converted to Chris-

---

* Jews were also involved in financing railroads in Brazil, Mexico, Turkey, and the United States.

tianity). The government, unable to decide, approved concessions for both. So Rothschild built his railroad on one side of the River Seine, and the Foulds on the other. The two railroads opened in 1839, but one year later, reality took over and the two companies merged. James Rothschild went on to other railway projects, obtaining the concession to build a northern rail line to connect Paris with industries in the north of France.

The Rothschild family were also involved in railroads in Belgium, where Nathan Meyer Rothschild and his sons helped finance state-built railroads from 1834 to 1843. They also helped raise funds for railroads in Italy, where they became large stockholders in the Lombard-Venetian line and the Central Italian Railway, and in Spain.

The Pereire brothers, Emile and Isaac,* were also enthusiastic about the potential of railroads. In the first phase of railroad development in Europe, between 1840 and 1870, they were second only to the Rothschilds. By the time they retired, they had made possible six thousand miles of railroads.

They began by building up France's railroads. When the Rothschilds built the northern line in the 1840s, the Pereires built one in the south. When the 1848 revolution financially ruined some of the new railroads, the Pereire brothers developed a "railroad bank" to help underwrite the companies. From 1852 to 1870, the Crédit Mobilier, as it was called, made possible the expansion of France's railroads from two thousand miles to eleven thousand miles, and financed Swiss railroads as well.

The Pereire brothers also contributed to the growth of railroads in Austria (they started the Austrian State Railroad Company), Spain, and Hungary (where they built the Franz-Joseph line).

Bethel Henry Strousberg, who owned locomotive

---

* Their grandfather, Jacob Rodrigues Pereire (1715-80), was the world's first teacher of deaf mutes.

factories and rolling mills for the production of rails, founded railway companies in Hungary and Prussia.

Another Jew became known as the "Railroad King of Russia." Born into a poor family, Samuel Salomowicz Poliakoff (1837-88) started his railroad career as a porter. After he settled in St. Petersburg about 1860, though, he got involved in railroading as a promoter. With his two brothers, he eventually constructed five of Russia's most vital rail lines and even opened a railroad school to provide workers with a technical education. For his service in helping Russia develop its railroads, Poliakoff was elevated to the nobility by Czar Alexander II. At his death, he owned one-fourth of the Russian railroad system.*

Irony, then, trails the Jewish people as a bridal train trails the bride. In all likelihood, neither the Nazis nor the Jews who rode their death trains realized the extent to which Jewish brains and money of the century before had contributed to the machinery of the Holocaust. This paradox is yet another reminder of how pervasive—and overlooked—has been the Jewish Connection.

And how did it come about? We're back again to the Diaspora. Indeed, the Diaspora is at the very center of the ironies implicit in the Jewish experience. It has been the Diaspora, with its enforced exiles, that has exposed the Jews to virtually all the hurricanes of history. But this rootlessness has also been central to a seemingly long-ordained role for the Jews, as though the Diaspora were history's wind, scattering not only Jews but the seeds of the Jewish mind throughout the world.

The exile of the Jews from Israel insured that the Jew did not remain in the Mideast, a part of the world

---

* Another Jewish Connection with Russia's railroads involves Yevzel de Gunzburg of St. Petersburg, a Jew who founded the first private banking house in Russia. After the Russian government tried and failed to raise sufficient capital to construct rail lines, the Gunzburgs took over and provided the funds to lay fourteen thousand miles of track.

that for centuries was outside the mainstream of civilization. The Diaspora thrust the Jewish people into the world. Jews profited from their dispersal, but the world profited, too, for the Diaspora made it possible for this one small people to spread the word about One Supreme Being and to teach the world about the Ten Commandments.

On a secular level, the Diaspora made possible the spread of cultural and technical advances. During the development of western civilization, Jews helped transplant the ideas of the East to the West, for after the dissolution of the Roman empire the Jews helped to link both hemispheres. The medical advances made by the Arabs were carried from the Orient to the Occident in large part by the Jews, who knew and studied the Aramaic, Arabic, and Greek texts and thereby became the leading physicians in Medieval Europe. As historians Will and Ariel Durant point out, the Jews' international connections facilitated world trade and built up multi-national banking houses. The Jew was, in a sense, civilization's bee, pollinating one culture with the ideas of another— and bringing his own special contribution to the mix.

That Jewish people would play the role of messenger is prophesied in two passages in the Bible. In Deuteronomy 4:27, 29: "The Lord shall scatter you among the peoples. . . . But from thence ye will seek the Lord your God and you shall find him." In Amos 9:9: "I will sift the house of Israel among all the nations, as corn is sifted in a sieve."

The dispersal of the Jews as part of a divine scheme has long been accepted by Jewish and Christian thinkers alike. In fact, this theory was one of the major reasons Jews were readmitted into England in the seventeenth century, after having been expelled centuries before.

Rabbi Manasseh ben Israel's argument to the English was that England must allow Jews to live on its soil or the Day of Judgment for Christian or Jew would never come. Said he in "A Declaration to the

Commonwealth of England" in 1655: "Before all be fulfilled, the People of God must be first dispersed into all places and countries of the world." Oliver Cromwell, agreeing that England should not stand in the way of destiny, set the stage for the readmittance of Jews into England.

With the creation of the modern State of Israel, the Diaspora appears to be coming full circle. Each new wave of persecution sends more Jewish refugees to Israel. Could this ingathering of the exiles, foretold long ago, be the next great stage in Jewish history? Again, a passage in the Bible emerges as ironic. Since 1949, when the Yemenite Jews were transported to Israel by airplane, virtually all Jewish immigrants to Israel first touch Israeli soil at Lod International Airport.

In the days of Joshua, Lod was a fortified city. Its motto has since become this prophecy from Jeremiah: "Thy children shall come again to their own border."

IV

Everywhere
You Turn

*Jewish Connections
from Abraham to Einstein*

FACT: The Sermon on the Mount delivered by Jesus was derived from a Jewish work.

FACT: The organ was originally used in the Temple—and early Christians were reluctant to use it in church services because they thought it "too Jewish."

FACT: All the writers of the New Testament were Jews, except Luke.

FACT: Mohammed, the founder of Islam, at one point called himself a "Jewish prophet."

FACT: Three of the four greatest thinkers dominating the twentieth century were Jewish.

FACT: Both Freud and Einstein built their momentous theories on backgrounds of Judaism.

THE FOUNDER OF THE Jewish nation is called Abraham, but Abraham was not his real name. The Bible tells us that he was originally known as Abram, which means "the father of Aram." Early in his life, Abram rejected the idol worshiping he saw around him and advocated monotheism, the belief that there can be only one Supreme Being ruling the world. Genesis 17 reports that as a result God came to Abram saying, "Behold, my covenant is with thee, and thou shalt be the father of a multitude of nations." God then changed Abram's name to Abraham, which in Hebrew means "the father of a multitude of nations"—a restatement of God's covenant with him.

Names are considered to be of great symbolic importance in Judaism,* and this episode is surely at the root of the belief. What makes this scene even more intriguing is that several sentences later God also changed the name of Abraham's wife. Her name was originally Sarai, which means "my princess," but was altered to Sarah, "princess to all." Along with her new name she is given a blessing and a prophecy parallel to that of her husband: "Yea, I will bless her, and she shall be a mother of nations."

A prophecy that Abraham and Sarah would be the parents of a single nation would have been startling enough. Indeed, later the prediction is made that their seed would multiply like the stars in the sky and the sand on the shore. But God's first—and most significant—blessing clearly indicates that their descendants will comprise not just one nation, but "a multitude."

---

* Jews hold names in such awe that the conversational Hebrew for God is *Hashem*, which means "The Name."

Has this prophecy come true?

In formulating an answer to this question, we will begin to understand why and how the Jewish Connection has permeated the world.

The tiny fraction of humanity known as Jewry has given birth to two other great religions. The Bible, the Ten Commandments, the concept of monotheism, the eradication of idol worship, the abhorrence of human sacrifices*—all are Jewish contributions that have traveled the world. Jewish minds have also fostered scientific and economic ideas that have changed the course of history. And all this has come about through two peculiarly Jewish concepts—monotheism and messianism—both operating in unnoticed ways.

The Jewish Connection received its first major impetus in the founding of the Christian Church. Today more than one billion people are Christians. While the relationship between Christianity and Judaism is often acknowledged, the depth of the Jewish-Christian tradition has often been left unexplored. If we probe the history of Christianity, we will be impressed anew with the pervasiveness of Jewish Connections in a faith now followed by nearly one-third of the world population.

We must start with one basic point: Jesus, the founder of Christianity, was a Jew. Although most Christians know this, the implications deserve a closer examination.

For instance, Jesus underwent circumcision, a practice of the Jews that the early Christians discarded because they felt it would be a deterrent to potential converts. Still, the fact remains that Jesus bore the sign of the Jewish covenant in his flesh, as his early followers were very much aware. Jesus' foreskin was

---

* Jewish abhorrence of human sacrifices was so strong that the Hebrew name for hell, *Gehenam*, comes from the Valley of Gehena outside the walls of the Old City of Jerusalem. At the base of this deep valley were held the child sacrifices of a Canaanite tribe. Even today, this valley is so detested by Jews that it is left undeveloped.

considered one of the most precious relics of the Middle Ages—and at one time there existed at least twelve of them in Europe! One was on display at the Church of the Holy Prepuce, which became a shrine for women who could not conceive; viewing the holy foreskin was said to bring fertility.

Jesus wore *tsitsiths*, the fringes that the Torah instructed Jews to display on the four corners of their clothing (today, religious Jews wear a special garment whose four sides are fringed to carry out this precept). The Christian scriptures recount that a woman was cured when those worn by Jesus were touched, but Jesus wasn't the only Christian to wear them. Early mosaics on display in churches in Italy show Apostle Matthew and some other early Christians with them on. *A History of Jewish Costume* says that, in the Church of Saint Vitale, a mosaic from the sixth century shows Apostle Matthew wearing *tsitsiths*. Other early Christians are shown with *tsitsiths* in mosaics of the fifth century in the Church of Saint Pudenziana in Rome, in the groups of Christian martyrs in the sixth-century basilica of Saint Apollinaire Nuovo, and on the cupola of the sixth-century baptistry of the Arians.

Many other elements of Christianity are Jewish. Like Jesus, all the apostles were Jews,* as was the first Pope. Jews wrote all of the books of the New Testament except for those written by Luke.

The structure of the Christian church was patterned after Judaism. Although now expanded, the College of Cardinals was set by papal decree in the sixteenth century at seventy members, with the Pope ruling as its seventy-first. This arrangement parallels that of the Great Sanhedrin, which consisted of seventy judges plus the High Priest, who presided over it. The position of Pope parallels the Temple High Priest, Judaism's highest religious office. The triple

---

* The apostles numbered twelve, which has been said to be a parallel of the Twelve Tribes of Israel.

crown of the Pope was derived from the High Priest's golden diadem and turban.

The Vatican has utilized architectural motifs of the Temple. When Constantine built the basilica above St. Peter's tomb, he used a twisted marble column that was said to be a type found in the Temple in Jerusalem. Such columns were called solomonicas because of their derivation from King Solomon's Temple. Some of them have been preserved, and when the architect Bernini was designing his baldachin (a canopy to be built over the altar) he adopted their style. Bernini's final design incorporated other Jewish elements, as this passage from *The World of Bernini 1598-1680* shows:

In his conception of the crossing of St. Peter's, Bernini had far more in mind than meets the twentieth-century eye. The twisted, Solomonic columns of the baldachin in his day had an immediate connotation: the city of Jerusalem, whence their prototypes were thought to have come. The mere placement of these columns in the crossing of the church was enough to establish, or at least to offer the pretense, that the area of the crossing *was* Jerusalem.

The Temple provided Christianity with another important feature—the organ. According to *The Jewish Book of Knowledge*, the Temple featured "a pneumatic pipe-organ worked by twin bellows, a prototype of the kind in use today." After the destruction of the Temple, the rabbis banned the playing of musical instruments in synagogues as a sign of mourning. The Church at first resisted incorporating organ music into church services because of this close link with Temple worship. Some early Church Fathers even felt that this "Jewish instrument" might "seduce some Christians" to Judaism.

Yet another Jewish feature that came to the modern world through Christianity was the Temple's most striking decoration—two great carved figures, each having a human face, the body of an animal, and two spreading wings. Described in Ezekiel 1:5-11, the creatures gave form to the angels depicted in Christian art. The Hebrew name of the figure, *kerubh*, became "cherub," a word used today to describe either a small winged angel or a child with a sweet disposition.

If we turn to the Christian calendar, we can see a marked Jewish influence. In Jewish tradition, circumcision takes place when the child is eight days old, with the day of birth counted as the first day. Start with December 25, the day Jesus' birth is celebrated; count eight days and you come to New Year's Day. This holiday originally commemorated the circumcision of Jesus.

Some Christians call New Year's Eve "Watch Night," a term introduced by John Wesley. The founder of Methodism wanted to usher in the new year with a religious service, so he patterned the event after the night of Passover, in which Jews usher in the holiday with a Seder, a religious service structured around a festive meal.

The Christian Sabbath is openly derived from that of the Jews. For centuries the early Christians conducted their Sabbath on Saturday. Seventh Day Adventists today follow this practice, and some Puritans tried to renew the practice in their day. Part of the reason for changing the day of the Christian Sabbath was to eliminate such an obvious connection to Judaism.

The Christians did not find it easy to shift their Sabbath. At a Council of Laodices meeting held sometime between 343 and 381, the Church had to forbid its members to rest on Saturday and order them to honor Sunday, but the Jewish influence was so strong that this Council allowed a special Christian religious service on Saturday. Still, according to Canon 29, "The Christians must not Judaize and sit idle on a Sabbath, but ought to work that day." Not until

Charlemagne in 789 did the Christian Sunday become like the Jewish Sabbath, a day not only of worship but of rest.

It is more than coincidence that Easter and Passover come so close to each other each year. In Asia Minor until 189, Easter was ritually observed on the day Passover began. But, in an attempt to sever the Jewish Connection, the Council of Nicaea decreed that Easter was to fall on a Sunday and should not be determined by the Jewish calendar.

The early ties between Christianity and Judaism were so complex that even theologians cannot determine if many documents from those years are Jewish or Christian in origin. Indeed, much of Jesus' teaching was rooted in Judaism. *The World Book Encyclopedia* states that, although Jesus added his own teachings, "much of what Jesus taught was already in the Hebrew Bible or was part of Jewish tradition." And, according to Michael Grant in *The Jews in the Roman World:* "Much of the Sermon on the Mount reputedly delivered by Jesus was shared with a slightly earlier Jewish work *The Two Ways.* . . . Indeed, on occasion, the Gospels go to great lengths to demonstrate the Jewishness of Jesus."

As Christianity developed, the Jewish Connection continued to operate. Martin Luther, the founder of the Protestant Reformation, did not know Hebrew well and often consulted rabbis of his day. He leaned heavily on the work of another Christian influenced by Jews—Nicholas de Lyra, an early fourteenth-century commentator on the Bible. De Lyra, in turn, depended on rabbinic sources, especially the writings of Rashi, the great Jewish commentator of the eleventh century, whom he sometimes translated almost word for word. Critics of de Lyra called him the "Ape of Rashi," but his critiques were valued so highly by Christian commentators that they were reprinted seven times between 1471 and 1660, and his system of biblical interpretation was being taught at the University of Erfurt when Martin Luther became a student there in 1501.

The course of the Reformation was affected by numerous Jewish influences, often in esoteric ways. A seven-hundred-page book on this topic—*Jewish Influence on Christian Reform Movements* by Dr. Louis Newman—was termed insufficient to cover such a broad topic. In a prefatory note, Richard J. H. Gottheil, then chairman of the Division of Ancient and Oriental Languages and Literatures at Columbia University, points out that the subject of Jewish influence on Christian reform movements "is a very rich one; it cannot be dealt with entirely in one volume."

Christianity's Jewish Connection was demonstrated in an unusual statement issued in the summer of 1973 by a group of eighteen Roman Catholic, Methodist, Baptist, Anglican, Greek Orthodox, Episcopalian, Reformed Church, and Lutheran theologians convened by the Commission on Faith and Order of the National Council of Churches of Christ in collaboration with the Secretariat for Catholic-Jewish Relations of the National Conference of Christian Bishops. As reprinted in *The Crucifixion of the Jews*, "A Statement to our Fellow Christians" started:

The Church of Christ is rooted in the life of the People Israel. We Christians look upon Abraham as our spiritual ancestor and father of our faith. For us the relationship is not one of physical descent, but the inheritance of a faith like that of Abraham, whose life was based on his trust in the promises made to him by God (Gen. 15:1-6). The ministry of Jesus and the life of the early Christian community were thoroughly rooted in the Judaism of their day, particularly in the teachings of the Pharisees. The Christian Church is still sustained by the living faith of the patriarchs and prophets, kings and priests, scribes and rabbis, and the people whom God chose for his own. Christ is the link (Gal. 3:26-29) enabling the Gentiles to be numbered among Abraham's "offspring" and therefore fellow heirs with the Jews according to God's promise. It is a tragedy of history that Jesus, our bond of unity with the Jews, has all too often become a symbol and source of division and bitterness because of human weakness and pride.

The very name Jesus Christ is Jewish. "Jesus" is Hebrew for "savior" or "help of the Lord." Christ is Greek (*Christos*) for the Hebrew word *Meshiach*, meaning "anointed one," a term derived from the fact that Jewish kings and priests were installed by being touched with holy oil. Since in Jewish tradition the Savior would be designated by being anointed, the Savior was called in Hebrew *Meshiach*. From this comes the word Messiah used by English-speaking Christians.

Our present concepts of monotheism* and messianism are distinctly Jewish contributions to the world. No other peoples of the past offered up such a combination of ideas; only the Jews renounced the worship of many gods, saw a world created and ruled by one Supreme Being, and awaited a Messiah who would usher in an age of peace. For the Jews alone, the golden age was not in the past but of the future.

So strong has been the idea of the coming savior that throughout history a number of people—both Jewish and non-Jewish—have come forward claiming to be the Messiah. The last great display of a messianic movement occurred in the seventeenth century. Sabbatai Zevi, a Turkish Jew, attracted so much attention with his claims to being the Messiah that bets on his authenticity were placed on stock exchanges.

---

* Some historians have declared the first monotheistic religion to have been one founded by the Pharaoh Akhenaton, husband of Nefertiti, who was opposed to the myriad gods of the Egyptians. But his religious reforms were rejected by the Egyptian priests and the vast majority of the populace. As a result, his reign was short-lived, and his ideas were never brought to the attention of other peoples. It may even be said his religion was not a true monotheism because it was centered on worship of the sun.

Diarist Samuel Pepys recorded having heard excited discussions about him in England. Various Christians believed he represented the Second Coming of Christ, Moslems worried that he was, and a number of Jews accepted him as the Messiah. Many of his adherents sold their homes and possessions and prepared for a journey to a new life in the Promised Land. His initials were carved in the stones of some synagogues, prayerbooks were inscribed in his honor, and marriages among children were quickly arranged in readiness for the messianic age.*

Eventually, Sabbatai was captured by the Sultan of Turkey, who did not know whether to believe him or not. A famed Polish rabbi traveled to see Sabbatai in his prison cell and, after three days of intensive interviews, proclaimed him an imposter. The Sultan then offered Sabbatai the choice of converting to Islam or being beheaded. He chose conversion, and his movement collapsed in disgrace. A diehead band of followers continued to believe in him and, following their master's example, converted to Islam. Members of this sect, called the Donmeh, can still be found in Turkey, where they practice a curious mixture of Judaism and Mohammedanism.

The Sabbatai Zevi movement is but one manifestation of the messianic ideal. During the sixteenth and seventeenth centuries, would-be messiahs also appeared among Christians throughout Europe.

1550. In Poland, Jacob Melstinski announces he is Christ and chooses twelve apostles.

1556. In Delft, David Jorries proclaims himself the true Christ.

1614. In Langensalza, Ezekiel Meth proclaims himself the Grand Duke of God and the Archangel Michael.

1615. Isaiah Stieffel announces, "I am the Christ, I am the Living word of God."

---

* In some congregations, Jews said the prayer usually recited for heads of governments for Sabbatai Zevi instead.

1624. Philippus Ziegler prophesies a messiah of the line of David will be born in Holland.

1654. In England, the Quaker Jacob Naylor says he heard a voice telling him to leave his farm. He arrives in Bristol in 1657 escorted by disciples, with two women leading his horse and singing the old Jewish chant, "Holy, holy, holy, Lord God of Israel."

While each of these messianic impulses failed, another religious movement—one that would extend the Jewish concept of monotheism through a substantial part of the world—took shape under the leadership of Mohammed.

Mohammed presented himself as a prophet to be followed rather than as a Messiah to be worshipped. He saw himself as completing the teachings of Abraham, Isaac, Jacob, and Moses, as well as Jesus, each of whom he also called prophets. But, significantly, at one point he termed himself a "Jewish prophet."

Here are some other aspects of Mohammed's Jewish Connection:

• He originally chose Jerusalem as the city to be faced in prayer, an exact parallel of the Jewish practice. The Moslems now pray toward Mecca because of Mohammed's anger when the Jews, whom he hoped to enlist as his followers, refused to join him.

• He set aside Friday as a special day with congregational prayer, patterning the observance after the Jewish concept of a weekly holy day and choosing Friday because on that day Jews began their Sabbath preparations.

• As the Jews had done, he abolished idol worship, which was still rampant in the East, and spoke out against it.

• He developed a religion that is strongly monotheistic.

• He spoke of restoring the "religion of Abraham," supported the teachings in the Hebrew Bible, and venerated its people. Of twenty-five prophets listed by

Mohammed in the Koran, nineteen are from Jewish scripture.

The Koran also shows the Jewish Connection:

• The Moslem is forbidden to eat the flesh of pigs or any other animal not slaughtered in the name of God—an obvious link with the Jewish precept of kosher food and ritual slaughter.

• The Moslem is enjoined to pray five times a day, in specified periods that mark the passing of the hours. The Jewish tradition calls for three prayer services at carefully demarcated times.

• The Moslem must undergo circumcision, a practice not widely observed in the Arabian lands of Mohammed's era, except by the Jews who lived there.

Just as Christianity rose from Jewish origins to become the major religion of the West, Islam sprang from Judaism to dominate the East. How was the faith Mohammed preached able to take hold so strongly among the Arabs? The answer lies in yet another twist of the Jewish Connection: the Arabs already viewed themselves as descendants of the founder of Judaism.

The Arabs traced their ancestry to Ishmael, Abraham's son by his concubine, Hagar. The growth of the Arab nation had therefore borne out another Biblical prophecy. In Genesis 21:18, God says of Ishmael, "I will make him a great nation." Mohammed built upon this connection by placing Abraham at the center of Islam. Indeed, the major shrine of Islam is the Kaaba, which contains the Kaaba stone, said to be the last remnant of a house of worship built by Abraham. Moslem pilgrims kiss this stone as part of their pilgrimage to Mecca. Outside the Kaaba is the zamzam, a well said to have been used by Hagar and Ishmael after they left Abraham's house.

Today in Israel we can see innumerable examples of the literal overlapping of the Christian and Moslem faiths with Judaism. The tomb of King David is located on Mount Zion, near the walls of the Old City of Jerusalem. In a building on top of the tomb, reached by a flight of stone steps worn by the foot treads of two thousand years, is the room where the Last Supper is said to have taken place.* The Moslems' Dome of the Rock now sits on the very spot on which the Temple stood, from which Mohammed's horse was said to have leaped to take his master to heaven, and to which Abraham reportedly bound his son Isaac in answer to a call from the Almighty.

Moses, the greatest Jewish prophet and leader, is a figure holy to all three religions, and the giving of the Ten Commandments is a colossal event in the history of each. This common tradition is perhaps best demonstrated by the ancient monastery of St. Catherine's, built about the year 340 at the foot of what was believed to be Mount Sinai, where God spoke to Moses out of the burning bush and later gave him the Ten Commandments. At the top of the mount there now stands not a synagogue, but both a Christian chapel and a Moslem mosque.

The disagreements among the three faiths over the ground of their common origins is vividly portrayed in a statement issued by the Israeli Embassy in the United States to explain the new policy initiated on August 5, 1975, to guarantee followers of each religion access to the Cave of Machpela at Hebron, the burial site for Abraham, Isaac, Jacob, and their wives.

The regulations spelled out in that document show vividly how differing modes of worship of the same God have converged on one site:

A. *Mode of Access and Egress*

1. Eastern Entrance—for entry and egress of Moslem worshippers.
2. Southwestern Entrance—for entry and egress of Jewish worshippers.

---

* The Last Supper was, of course, a Passover Seder.

3. Western Entrance—for entry and egress of tourists and visitors of all faiths.

B. *Areas of Worship*

1. For Jewish worshippers: Hall of Abraham and Sarah; Hall of Jacob and Leah; balcony and courtyard connecting the two halls.
2. For Moslem worshippers: Hall of Isaac and Rebecca; Jawliyya Hall; Halls of Yusufiyya.
3. Visitors and tourists will be able to visit all areas at times when no prayers are in progress.

C. *Times of Worship*

1. Moslems will be able to pray in their areas 24 hours a day, every day of the week.
2. Jews will be able to pray in their areas on weekdays and on the Sabbath, as well as on Jewish Holy days, in accordance with the accepted hours of prayer. However, on Fridays—the Islamic special day of prayer—Moslems will be able to pray throughout the whole day, whereas Jews will be limited to evening prayers only, to greet the incoming Jewish Sabbath.

This complex arrangement, though a poignant commentary on the tangled lines of the Jewish Connection, provides modern evidence that the prophecy made so long ago to Abraham has proven true: he did indeed father a "multitude of nations." Throughout history, scores of countries—even entire empires —have been dominated by the faiths built on ancient Judaism. Today more than half of the world's population follows one of these three great religions.

The Jewish Connection goes far beyond religious ties. With their emancipation in the nineteenth century, Jews were able to thrive among the nations of the world as never before. As a result, in the secular areas of life, the thinking of Jews has shaped another "multitude of nations." Nowhere is this better seen than in the realm of economics.

One-third of the world now lives in countries that operate according to political systems inspired by a Jew—Karl Marx. Yet the Jews themselves have suffered much from the spread of communism and the atheism it mandates. Red China, after all, refuses to recognize the existence of Israel in United Nations debates, and the Soviet Union represses Judaism within its borders and supports the Arabs in the Mideast conflict. Lewis Mumford, in *The Condition of Man*, has even suggested that "the Jew-baiting of the Nazis was a sinister game that Marx himself actually began."

Still, a case can be made that the communism of today—filtered through the influences of his disciple Lenin—is hardly the stuff of which Karl Marx dreamed. He viewed socialism as a noble campaign to free the working man from the abuses of capitalism, which in his day sought profits by any means. Jacques Barzun in *Darwin, Marx, Wagner* put Marx's ideas in perspective when he wrote: "It was surely out of a passionate hatred of injustice that Marx spoke of exploitation." His ultimate aim was probably a world similar to the Jewish messianic view in which "lion would lie down with the lamb," for in Marx's vision, as Louis Untermeyer said, "the world would no longer be divided between the exploiters and the exploited, and class antagonisms would therefore vanish."

Heinrich Karl Marx, born on May 5, 1818, in Trier in the German Rhineland, came from a family whose ancestors had been deeply religious Jews. Almost all of the rabbis of Trier from the sixteenth century to his birth were ancestors of Marx. His father's father had been a rabbi; his mother's father had been a rabbi, and her family for centuries had been rabbis. In *Karl Marx: His Life and Thought*, David McLellan notes that "it would be difficult to find anyone who had a more Jewish ancestry than Karl Marx."

But Marx's father, an able, ambitious lawyer, converted to Christianity since Jews could not practice in the higher courts. Who can doubt that his father's opportunism soured Marx on all religion? Karl Marx was baptized as a Protestant at the age of six. In 1843, he would write that he found "the Israelite beliefs" to be "obnoxious."

When Marx died in 1883, after years of poverty, he left behind writings that filled forty volumes. In an ironic link to Jewish tradition, he came to be hailed as "the workers' Messiah," and *Das Kapital*, his major work, has been called a "modern testament" and the "Bible of the working classes." He, however, has sometimes been called "the Father of Lies" and "the Antichrist."

Although Marx repudiated all religion as a weapon used against the worker to keep him in his place—"the opiate of the masses"—the spiritual approach to life influenced his ideas and, ironically, helped him capture a following. Today Marx's writings are studied in Communist countries with the fervor of scholars poring over the Bible. His theories are espoused by even more people than the Holy Scriptures, and with comparable intensity. If Communists believed in saints, Marx would be canonized as their patriarch.

Karl Marx is really the black sheep of the Jewish Connection. But could his indignation at social injustice have been fueled by his deep blood-line links with the morality of ancient Judaism?

"The characteristic genius of the Jew," wrote Edmund Wilson in *To the Finland Station*, "has been especially a moral genius. . . . It was here that Karl Marx as a Jew had his great value for the thought of his age. . . . Nobody but a Jew could have fought so uncompromisingly and obstinately for the victory of the dispossessed classes."

Marx simply didn't realize how difficult it is to sever one's Jewish Connection.

Whereas Karl Marx is universally termed the father of communism, other economic theories seem to have had multiple founders. Newton once said that to make his discoveries he "stood on the shoulders of giants," and history is studded with cases in which different people arrived independently at the same discovery at almost the same time.

Adam Smith, author of *The Wealth of Nations*, is surely due an important place in the development of capitalism. But what about a Jew by the name of David Ricardo? If he isn't the father of capitalism, he is surely one of its uncles.

The World Book Encyclopedia refers to Ricardo as "the leading British economist of the early 1800's" who "helped establish the theories of *classical economics*," and goes on: "Ricardo's theories influenced other economists. His theory of comparative advantage is still the basis for the modern theory of international trade." The encyclopedia then reports that Karl Marx was influenced by Ricardo's labor theory of value, Henry George was affected by Ricardo's theory of rent, and John Stuart Mill used Ricardo's ideas as the basis for a philosophy of social reform.

The *Encyclopaedia Judaica* places Ricardo even more firmly among the early figures of capitalism, terming him "one of the founding fathers of modern economics," and says that "much of today's knowledge about currency, taxation, and international trade is based on Ricardo's analysis."

Who was this David Ricardo?

Born in 1772, he was a Sephardic Jew raised in England with a traditional Jewish education. His father was a religious Jew who had amassed a fortune (he was a good capitalist, too), and young David became a broker. Rising fast in London society, he married a non-Jew of the English gentry, Priscilla Anne Wilkinson. His marrying outside the faith so offended his family that his father went into mourning and stopped supporting him. Within twelve years, though, Ricardo had speculated in the stock market so successfully that he had become a millionaire. He eventually was elected to Parliament. Since not until

1858 could a professing Jew sit in Parliament, he must have converted, although there is no evidence of this. Still, the record is clear that throughout his parliamentary service he used every opportunity to press for Jewish rights.

Ricardo's chief work, published in 1817, was *Principles of Political Economy and Taxation*, which has been termed by *The Standard Jewish Encyclopedia* "one of the most influential books of the nineteenth century."

The impact of Ricardo's theories has led Paul Samuelson, Nobel Prize winner in economics, to place Ricardo with John Stuart Mill as "the principal exponents of the classical school of economics." In a diagram of "The Family Tree of Economics" on the inside back cover of his famous book *Economics: An Introductory Analysis*, Samuelson includes Ricardo as one of five major figures in the classical school of economics that is the foundation of present-day theory. Interestingly, Samuelson shows the tree of economics as starting on one side with Aristotle and on the other with the Bible.

In the twentieth century, the "multitude of nations" have been greatly affected by two more Jews. The religious heritage of these two men played a critical role in their own lives—and in the ideas that have so influenced modern society. Their names: Sigmund Freud and Albert Einstein.

Ernest Van den Haag, author of *The Jewish Mystique*, has written that four men are widely regarded as having most dominated the thinking of the twentieth century: Freud, Einstein, Darwin, and Marx. Of these four, only Darwin was not born a Jew.

Sigmund Freud (1856-1939), founder of the modern theories of psychiatry, creator of the technique of psychoanalysis, first to chart the subconscious mind, has been described (in *Freud: The Man, His World, His Influence*) as probably representing "the single most important intellectual force of the twentieth century." In an essay in that book, Friedrich

Heer calls Freud's work "one of the landmarks of the twentieth century."

Freud was the son of a Jewish tradesman, who moved the family when Sigmund was four from Freiberg, Moravia, to Vienna. The Austrian capital was then a hotbed of anti-Semitism,* and when Freud entered medical school at seventeen he encountered open hostility. Thus began the special role Judaism would play in Freud's life. His theories were attacked as "Jewish" and his books were burned by the Nazis, who also seized his money, destroyed his publishing house, and hounded him out of Austria when he was eighty-one.

But anti-Semitism may have been an important ingredient in Freud's successful pursuit of the uncharted mysteries of the mind, for as an innovator he was upsetting comfortable ways of thought and had to be prepared to suffer the hostility of those his theories disturbed. As a victim of anti-Semitism, he had already had to deal with rejection; his Jewishness therefore prepared Freud for the exclusions that his theories provoked. In his *Self Portrait*, Freud himself wrote that his exposure to anti-Semitism in medical school "produced one important result. At a rather early date, I became aware of my destiny: to belong to the critical minority as opposed to the unquestioning majority. A certain independence of judgment was therefore developed."

Freud's statement points to one good reason why Jews can be found so frequently in movements that challenge preconceived notions. Often placed outside society by religious discrimination, Jews can serve society as intellectual rebels, questioning the theories and exploding the ignorances of the past.

Although Freud openly questioned all religion, including Judaism, he always thought of himself as a Jew and raised his six children as Jews. In a letter to

---

* In *The Interpretation of Dreams*, Freud says he could never forget that when he was young his father told him his hat had been knocked off by a Christian who exclaimed, "Get off the pavement, Jew."

his fiancée written in 1882, Freud concluded that "something of the core, of the essence of this meaningful and life-affirming Judaism will not be absent from our home." And later in his writings, when mentioning his first exposure to anti-Semitism, he said, "I could never grasp why I should be ashamed of my origin."

According to Friedrich Heer, Bible reading had made a deep impression on Freud as a boy (later, on his thirty-fifth birthday, his father presented him with a Hebrew Bible). Freud, says Heer, openly admitted that the scriptures had "a decisive influence on his intellectual and spiritual development." Especially important to him was the fact that in the Bible of the Jews there is no concept of hell: "one's life on earth was a scene of all one's striving, an important consideration for a man seeking to explain man to himself on this earth."

Freud began his medical career in research in 1876, when at the age of seventeen he conducted a search for the concealed testes of the eel—and found them. Success did not come as easily afterward. His first and most important work—*The Interpretation of Dreams*, termed by one reviewer "a milestone in the advancement of human knowledge"—took eight years to sell a first printing of six hundred copies, from which he earned only $250. Throughout the last sixteen years of his life, he suffered from cancer of the jaw and underwent 33 operations. And yet Freud insisted on continuing his ground-breaking work until his death at eighty-three.

Freud's importance is well described in a passage from Lawrence Wilson's book, *100 Great Events That Changed the World:* "Since Freud we know not only what we do, but approximately why we do it. The consequences have been immense. There is hardly a sphere of modern life which has not been influenced by Freudian thought—sociology, social welfare, politics, the law, the family, education, the treatment of delinquency and mental illness, medicine, the arts, propaganda, advertising, entertainment and even religion."

Would Freud have made such an impact if he had not been Jewish? Perhaps the answer lies in the answer he gave when asked about the problems of bringing up his children as Jews in Vienna's climate of anti-Semitism. "Life is a problem for everybody," he retorted. "Besides, you can't expect to be a Jew for nothing!"

On May 20, 1919, a total eclipse of the sun set the stage for testing a theory that, if proved true, would overshadow old ways of thinking. On that day, Einstein's theory of relativity was put to the proof, using instruments to determine if a light ray would bend when passing through the gravitational field of the sun. Einstein had calculated the deviation at 1.75 seconds of an arc and staked his years of work on it. When pictures of the eclipse were developed and examined, the deflection was found to be 1.64 seconds—as close to perfect agreement with Einstein's prediction as instruments allowed.

Amid the international acclaim that followed, Einstein underlined the problem inherent in the Jewish Connection as it affects "the multitude of nations." Said he, "Today in Germany I am hailed as a German man of science and in England I am pleasantly represented as a foreign Jew. But if ever my theories are repudiated, the Germans will condemn me as a foreign Jew and the English will dismiss me as a German."

Albert Einstein—physicist, mathematician, creator at twenty-six of the theory of relativity that ushered in the atomic age, supplanted Newtonian physics, and "caused the greatest revolution in science since Galileo"—was influenced by his Jewishness throughout his life.

Born March 14, 1879, in Germany, Einstein came to see his theories outlawed by the Nazis, who forced him to leave Germany, took his possessions, and confiscated his books. Although in his later life he did not observe the rituals of Judaism, he was a keen supporter of Zionism and other Jewish causes. He was a trustee of the Hebrew University and donated to it his manuscripts on relativity. He wrote on a number of Jewish topics and helped various Jewish charitable causes, once wearing the traditional skull-cap while playing a violin in a synagogue performance. He went on a fund-raising tour of America with Chaim Weizmann in 1921 and helped raise millions of dollars for the Jewish National Fund. When Weizmann, who had become the first President of Israel, died in 1952, Einstein was asked to stand for election as President of Israel, but he modestly declined.

He retained a deep respect for the power of religion. "The most beautiful thing we can experience is the mysterious," he once said. "He to whom this emotion is a stranger, who can no longer pause to wonder and stand rapt in awe, is as good as dead. . . . To know that what is impenetrable to us really exists, manifesting itself as the highest wisdom and the most radiant beauty which our dull faculties can comprehend only in their most primitive forms—this knowledge, this feeling, is at the center of true religiousness. In this sense, I belong in the ranks of devoutly religious men."

According to Banesh Hoffman, author of *Albert Einstein: Creator and Rebel*, Einstein was in his youth "intensely religious, both spiritually and ritualistically. For years he refused to eat pork, for example, and he took it amiss that his parents were lax in their Jewish observances."

Later, though, he moved away from organized religion, but never gave up his strong sense of the existence of a Supreme Being. His allegiance to the Jewish people grew stronger as both his fame and German anti-Semitism grew. As early as 1933, he resigned from the Prussian Academy, citing what he called "the war of annihilation against my fellow Jews" and vowing "to employ, in their behalf, whatever influence I may possess in the eyes of the world." Following World War II, Einstein refused an invitation to rejoin the Academy, saying that "the Germans slaughtered my Jewish brethren; I will have nothing further to do with the Germans."

But it is in Einstein's style of thinking that we can see the importance of his Jewish Connection. In fact, one might say without exaggeration that certain aspects of the Jewish religion were, even without his realizing it, responsible for his ability to perceive the order of the physical world in a new way. Biographer Banesh Hoffman emphasizes the influence of Einstein's spiritual beliefs on his history-making theories:

Perhaps in a brief biography it seems almost irrelevant to dwell on the religious evolution of one who was to become famous as a scientist. But Einstein's scientific motivation was basically religious, though not in the formal, ritualistic sense. "The most incomprehensible thing about the world," he said, "is that it is comprehensible." When judging a scientific theory, his own or another's, he asked himself whether he would have made the universe in that way had he been God. This criterion may at first seem closer to mysticism than to what is usually thought of as science, yet it reveals Einstein's faith in an ultimate simplicity and beauty in the universe. Only a man with a profound religious and artistic conviction that beauty was there, waiting to be discovered, could have constructed theories whose most striking attribute, quite overtopping their spectacular successes, was their beauty.

Indeed, Einstein's immersion in his Jewishness helped him unlock doors to new worlds. Elsewhere Hoffman writes that Einstein's search for a unified field theory—a long, arduous, often frustrating enterprise that took thirty years—was sustained by "his profound conviction that there *ought* to be such a theory—that, as the ancient Hebrews put it, the Lord is one."

The monotheism of Judaism and its effect on Einstein explain much about the central role of the Jewish Connection in the dawning of the modern age and its influence on a "multitude of nations." The cohesiveness Einstein perceived is the same order described in the Bible and taught in the very tenets of the Jewish religion. The philosopher Alfred North Whitehead once asked why so many technological advances occurred in the West, rather than the East, and concluded that the West had two factors absent from the East—the religious development of Judaic monotheism and the existence of the Greek civilization.

Mentioning Whitehead's observation, Cecil J. Schneer, in *The Search for Order*, underlines this point:

> The belief in a supreme Deity, in one God, the Creator, is a belief that the universe exemplifies purpose and not aimlessness. Natural law governs the world of events because the world of events is the creation of a supreme power. Order, regularity, law and purpose are attributes of a single Deity. Westerners could search for an explanation of events because their religious heritage had predisposed them to expect that explanations exist.

When Einstein died in 1955 at the age of seventy-six, his theories were internationally famous. What had once been said to be understood by only twelve people in all the world was now affecting the ways scientists thought and governments acted. "The ideas of relativity form a framework which can embrace all laws of nature," says the *World Book Encyclopedia*. "Relativity has changed the whole philosophical and physical notions of space and time. It has influenced our views and speculation of the distant worlds and the tiny world of the atom." His theory, and the pivotal equation, $E = mc^2$, has become so much a part of our culture that CBS television, in a film on his life, used it as the simple title to the program. Einstein's visage became so well known that, according to William Manchester in *The Glory and the Dream*, his shaggy mane gave rise to a new word for the brainy people of the world—"longhairs."

Einstein had been slow to speak as a child and had a poor memory as a student. One teacher told him bluntly, "You'll never amount to anything." Perhaps this is but another link in the long chain of irony binding the Jewish Connection.

V

Jews on First:
Inventors and Explorers

*Jews who gave at the office . . .
and in the laboratory*

FACT: A Jew invented the telephone—and exhibited it publicly fifteen years before Bell patented his invention.

FACT: Almost two hundred years before Columbus, a rabbi wrote that the world is round.

FACT: Columbus's life was saved by a prediction in a book written by a Jew, who also devised navigational aids for a number of other explorers.

FACT: Orville and Wilbur Wright were influenced in their invention of the airplane by a Jew who had made two thousand controlled glider flights.

FACT: The first American scientist ever awarded the Nobel Prize was a Jew.

FACT: The first planet discovered since prehistoric times was found by a Jew who was a musician by profession.

WELCOME TO THE Goldbergian Institute, which houses the many overlooked inventions and innovations that Jews have given to mankind. In the twelve floors (one for each tribe) of this museum of the Jewish Connection are displayed the work of Jews who, although not as well known as Freud, Einstein, and Marx, have in their own ways shaped the world.

In the lobby is a small glass case containing three books. The first, by Moses de León (1250-1305), is a mystical commentary on the Bible entitled the *Zohar* (*Book of Splendor*), and it is opened to the page in which he asserted, almost two hundred years before Copernicus and Columbus, that the earth is round and that it rotates! Wrote de León, "The earth revolves like a ball . . . when it is day on one-half of the globe, night reigns over the other half." He also speculated that people lived on the other half of the globe.

The second book is by Isaac B. Solomon Sahula, written in 1281 and published about 1490—two years before Columbus's voyage. Sahula declared that "the globe 'beneath us' is inhabited by people" and that "when it is day on this side of the globe, it is night on the other side." The third book is the Palestinian Talmud, opened to the page in the volume *Abodah Zara III* in which—centuries before Columbus—it is proclaimed that the "world is round."

This sets the tone for the exhibits on the first floor, which is devoted to a survey of Jewish discoveries and inventions.

On the right, for instance, a display shows that present-day copyright law is based on a regulation evolved by medieval rabbis. Here on view is a book published in Rome in 1518—the *Grammar of Elias*

Levita, a Jew who taught Hebrew to a number of Christians, including a cardinal. The *Grammar* contains virtually the first copyright statement in a written work; it set the stage for international copyright law as we know it today.

As the exhibit explains, in the centuries following the invention of printing, copyright protection proved a problem in the non-Jewish world. Nathan Isaacs, in an essay entitled "The Influence of Judaism on Western Law" in *The Legacy of Israel*, describes a copyright notice in a Hebrew book printed within a few years of the first English statute on the subject. Here, in the place of a copyright notice, is a *haskamah* of the president of the Rabbinate of Frankfurt, which praises the editor, tells of the editor's fear that others will "remove his boundary" (the equivalent of infringement), and then "pronounces a ban against anyone who raises a hand to reprint this work within fifteen years of the date of completion of the current printing." Isaac notes, "This type of clause was practically universal in Hebrew books of this time."

Since Jews were in direct contact with non-Jews in the early days of printing (indeed, Christians published many of the Jews' early books), the world must have learned that the Jews had an effective device to prevent literary piracy. Interestingly, in anticipation of the present-day problems raised by copying machines, the Jewish ban on reprinting of books extended not only to publishers but to readers as well.

Next to this display is a framed picture containing simply two hand-lettered quotation marks. A notation points out that the use of such punctuation may very well have been derived from the Talmudic decree that forbids writing a passage from the Torah without showing by a symbol that the statement is not an original thought of the writer. In this way, a person would both honor the Torah and not fall into the trap of falsely ascribing to himself what he learned from another source.

The visitor proceeds across the room to a waist-high pedestal, which holds a pop-art replica of a common sandwich. A small card tells us that, although the Earl of Sandwich is credited with its invention, the great Jewish teacher Hillel (60 B.C.E–9 C.E.) actually made the first. For a Passover Seder meal he put bitter herbs between two pieces of matzoh to eat as a remembrance of the difficult times the Israelites had in Egypt. To this day, a part of every traditional Seder service is the making and eating of what is now called the "Hillel sandwich."

The visitor now enters the first wing of the museum. Across the entrance are the words "Jews with Stars in Their Minds." Inside is evidence of the surprising Jewish Connection with astronomy.

The first display shows a Jacob's staff, a nautical instrument that enabled sailors in the Middle Ages to chart their positions. The Jacob's staff was invented by a rabbi, Levi Ben Gershon (1288-1344). Known also as Gersonides or by his Hebrew initials, which were transcribed as *Ralbag*, he was not only a leading Jewish philosopher and Bible commentator but a mathematician and astronomer as well. He wrote important works on arithmetic, geometry, harmonic numbers, and especially trigonometry. His thinking, expanded upon by Regiomontanus in 1464, formed the basis for modern trigonometry.* His description of an instrument to fix the position of the stars attracted the attention of Pope Clement VI, who ordered a translation of the passage from Hebrew into Latin. This led to the construction of the Jacob's staff.

In the next display case is a copy of the famous Catalan Atlas, a map of the world that incorporated the information collected by Marco Polo. The atlas was the work of Abraham Crescas of Majorca, a fourteenth-century cartographer, who served as the

---

* Another Jew helped develop calculus. Immanuel Bonfils, a fourteenth-century Frenchman who taught mathematics and astronomy at Orange and drew up important astronomical tables, did work on the extraction of square roots and decimals that anticipated exponential and decimal calculus.

Master of Maps and Compasses to the King of Aragon. Considered to be the best map of the world in 1377 when it was made, it was sent as an important token of friendship to the King of France, Charles VI. The original is now in the Bibliothèque Nationale in Paris.

Another Jewish cartographer was Crescas' son, Judah. Known as the Map Jew, he was forcibly converted to Christianity in the persecutions of 1391, and later, as the first director of Henry the Navigator's nautical observatory at Sagres, helped chart the voyages of Portuguese explorers.

The mathematician and cosmographer Pedro Nunes (1492-1577) was a Jew who, though forced by the Inquisition to live as a Marrano, remained secretly attached to Judaism. Nunes was the most distinguished of Portugal's nautical astronomers, and his *Treatise on the Sphere*, written in 1537, is considered by historians to have opened the way for Gerhardus Mercator (1512-1594), whose work launched modern cartography.

A prominent feature of the Goldbergian Institute is a large world map showing the routes of the great explorers. Across the top is the sign: "Zacuto Helped Make It Possible."

Abraham ben Samuel Zacuto (1450-c.1525) was an astronomer and rabbinical scholar who compiled tables used as navigational guides by Columbus, Vasco da Gama, Alfonso de Albuquerque and Cabral on their historic voyages. A professor of astronomy at the universities of Salamanca and Saragossa, he wrote a vital work on the stars that was translated into Spanish and Latin and played a key part in Columbus's discovery of the New World and the opening of new sea routes.

Zacuto's book actually saved Columbus's life. On his last voyage, when he and his crew fell ill in Jamaica and natives refused to help, Columbus used Zacuto's accurate prediction of a moon eclipse to frighten the local populace into supplying critically needed food. Columbus's copy of Zacuto's tables, with notes by the explorer himself, is preserved today in Seville.

When Spain expelled its Jews, Zacuto traveled to Portugal, where he became Royal Astronomer and was consulted about the voyages of Vasco de Gama, Alfonso de Albuquerque, and other explorers. There Zacuto developed a new astrolabe, made of iron instead of wood, and the Portuguese explorers used this too—especially da Gama, who was the first to employ the improved instrumentation in his search for new sea routes to India.

Because of continuing persecution of Jews in Portugal, Zacuto eventually had to flee to Tunis, where he wrote a history of the Jews entitled *Sefer ha Yuchasin (Book of Records)*. He remained on the move throughout the rest of his life, and the date and place of his death are uncertain.

Also on view at the museum is an old fragile telescope, and behind it a painting of a bewigged man viewing the heavens. In 1781, a Jew, William Herschel (1738-1822), used a telescope he had made himself to discover Uranus, the first planet to be found since prehistoric times. In addition, Herschel discovered two of the satellites of Uranus, that the planet rotated in the opposite direction to the others, and that its satellites also revolved around it in the opposite direction. He discovered two satellites of Saturn, became the first astronomer to attempt a comprehensive survey of the heavens, fixed the position of 2,500 nebulae, of which 203 had been unknown, founded the modern system of star astronomy, provided the basis for today's theories of astrophysics, and discovered infrared radiation—surely an interesting series of discoveries for a person who was a musician by profession.

Nor was the Herschel family's scientific achievement limited to William. His sister, Carolina Lucretia

Herschel (1750-1848), was the first woman to discover a comet.

The next wing of the Goldbergian Institute is entitled "The Jews Who Brought You the Twentieth
Century." Its first series of exhibits, plaques, and
audiovisual devices is devoted to the Jewish Connection in the field of atomic research.

The widespread influence of the Jews in the twentieth century can be traced to the liberating effects
of the American and French revolutions* of two
hundred years ago. Once they were released from the
ghettos, allowed to attend universities, and given
the right to serve in armies, to vote, and to hold
public office, Jews responded with a great release of
their creative and intellectual powers.

In the nineteenth century, Jews proposed a flood
of inventions, new ideas, and technological advances.
For a world that had for so long excluded such a
natural resource, the discovery of the Jew was comparable to finding another New World, largely un-
tapped, yet brimming with something even more
vital than raw materials—innovative thinking.

Nowhere is the Jewish Connection more evident
than in the development of the theory of atomic energy. Indeed, atomic research is almost exclusively
the work of Jews. The tale begins with Albert Abraham Michelson.

Born in Prussia in 1852, Michelson came to America as a youngster with his parents. After graduation
from high school, he sought a career in the U.S. Navy.
Hoping for an Academy appointment, he approached
President Ulysses S. Grant on the White House steps
one morning as the chief executive came out to walk
his dog. Grant had already used up his allotted ten
appointments-at-large at Annapolis, but was im-

---

* Yet even among the revolutionaries, the Jews faced hurdles. The
ghettoized Jews of Alsace-Lorraine had to wait two years after the French
Revolution before the rights accorded all other groups were extended to
them.

pressed with the young man and was later moved to action by a letter from Michelson's congressman in Nevada.

His father is a prominent and influential merchant of Virginia City [wrote the representative] and a member of the Israelite persuasion, who by his example and influence has largely contributed to the success of our cause, and induced many of his coreligionists to do the same. These people are a powerful element in our politics, the boy who is uncommonly bright and studious is a pet among them, and I do most steadfastly believe that his appointment at *your* hand would do more to fasten these people to the Republican cause, than anything else that could be done. The Union people of Nevada. . . . will demonstrate to you hereafter that the "strong box" of the nation will be the strong-hold of your administration on this coast. I know you can greatly please them and strengthen us by making this appointment.

Grant soon created an additional opening and Michelson was given the "eleventh appointment." Michelson actually was helped by the fact he was a Jew, and his career as a scientist was launched, as he himself later noted, by "an illegal act."

After graduating from the Naval Academy in 1873 and serving several years as an officer, Michelson turned to scientific research, his primary interest, and began a career of teaching and experimentation that would take him to several colleges. Michelson's work led to such outstanding discoveries that in 1907 he became the first American scientist to be awarded the Nobel Prize.

What had Michelson done to win this high honor for himself and for his country? Put simply, he had measured the speed of light with such accuracy that even today's more sophisticated instruments have shown his figures to be off by only four kilometers per second!

Working with E. W. Morley, he had also devised a test, known as the Michelson-Morley experiment, that according to science writer Isaac Asimov was "probably the most important experiment-that-did-not-work in the whole history of science." This technique used rays of light to determine the extent of the universe's "ether," a substance scientists then believed permeated the cosmos and explained how light traveled. The Michelson-Morley research proved that no such ether existed, a finding that shook the scientific world.

The exact effect Michelson's work had upon Einstein and the theories of relativity that launched the atomic age is somewhat unclear because of conflicting statements made by Einstein in his later years. However, Einstein many times publicly acknowledged his debt to Michelson and mentioned having used his findings either in calculations or as corroboration. A major biographer of Einstein, Ronald W. Clark, terms the Michelson-Morley experiment "a linchpin of the whole theory of relativity." Einstein himself told Sir Herbert Samuel, "If Michelson-Morley is wrong, then relativity is wrong." And in a speech at a dinner held in 1931, Einstein turned to Michelson and, in a celebrated statement, said: "You, my honored Dr. Michelson . . . led the physicists into new paths, and through your marvelous experimental work paved the way for the development of the Theory of Relativity. . . . Without your work this theory would today be scarcely more than an interesting speculation: it was your verifications which first set the theory on a real basis."

Michelson is a largely overlooked figure now, but Einstein's name continues to glow in the history of atomic research. Interestingly, Einstein denied being responsible for the actual release of atomic energy, and he was much distressed by the military uses to which his theories were applied. Moreover, he was concerned that Hitler would eventually press German scientists to develop an atomic bomb. It was therefore

Einstein to whom American physicists turned in 1939 after they had failed to convince America's military leaders of the need for an atomic project. The scientist agreed to send a letter to Franklin Roosevelt to describe the potential of atomic energy, and his position persuaded the President to launch America's project to build the atomic bomb before the enemy did. This was no easy decision, and Einstein's prestige may have been all-important. The Manhattan Project was a $4 billion risk at a time when America had not yet recovered from a deep depression.

The irony of a German-born Jew being responsible for the development of the atomic bomb in the United States during a world war with Germany has not been lost on observers. At the end of that war, the Americans discovered that the Nazis, incomprehensibly, had no atomic weapons. This glaring oversight has been largely credited to Hitler's anti-Semitism, for he had driven out many important Jewish physicists who could have been tapped to work on atomic weapons. In fact, Hitler called all physics "Jewish physics"* and disliked the field in general.

One of the Jewish physicists who fled Germany and worked on America's atomic research was a woman, Lise Meitner. She was born in Vienna and taught in Berlin until the Nazis came to power. In 1917, she had helped discover one of the radioactive elements and later proved the existence of others. During World War II she worked at the Los Alamos, New Mexico, atomic power development project, where she collaborated with the Nobel Prize winner Niels Bohr on his uranium fission theory. Bohr himself is part of the Jewish Connection; his mother was Jewish.

The entire Los Alamos project was under the di-

---

* In *The New Israelis*, David Schoenbrun writes that although people named Cohen—a totally Jewish name derived from the Hebrew *Kohain*, which means "priest"—number only "two out of every twenty-four thousand people in the world," Cohen is the name of "two out of every thousand physicists in the world." And that accounts only for Jews named Cohen!

rection of another Jew—Dr. J. Robert Oppenheimer, a physicist and the descendant of one of New York's first Jewish families. Secretary of War Stimson said of him, "The development of the atomic bomb has been largely due to Dr. Oppenheimer's genius and the leadership he has given his associates."

Among those associates were such Jewish refugee scientists as Dr. Otto Frisch, Professor Rudolf Peierls, Dr. Frank Simon in Britain, and one of the most important of all, Dr. Edward Teller. A Hungarian refugee who had done his graduate education in Germany, Teller had been forced to flee to Denmark. From 1939, while professor of physics at George Washington University, he was deeply involved in the United States' atomic research, working also on the Los Alamos project. In 1952, he headed America's project on the hydrogen bomb and has been given credit for its development. Another important figure in atomic research was the Hungarian-born Jew John von Neumann, a brilliant mathematician whose work was crucial to the efforts at Los Alamos.

While mankind has come to regret the destructive potential of the atom, it has also been seen as the key to many peaceful uses. Here too Jews have played a part. The first chairman of the U.S. Atomic Energy Commission, appointed in 1946, was David Lilienthal. The chairman of the American delegation to the United Nations Atomic Energy Commission, also appointed in 1946, was Bernard Baruch. The first person to turn atomic energy to nondestructive purposes was a Jew, Admiral Hyman Rickover. Known as the originator of America's nuclear fleet, Rickover successfully pressed for the use of atomic power in ships, and in 1952 the world's first atomic-powered submarine was built. And Leo Szilard, the Hungarian Jew who, with Enrico Fermi, made possible the first self-sustaining nuclear reactor in 1942, campaigned so energetically against the military use of atomic energy he was presented the Atoms for Peace Award in 1959.

Why such a connection between Jews and atomic energy? One reason is that, from the time of the medieval astronomers, Jews have exhibited a fascination with the material universe. Judaism emphasizes life on earth; the Hebrew scriptures barely refer to the afterlife, and the world is regarded as God's creation, to be explored and enjoyed by all. Also, atomic research is basically an intellectual pursuit and Jews are, by history and training, an education-oriented people. The most respected people in a Jewish community throughout the ages have been scholars. Education was pursued as the bond holding together not only families and communities, but a far-flung people, all of whom studied and treasured the same books.

But that can be only part of the explanation; intellectual interests do not guarantee intellectual success. The Jewish Connection in atomic research is more likely an indication that, as much as the Jewish personality is rooted in an allegiance to the past, the Jewish mind is oriented to the future. With no vested interest in preserving the status quo, Jews, especially Jews with brilliance, may very well find it easier than others to question old assumptions. Jewish physicists could seize on the idea of atomic power as a vast new energy source precisely because it looks to the future. The Jewish concept of messiah is also oriented to the future; it represents hope for a better world. Surely this outlook helped enable Jews to see that the world is round, that there could be new worlds, and that the pursuit of astronomy and navigation could open up great possibilities.

There is one other possible explanation for the Jewish Connection here: Jews just seem to have an uncanny knack for being where the world's action is. Consider two surprising facts about the dropping of the atomic bomb. A Jew, Lieutenant Jacob Beser of Baltimore, was on the atomic bomb missions to both Hiroshima and Nagasaki—the only times it was used for military purposes. He received the Distinguished Flying Cross. Ironically, when the atomic bomb was dropped on Nagasaki, overlooking "ground zero" from atop a hill was the cemetery that until the 1900s had served Nagasaki's Jewish community.

The Goldbergian Institute also offers extensive displays of the unusual ways in which Jews were involved in some of the most influential inventions of the twentieth century. Let's begin with the field of aviation.

Otto Lilienthal, a German Jew, is listed in *The Book of Firsts* as the man who made history's first series of controlled glider flights, using a 44-pound machine of his own design, with a wing area of 150 square feet. In the summer of 1892, in a suburb of Berlin, Lilienthal began his work with the glider by jumping off a high dirt mound formed by construction work on a canal. During the next four years Lilienthal made more than 2,000 powerless glider flights as he sought to develop theories on aerodynamics. People thought he was crazy, but he persisted in his efforts. By shifting his body to alter the center of gravity, he learned to control the glider enough to make brief, but successful, flights. He soon considered powering his flight with a motor. On August 10, 1896, just moments after telling a friend that "sacrifices must be made" if man were to learn to fly, a sudden wind made him lose control of the glider at a height of 25 feet, and he fell to his death.

Lilienthal's sacrifice did indeed help man to fly, for his death—as well as his life—inspired the Wright brothers. In an article that appeared in *Century Magazine* in September, 1908, Wilbur and Orville recalled that they had been interested in flying as boys, but had not pursued it. "It was not till the news of the sad death of Lilienthal reached America in the summer of 1896 that we again gave more than passing attention to the subject," they wrote. The brothers then began reading various studies on flying, concentrating on Lilienthal's theories and findings, especially those recorded in *The Problem of Flying and Practical Experiments in Soaring*. Noting some of the people who had worked on flying, the Wright brothers termed Lilienthal among the "great missionaries of the flying cause" and one who with his "unquenchable enthusiasm" had "infected us" and had "transformed idle curiosity into the active zeal of workers."

It is interesting to note that when the Wright brothers started to build one of their first airplanes in 1901 they proceeded, they wrote, "with the shape of surface used by Lilienthal."

Lilienthal's place in aviation history is so important that *The American Heritage History of Flight* says his influence "can hardly be overestimated. He was the first to demonstrate beyond question that, with or without power, the air could support a man in winged flight."

Our next museum exhibit is a model of a rigid airship or dirigible, of the kind made famous by the *Hindenburg*. We often call this aircraft a zeppelin, after Count Ferdinand von Zeppelin, but strictly speaking it should be called a schwarz, to honor its actual inventor.

The Austrian Jew David Schwarz was an engineer who in 1890 devised the idea for an airship with a gas-filled metal container to carry it aloft. He presented his plans to the minister of war of Austria, who turned the idea down for financial reasons. After Schwarz had constructed a prototype in Russia in 1892, his invention came to the attention of the German government, which sent him a telegram with the go-ahead to begin production. When Schwarz received the good news he did what any overjoyed inventor might do at such a moment: he dropped dead in the street from shock.

The German government proceeded anyway, with Schwarz's widow in charge of the construction. Count Zeppelin, a retired German army officer, became intrigued with Schwarz's ideas and eventually bought the patents from his widow. The contract of purchase has been placed in the archives of the Hebrew University in Jerusalem.

The Germans used Schwarz's airship idea in many ironic ways. Between 1910 and 1914 they carried passengers between several German cities—an innovation credited as the world's first airline. During World War I, Germany used the dirigible to carry out reconnaissance, supply its troops, and even drop bombs. Over fifty airship raids were made on England. In 1929, the *Graf Zeppelin* flew around the world. And the Nazis used the largest zeppelin of them all, the *Hindenburg*, for propaganda purposes.

Guglielmo Marconi is credited with being the inventor of radio, but his contribution could better be viewed as that of turning someone else's discovery of a physical principle into a commercially feasible instrument. For the truth is that radio waves were discovered by a German with a Jewish Connection whose work directly influenced Marconi.

Heinrich Rudolph Hertz was a scientist who in lab tests showed the way radio waves behave, based upon the known behavior of light. To carry out his work, he had to generate radio energy, transmit it, and detect it. To do this, he in effect invented radio. In fact, radio waves were first called "Hertzian waves" to honor him.

The Book of Firsts says: "Credit for making known the existence of radio waves must therefore be accorded to the German electrical scientist Heinrich Hertz, whose brilliant researches on the subject in

1887-9 paved the way for practical radio telegraphy and broadcasting."

Marconi, of course, was the one who made Hertz's work practical. But, just as the Wright brothers were inspired by the work of Lilienthal, Marconi developed his first serious interest in radio because of Hertz. According to Marconi's daughter, on a summer day in 1894 her father picked up an Italian electrical journal containing a piece about Hertz, who had died the first of that year. The article, wrote Marconi's daughter, was "about his [Hertz's] extraordinary work with electromagnetic waves. In Hertz's radiant discovery was the spark that lighted up everything young Marconi had been groping toward. If this was the turning point in my father's life, it was also, in a real sense, a turning point in the evolution of the world we know and take for granted."

Inspired by this magazine article, Marconi learned as much as he could about Hertz and Hertzian rays. In his first experiments, Marconi used, as he himself acknowledged in a speech years later, "a form of oscillator . . . which itself was a modification of Hertz's oscillator." A biography of Marconi acknowledges that Hertz's "contribution to the discovery of radio cannot be overestimated."

Indeed, the development of television also stems from Hertz's discoveries, and he would no doubt have gone on to even greater feats, for he was well on his way to discovering X-rays when he died at the age of thirty-seven.

There has been some question about Hertz's Jewishness, since he was the son of a baptized Jew. But the Nazis had no doubts about Hertz's origins. When Hitler came to power in Germany, universities were ordered to stop using the word "hertz" to label a unit of physical measurement.

When the word "phonograph" is mentioned, do you first think of Thomas Edison? Well, you really should think of Emile Berliner, because he is the man who developed the modern-day phonograph—along with the kind of records, recording studios, and record shops we have today.

Emile Berliner was brought to America from Germany by his parents at an early age and grew up in Washington, D.C. His father was a Talmudic scholar, but Emile was interested in science. While Edison was working out a type of phonograph that used a cylinder as a record, Berliner invented a machine that would play a disc. The machine he patented was called the gramophone, and the famous RCA trademark is a picture of a dog listening to "his master's voice" on Berliner's device.

The gramophone was superior to Edison's machine. Besides, Berliner saw the popular entertainment uses of a record player, while Edison did not. Edison saw the phonograph—which, by the way, was his favorite invention—as primarily for use in offices to record dictation. As a result of Berliner's foresight, his company grew to dominate the field. The Berliner Gramophone Company introduced the idea of paying royalties to singers and other artists for exclusive recording contracts, produced and placed on the market a low-priced record player, and made the first shellac records in 1897. In the same year it opened in Philadelphia the first commercial recording studio and the first record shop—in adjoining buildings, so that what the studio produced the shop could sell.

In short, Emile Berliner made possible the modern record industry. His company was eventually absorbed by the Victor Talking Machine Company, now known as RCA.

Although Berliner's name is not well known today, Berliner and his company were quite successful. Berliner had persuaded a mechanic in a bicycle repair shop to make a spring movement for his original gramophone, and later that man was made president of the Berliner Company. According to the personal secretary to Thomas Alva Edison, the former bicycle mechanic alone "amassed a fortune nearly ten times greater than the one accumulated by Edison during his whole career of inventive production."

Berliner also played an important role in the development of the telephone. In 1877, just one year after Alexander Graham Bell patented his invention, Berliner patented a device that made the telephone into the modern convenience we know today. He developed a carbon microphone transmitter that carried the human voice clearly and thereby increased dramatically the distances the telephone could cover. Bell's original telephone, using magnetic induction, reproduced the voice in weak undulating currents, and employed the same instrument for talking and listening. Berliner's transmitter introduced the concept of talking and listening in separate parts of the phone. Such a transmitter also became the basis for the modern microphone. You could say that Berliner, with his contributions to both the record industry and the microphone, invented the disc jockey.

Our next Goldbergian Institute display is a re-creation of Johann Philipp Reis exhibiting his telephone to scientists in Europe in 1861—fifteen years before Bell patented his. Reis, a German Jew, is listed in *The Book of Firsts* as number one to publicly demonstrate the telephone.

Reis's original model used "a violin case for a resonator, a hollowed-out beer-barrel bung for a mouthpiece, and a stretched sausage-skin for a diaphragm" in a crude attempt to copy the design of the human ear. He showed an improved model of this in a public demonstration before the Physical Society of Frankfurt on October 26, 1861, at which time he was able to transmit verses of a song over a three-hundred-foot line between the room he was in and a hospital. Says *The Book of Firsts*, "In view of modern tests made with Reis telephones under controlled conditions, it seems likely that they were capable of transmitting articulate speech spasmodically."

Reis's instrument could not reproduce varying degrees of loudness, and he was unable to develop his work further. A sickly man, born of poor parents, he had neither the stamina nor the means to commercialize his invention. He died in 1874 at the age of forty, but his work was well known by that time. Alexander Graham Bell knew of his work, was even shown a Reis machine transmitter, and gave credit to Reis for his ideas. So did others trying to perfect a telephone-type invention, including Edison, who tinkered with Reis's approach. In fact, inventors were so hot in pursuit of a telephone that in 1876 when Bell finally did apply for a patent for his telephone he beat another inventor by only hours.

After Bell's patent was granted, he was accused by many of having stolen the idea. When Bell sought a British patent, several letters to the *Times* charged him with thievery from Reis. An article in *Munsey's Magazine* in 1900, "The Romance of the Telephone," charged Bell and his company with having cheated Reis and two other inventors out of their claims to the telephone. The United States government under President Grover Cleveland even brought suit against Bell for, according to one biographer, "claiming the invention of something already widely known to exist in the form of the Reis 'telephone' and also with somehow concealing the existence of the latter from the Patent Office's expert examiner in that field."

On March 22, 1876, twelve days after Bell's first intelligible speech transmission, the *New York Times* ran an editorial entitled "The Telephone." It was not about Bell, but about Philipp Reis, whom the writer termed the reputed inventor of a "remarkable instrument." The writer obviously did not know about Bell.

Bell survived the lawsuits and the challenges, but Reis has a special place in the history of the telephone.

In Europe, he was recognized as its inventor, and a monument to his memory was built by physicists in 1878.

A Jew can also be found in the early history of the automobile—in fact, until the 1960s historians believed the gasoline-driven engine was invented by a Jew. German-born Siegfried Marcus was said to have patented in 1864 a motorcar powered by an internal-combustion engine that drove it at four to five miles per hour. That vehicle is still in perfect running condition today.

The Book of Firsts reveals that the correct date for Marcus's invention was 1888, three years after Karl Benz of Mannheim, Germany, built the first car successfully powered by a gasoline engine in 1885. But Marcus is still considered an important figure in the development of the automobile, and his contributions are credited in most histories of motoring.

Atomic energy, flight, broadcasting, recordings, communications, transportation—each is an integral part of the modern age; and, incredibly, each has been brought about by the help of Jews.

You may be asking yourself why so much of this Jewish involvement has been overlooked. Why do we know so well the names of the Wright brothers, Zeppelin, Edison, Marconi, and Bell, yet hear little about Lilienthal, Schwarz, Hertz, Berliner, and Reis?

One very mundane reason is that, in these cases at least, the Jewish innovators died early. Hertz died at thirty-seven, Reis at forty. Lilienthal was killed at the peak of his career, and Schwarz died before his work had really begun. Only Berliner lived a full life of seventy-eight years, and he was the only one who reaped financial rewards during his lifetime. Also, for the most part these were men of humble beginnings, without the means or connections to bring their work to full fruition. Although Edison, Marconi, and Bell were not heavily financed at first, their later circumstances were far more comfortable than those of their Jewish counterparts.

Since the days of the Bible, it seems that the lot of the Jew has been to make his contribution behind the scenes. Other nations have grown more prosperous and powerful; other religions have become more popular. But the Jewish people have helped those other nations and religions to grow and flower. The important thing is that the Jewish contribution is being made, the influence is being felt, and the Jewish people are making an impact far out of proportion to their numbers. (That's why new exhibits are constantly being added to the Goldbergian Institute.)

VI

It Just Seems
the Whole World Is Jewish

*How the Jewish Connection
can be found in so many people,
places . . . and even animals*

FACT: Adolf Hitler thought he was Jewish.

FACT: Rembrandt's contemporaries believed he was a Jew.

FACT: There once was a Jewish Pope.

FACT: A widely used automobile is named after a Jew.

FACT: The name of a German Jew can be found on the front pages of many of the world's newspapers—every day.

FACT: The American Indians were once thought to be descended from the Lost Ten Tribes of Israel—and evidence supporting this theory is still being cited today.

MARK TWAIN, SURVEYING the wide-ranging activity of Jews in his day, once cracked that there must be at least 25 million Jews living in America. Of course, at no time during Twain's life were there more than 2 million Jews in the country. Twain, generally friendly to Jews, was simply expressing a feeling shared by friend and foe alike—Jews just seem to be all over.

Jews seem to be unrestricted by limitations of space, time, or numbers. For instance, today in Israel 3 million Jews somehow manage to build lives for themselves, develop a modern technology, enjoy a smattering of luxuries, work hard six days a week, and at the same time maintain a modern army that can fend off 200 million Arabs. It's as if the state of Kentucky were to take on the rest of the United States—and beat it in four wars.

The Diaspora is at least partly responsible for this feeling that Jews are all over the place—in fact, the Jews *are* all over the place. Jewish congregations have been set up from the Arctic Circle (Greenland Air Force Base) to the southern tip of New Zealand's South Island, near Antarctica. A Jew has been called "father of the ballet": during the Renaissance, Guglielmo of Pesaro wrote the first known theoretical work in the field. Other Jews have held championships in every classification of professional boxing, from flyweight to heavyweight.

The Jew has been accused of many things, but never of being lazy. On the contrary, Hitler accused the Jews of doing too much, of trying to take over the world—which naturally upset the Nazis since they wanted to take over the world themselves.

As an example of how active Jews can be, consider

Dr. Hirsch Loeb Gordon, the first American to earn ten higher academic degrees—all through actual study. As told by Tina Levitan in *The Firsts of American Jewish History*, Gordon was born in 1896 in Vilna, Lithuania, came to America in 1915, and by 1917 was working on his first doctorate. He entered graduate school at Yale University that year and received a Ph.D. in Semitic languages and literature with highest honors in 1922. During the next twelve years, while holding teaching positions in history, archeology, philology, philosophy, and psychiatry, Gordon earned the following degrees: 1923, doctorate in Egyptology from Catholic University in Washington, D.C.; 1924, master's degree in diplomacy from the American University in Washington, D.C.; 1926, master's degree in educational psychology from Teachers College, Columbia University; 1927, master's degree in Religious Education from the Jewish Theological Seminary of America; 1928, doctorate in Hebrew Literature from the Seminary; 1928, master's degree in Fine Arts from New York University; 1931, doctorate with high honors in Classical Archeology from the University of Rome; and 1934, doctor of medicine and doctorate in natural science from the University of Rome.

Perhaps there seem to be more Jews than there are because Jews have shown a distinct propensity to be where things are happening. On the night of April 14, 1912, one young man was on duty at a New York wireless, and it was through him that the world first learned of the sinking of the *S.S. Titanic* and was kept informed throughout the entire tragedy. Rescue efforts were coordinated by means of this wireless, and Marconi cited its use as a major impetus to the commercial development of the radio. The young man who stayed on duty for seventy-two straight hours in the telegraph station at John Wanamaker's New York store was David Sarnoff, a Russian-born Jew, who later went on to head RCA and NBC.

Even the names of Jews are part of our lives in ways

we take for granted. You will find, for instance, a
Jew's name listed on the front pages of many of the
world's newspapers every day. The Reuter's News
Agency is the European counterpart of the American
Associated Press and United Press International wire
services, and each day newspapers all over the world
carry its dispatches. The company was founded by
Paul Julius Reuter (1816-1899), a German Jew who
launched his career in 1849 using homing pigeons. He
soon went to more sophisticated methods to speed the
news, and the agency received a big boost in 1858
when it relayed a speech by Napoleon III. Reuter was
eventually made a baron, and his name is now syn-
onymous with a great journalistic enterprise.

An automobile has made another Jewish name
world famous. The Citroën, one of France's most popular cars, is named for a Jew who was a pioneer in
France's automotive industry. Termed the "Henry
Ford of France," André-Gustave Citroën (1878-1935)
started as a bicycle manufacturer. During World War
I he produced munitions for the French government,
but at the war's end he turned to the mass production of automobiles. Within ten years, he was turning out a thousand cars a day.*

How many of today's dramatic actresses have been
compared with Sarah Bernhardt? She was considered
the greatest actress of her day, with a career that
spanned sixty years and earned her $25 million. Yet
few people realize that she was Jewish. Her real
name was Rosine Bernard and, although baptized
and raised as a Catholic, she was the illegitimate
daughter of a Jewish prostitute.

The Jewish Connection has been spread by the fact
that centuries of persecution have forced many Jews
to convert, either to save their lives or to escape discrimination. The result: a number of surprising people

---

* The largest name in history may have been that of a Jew. According
to the *Guinness Book of World Records*, the greatest advertising sign ever
erected was the name Citroën on the Eiffel Tower from 1925 to 1936. The
n alone was more than 68 feet high.

in history have had Jewish ancestry. Consider just two ironic examples. King Ferdinand of Spain, the Catholic king who expelled the Jews in 1492, had Jews in his ancestry. And, as hard as it is to believe, Torquemada, the Grand Inquisitor of Spain, also had Jewish ancestors.

During the Inquisition, many Marranos—the Jews who were forced to convert but maintained secret allegiance to Judaism—adopted careers in the Christian church, hoping to avoid detection. But this technique did not always work. At one auto-da-fé, the victims included priests, canons, curates, vicars-general, friars, nuns, and even an unfrocked Franciscan, whose monastic order contained the fiercest fighters of heresy. In Portugal, where the Inquisition was especially ruthless, from 1619 to 1627 the public executions condemned 231 persons—of whom 44 were nuns and 15 clergymen, and among them 7 canons.

Living under the Inquisition caused Jews to make some curious adjustments, as can be seen in the family of Manoel Pereira Coutinho, who had five daughters—all nuns in a convent in Lisbon—while in Hamburg his sons were living openly as Jews.

Many of those Jews who entered the Christian clergy were able to rise high in the Church; some even became bishops and cardinals. Juan Pérez de Montalván, a Marrano, was priest and notary of the Inquisition. The Society of Jesus founded by Saint Ignatius of Loyola had numerous monks of Jewish descent. When Saint Ignatius chose a successor to lead the order, he appointed Diego Lainez, who had been born a Jew.

The Inquisition and its forced conversions have given rise to one of the most intriguing speculations about a Jewish Connection: that concerning Christopher Columbus. The debate about Columbus's origins has raged for a number of years. Among those who have claimed that he was a Jew are at least half a dozen writers, most of them Spaniards trying to show Spanish blood in a man celebrated as Italian. They explain that he was really a Spanish Jew who had to keep his heritage secret because of the Spanish Inquisition. Talk about irony!

The most comprehensive work on Columbus's Jewishness is by a former Spanish Ambassador to the United States and France, Salvador de Madariaga. In a five-hundred-page book first published in 1940 and reprinted in 1967 (with replies to several critics of his theory, such as Professor Samuel Eliot Morison), de Madariaga presents the thesis that Columbus was a Marrano born of Spanish parents who had emigrated to Italy.

The official view of history has been that Columbus was born of an ordinary Catholic family of weavers in Genoa, Italy. But he himself never stated that he was a Genoan and—in 1497—even fought against Genoa at Cape St. Vincent. Also, he used Spanish in virtually all of the voluminous material he wrote, and there is no evidence he ever wrote in Italian. Indeed, Columbus's origins are a mystery that he himself seemed to have wanted to keep—a survival technique common among the Marrano Jews of the day. But consider some of the facts that we do know.

His real name was not Columbus—in fact, he was never called Columbus during his lifetime! His family name was Colon, which was common among Jews. The leading rabbi in Italy in the fifteenth century, for instance, was Joseph Colon (c.1420–1480).

Columbus's actions showed he had an affinity for Jews. In the opening of his journal on his expedition, he refers to the expulsion of Jews from Spain as though it were uppermost in his mind. He delayed the start of his voyage by one day until August 3, 1492, even though his ships were manned and ready to sail. The previous day was the ninth of Av, the fast day marking the destruction of the Temples and therefore, for Jews, an unpropitious day to launch an important undertaking.

His signature is a strange one and it has been given a Hebraic interpretation. Mysteriously, he charged his

son always to use this type of signature. In his letters
and documents, Columbus refers to Jewish concerns
and makes numerous references to ancient Jewish history, even once reckoning chronology by using the
Jewish and not the Christian approach.* He refers to
the Second Temple by the Hebraic term, "Second
House," and in one of his letters declares, "I am
not the first admiral of my family. I let them give me
what name they please; for when all is done, David
the most prudent king, is first a shepherd and after-
wards chosen King of Jerusalem and I am a servant
of that same Lord who raised him to such a dignity."

Jews were so involved in the funding of Columbus's
voyage that one historian, Professor Herbert B.
Adams, has noted that "not jewels, but Jews, were the
real financial basis of the first expedition." Columbus had to plead and bargain with the Spanish king
and queen over a period of seven years before being
allowed to conduct his voyage on his own terms. Instrumental in getting final agreement from the monarchs, who balked at spending the money, was Luis
de Santangel, the chancellor of the royal household,
a Marrano who said that he would lend the necessary
funds for Columbus. At the fateful meeting at which
Santangel convinced Ferdinand and Isabella to permit
the voyage were two other Marranos, who also supported Columbus—Gabriel Sanchez, the chief treasurer of Aragon, and Juan Cabrero, the king's cham-
berlain. The only high official intimately concerned
with Columbus's expedition who wasn't Jewish was
the royal secretary—and his wife was Jewish.

Santangel, according to account books preserved in
the Spanish archives, advanced 1,400,000 maravedis
to the Bishop of Avila for the voyage. Santangel at
the time was treasurer of a secret fraternity called
the Holy Brotherhood, and it was from this group
that he was able to secure the money. On May 5,

---

* When the Jewish historian Cecil Roth met de Madariaga in a library
one day and pointed out this fact to him, de Madariaga said, "That
clinches it."

1492, Santangel was reimbursed with 1,140,000 mara-vedis for the money "which he advanced to equip the caravels ordered by their majesties for the expedition" and to pay Christopher Columbus, "the Admiral of the fleet." A year later, May 20, 1493, the treasurer, Gabriel Sanchez, paid 30,000 gold florins to San-tangel on the money still owed for his loan.

For this reason, Columbus's first letters after his discovery were addressed not to the king and queen but to the two Jews, Santangel and Sanchez.

Speculation about the number of Jews sailing with Columbus has ranged from one to "a large number." But since Jews were being expelled from Spain at the time Columbus was enlisting a crew, it is possible that Marranos considered the voyage less hazardous than staying home. Of the 120 men on Columbus's three ships on the first voyage, 5 crew members are generally identified as Jews: Rodrego Sanchez of Se-govia, a relative of Gabriel Sanchez who was prob-ably sent along to oversee the investment; Alonzo or Alfonze de la Calle, whose last name was derived from the "Jews' lane," the name given to the Jewish quarter of Spanish cities; Maestro Bernal, ship's sur-geon; Rodrego de Triana, a sailor; Marco, a cook; and Luis de Torres, an expert in numerous languages, especially Hebrew and Arabic, who was a Marrano baptized shortly before the voyage.

Of course, the involvement of Jews in Columbus's voyage does not mean that Columbus himself was a Jew. But it does underscore that tendency of Jews somehow to be present even if only behind the scenes, in history's most important events.

Still the debate rages: was Columbus a Jew? His son, Ferdinand, once said cryptically that Columbus's "progenitors were of the blood royal of Jerusalem, and it pleased him that his parents shall not be much known." When Columbus died, a strange bequest was found in his will: "half a silver mark to a Jew who usually stands at the entrance to the Ghetto of Lisbon, or to another who may be named by a priest."

The executive editor of the *Encyclopaedia Judaica*, Dr. Frederick Lachman, wrote in 1975 that a recently discovered document "makes it almost certain that Columbus belonged to a Marrano family of Majorcan origin." He notes, however, that the "authenticity of this document has still to be proved." Dr. Lachman feels that, in light of this, the debate over Columbus's origins is still to be resolved, but the issue is very much alive: "The hypothesis that he was descended from a Jewish or formerly Jewish family cannot be confirmed, but neither can it be denied."

While many speculate as to whether Columbus was a Jew or not, there is another figure from history who himself wondered if he was Jewish: Adolf Hitler.

This bizarre twist emanates from the fact that Hitler's father was illegitimate, and the identity of Hitler's grandfather has never been established. Since Hitler made such an issue of everyone else's ancestry, it surely must have crossed his mind that his own family tree could come to haunt him. And haunt him it did, for he had reason to fear that his father's father was a Jew.

During Hitler's rise, his half-brother's son supposedly threatened in a letter to divulge Hitler's Jewish ancestry. Toward the end of 1930, Hitler asked Hans Frank, who was at the time serving as lawyer to Hitler's political party, to investigate the basis for the threat. Frank, who became the Governor General of Poland when it was taken over by the Nazis, reported as part of his confession at Nuremberg that, when he looked into the matter, he was able to substantiate that Hitler's grandfather was Jewish. He said he discovered that Hitler's grandfather had been the son of a Jewish family called Frankenburger, living in Gratz, who had employed Hitler's grandmother as a maid. Frank said that he uncovered letters written by the Jewish family to Hitler's grandmother, Maria Anna Schicklgruber, who had become pregnant by the son, then nineteen, while working in their home, and that the family made regular payments to her during the first fourteen years of her child's life to help support him.

Lucy Dawidowicz, in *The War Against the Jews*, also relates this story, but discounts it since an investigation after the war showed that no Jews had been living in the area where Maria Schicklgruber was working as a domestic.

But the plot thickens. Dr. Walter C. Langer, in his secret psychological report on Hitler done in the 1940s for the United States government, writes that Austrian police had "proved" that Maria Anna Schicklgruber was "living in Vienna at the time she conceived." This, of course, conflicts with Frank's statement, which placed the investigation in Gratz. However, Langer says—and here the story really becomes incredible— Hitler's grandmother was employed in Vienna as a servant in the home of Baron Rothschild. Although this could have meant that the maid was seduced by a butler, gardener, or guest, in Hitler's fiery imagination the seducer would have been a Rothschild. Langer's own insight into this subject may be clouded, because he also matter-of-factly states that Adolf Hitler had a Jewish godfather, a man by the name of Prinz, in Vienna, and this is disputed in the Afterword to Langer's report by Robert Waite.

While the accuracy of these facts is in doubt, one thing is clear: Hitler was concerned about who his grandfather was and initiated searches to find out. According to Langer, Hitler knew of a study that had been made by the Austrian police and tried to get the incriminating evidence. But Austrian Chancellor Dollfuss had hidden the report, so Hitler never found it.

Robert Waite puts the whole issue into stark perspective in his Afterword, saying, "The point of overriding psychological and historical importance is not whether it is true that Hitler had a Jewish grandfather; but whether he *believed* that it might be true. He did so believe, and that fact shaped both his personality and his public policy."

The delicious irony in this story is that because
Jewish law states the religion of the mother deter-
mines the religion of the child Hitler was not Jewish.
But according to Hitler's own perverted racial con-
cepts, which searched back through generations for
Jewish ancestors, he would have been tainted with
Jewish blood.

History records yet another incredible case of an
important figure with Jewish ancestry, and there is
no question about this Jewish Connection. Let's turn
our attention to the Jewish Pope.

Anacletus II was elected Pope in 1130, but to find
his Jewish Connection we must go back a few generations. The great-grandfather of Anacletus II was Baruch, a successful Jewish businessman who lived in
the Jewish quarter of Rome, where his contributions
maintained a synagogue. He also served as an adviser,
financier, and steward to Pope Benedict IX. Informed
by the Pope that to continue their business relationship he would have to convert, Baruch eventually
agreed, taking as his Christian name that of the Pope,
so that Baruch became Benedict.* But Benedict-Baruch
continued to associate with the synagogue he funded
and was still known as Baruch, so his conversion was
obviously more commercial than religious.

Benedict-Baruch's son served as steward to another
Pope, Leo IX, and as his father had done, converted
and took the name of the Pope, becoming known as
Leo.

It was Leo's son, Petrus Leonis, who first used the
name Pierleone. By the late eleventh century, the
Pierleone family, which has been termed "the Rothschilds of the Middle Ages," had become a force in the
financial world of Rome. Naturally, having acquired
power, they soon wanted more. And, since power in

---

* In a sense, Baruch did not really change his name. Benedict, which in
Latin means "blessed," is the Latin version of Baruch, which in Hebrew
means the same thing.

that day was in the hands of the Pope, they took an active interest in the affairs and politics of the Church. Young Pietro, one of Petrus Leonis' sons, was enrolled in the monastery at Cluny to study for a career in the Church. Over the years, he worked his way up to the position of cardinal.

Then came the time when Pope Honorius II (1124-1130) was about to die and a new Pope had to be chosen. The Pierleone family, of course, advanced the name of their very own cardinal, Pietro. Another family also influential in Church affairs—the Frangipani, an old-line Christian family—also offered a candidate. The rivalry became so heated that the Frangipani spirited the Pope away, waited until he died, and, in a hurried rump convention of only a segment of the cardinals, elected their own man, who adopted the name Innocent II. The Pierleone supporters among the cardinals, incensed at the quick election, held an election that same day with a greater number of cardinals present and elected Pierleone, who took the name Anacletus II (Anacletus I had been the name used by the third Pope, 76-88, who was later named a saint).

What then took place is revealing. The nobility and populace in Rome sided with Anacletus, and Innocent II found it wise to leave for France. From there and in tours to other parts of Europe, Innocent II strenuously worked to enlist support for his claim to the papacy, accusing Anacletus of being an "anti-pope."

Anacletus, meanwhile, succeeded in enlisting support from Roman nobles, the Duke of Aquitania and Roger of Sicily (who was Anacletus's brother-in-law). The fact that he was firmly entrenched in Rome while Innocent was touring Europe gave him an advantage. Still, as the years passed, the arguments grew so heated that eventually each Pope excommunicated the other.

One important element in the continuing struggle was Anacletus's Jewish ancestry, which, when it became known, aroused the ire of the Christian world outside Rome. Dr. Louis Newman, in *Jewish Influence on Christian Reform Movements*, says, "It is undubitable that the burden of accusation against Anacletus lay in his Jewish descent. If so recent a writer as Voltaire could not forgive him his Jewish ancestry, how much the less his contemporary opponents."

Innocent II found his greatest supporter to be Bernard of Clairvaux, who, while opposed to persecution of Jews, declared that it was "to the shame of Christ that a Jewish offspring had come to occupy the chair of Saint Peter"—forgetting, of course, that Peter himself had been born a Jew.

The opposition to Anacletus denounced his family's Jewish characteristics. One writer noted that "the antipope preserved the Jewish type of face" and that one of the Pierleone family was "a young man of dark but pallid complexion, who looked more like a Jew or a Saracen than a Christian." Others claimed that the family had practiced usury and had bribed Roman nobles to support Anacletus's claim to the papacy.

Bernard of Clairvaux, while noting that "the life and character of our Pope Innocent are above any attack even of his rival," charged that "the character of Anacletus is not safe even from his friends." Furthermore, Bernard pointed out that "if what is commonly said of Anacletus be true, he is not fit to have the government of a single hamlet."

In spite of all the scandalous charges made against him, Anacletus II ruled as Pope in Rome for the rest of his life; he died in his sleep in 1138. Innocent II then returned to Rome and successfully overcame another challenge (by a Pope who called himself Victor IV and ruled less than a year). Innocent ruled as the unquestioned Pope for five years, until his death. However, he is listed in papel history as Pope from the day on which he and Anacletus were both elected in 1130 until his death in 1143. Anacletus II is mentioned as an antipope.

The New Catholic Encyclopedia, in discussing the

term "antipope" ("one who uncanonically claims or exercises the office of Roman pontiff"), notes that "historically, this situation has occurred as the result of various causes, not all of which imply bad faith." To illustrate some of the ways antipopes have arisen, the encyclopedia lists "double election (Anacletus II, Innocent II, 1130)." Altogether, according to the encyclopedia, there have been thirty-seven antipopes. As for the legitimacy of Anacletus's claim, *The New Catholic Encyclopedia* states: "The double election of February 14, 1130, is so difficult to appraise that the historian cannot say whether from 1130 to 1138 legitimacy lay with Innocent II (1130-43) or with his rival Anacletus II (1130-38) and his successor Victor IV (1138), although Victor's resignation May 29, 1138, either gave or confirmed Innocent's canonicity thereafter."

In a fascinating book on the Pierleone family entitled *Popes from the Ghetto*, Dr. Joachim Prinz, who spent thirty years researching the subject, presents astonishing evidence that, besides Anacletus, two other popes were members of the Jewish Pierleone family: Gregory VI (1045-46) and his disciple and close relative Gregory VII (1073-85). Known also as Hildebrand, this Pope was descended from a daughter of Leo, the son of the founding father of the Pierleones.

There is one final irony. Gregory VII, a brilliant proponent of the supremacy of the office of Pope, was later made a saint. Which means there has been not only a Jewish pope, but a Jewish saint.

The most pervasive Jewish Connection—and the one that makes one wonder about just how Jewish is everybody—involves the many legends surrounding the Lost Ten Tribes of Israel.

The story of what happened to ten of the twelve tribes of Israel is a bona fide mystery. These ten constituted the Northern Kingdom of Israel, which, in a series of wars and political intrigues with Assyria in 745-705 B.C.E., were expelled or carried into captivity and dispersed through other parts of the Assyrian empire. The Jews remaining in Israel lost contact with these uprooted Jews, and in the ensuing years they seemed to vanish without a trace. What remains to-day of the Jewish nation is descended from the two tribes that constituted the Southern Kingdom of Israel.

Speculation about what happened to those Lost Ten Tribes has been rampant, at first only among Jews, then—because of the Christian concept that Jews must be spread throughout the world before the Second Coming could take place—among Christians as well.

Several countries supposedly have been inhabited by descendants of one, if not all, of the lost tribes. Many believe, for instance, that the American Indian was descended from them. In the early days of Amer-ica, James Adair wrote *History of the North American Indians*—and on every page was the heading: "On the Descent of the American Indians from the Jews."

John Eliot, a missionary who preached the gospel to Indians, wrote in 1649 to Reverend Thomas Thorowgood in England that the American Indians were descendants of the Lost Ten Tribes of Israel. Thorowgood then wrote in 1650 a book published in England entitled *Jews in America, or Probabilities that the Americans are of that Race, With the removal of some contrary reasoning, and earnest desires for ef-fectual endeavors to make them Christians.* Among other early American leaders who shared this belief were Cotton Mather, Roger Williams, and William Penn.

Some of the facts used over the years to support this contention have been that the Indians are sepa-rated into different tribes similar to the Lost Ten Tribes, that they have many dialects, but one basic language, and that that language, as Ethan Smith writing in 1823 said, "appears clearly spoken Hebrew, because both languages have no prepositions and are formed with prefixes and suffixes."

One Indian group in particular has been cited for its remarkable connections with the Jews. This is the Yuchi tribe, which lived in Georgia until 1836, when they were forcibly resettled in Oklahoma. The Yuchi are physically and linguistically different from other tribes, and many of their cultural habits parallel Jewish practices. They celebrate a festival very similar to that of the Jewish Feast of Tabernacles, or Succoth, in which they live in booths for eight days with roofs open to the sky and covered only by foliage and branches. The Yuchi tribesmen, again like the Jews during Succoth, carry long branches and conduct a procession in which the branches are shaken. Wedding and marriage practices also show parallels. The Yuchi women, for instance, are isolated from their husbands during their menstrual periods. An item in *Newsweek* magazine of June 9, 1975, notes that "some specialists in American Indian folklore think the customs, language, and appearance of the Yuchi, an old Georgia tribe, imply an old Jewish heritage." The article goes on to say that "stone inscriptions unearthed in Tennessee and Georgia have been cited as evidence that the Hebrews journeyed to America from Palestine perhaps 3,000 years ago."

Other evidence of this early Jewish Connection between the New World and the Old comes from a Colombian doctor of theology, Father Miguel Santa María Puerta, who, based on thirty years of research, claims that America was discovered thousands of years ago by the Jews, probably sailing under King Solomon. He also states that the Chibchas Indians, who built up two rival states in Colombia, are descendants of Jews. To prove this, he has found Hebraic elements in their language in the names of villages and plants.

Not long ago Father Miguel came up with some new proof for his claims. An article in the July 7, 1974, issue of a European magazine, *To The Point International*, relates how the Father discovered an earthenware jar of the kind used by Jews in ancient times to keep letters and important documents. Although many of these have been found in the Middle East, this is the first to be discovered in South America. Father Miguel's jar has a three-word Hebraic inscription and is similar to those uncovered in Beersheba, Israel. It comes from the small village of Chivata. Father Miguel says this is derived from the words "Shivat Zion," which come from the 126th Psalm telling of "returners to Zion."

One jar, of course, does not make a history. The jar could have been transported from the Middle East by a later traveler. But Father Miguel has other evidence. Letters chiseled in a stone discovered in the late 1960s in southern Colombia are Hebrew, and since then Father Miguel has also found ten huge stones engraved with Hebrew letters and words. The tip of one stone, according to the magazine article, shows clearly the word "Lev" (heart) as well as twenty-two other Hebraic letters. It was this last discovery that, according to the magazine, "has brought credibility and interest to Father Miguel's theories."

Another country whose inhabitants have been the subject of lost-tribe speculation is England—which was, ironically, the first nation to expel the two tribes of Israel. *The World's Most Intriguing True Mysteries* includes a whole chapter on "British Israel." The speculation in it is half-hearted and, in the end, deflated. However, this undoubtedly won't be the last discussion of the subject, for nearby Ireland has also been mentioned as a possible resting place for the Lost Ten Tribes.

Japan is yet another country where the lost tribes are said to have settled. This is the belief of a Japanese organization, called the Makuya Society (*Makuya* means "tabernacle"), whose members believe that the Japanese are descended, in part at least, from the Lost Ten Tribes. The society, founded by the late Professor Abraham Ikuro Teshima in the 1940s, has a strong feeling for Israel. Its members visit Israel, work in kibbutzim, and show their friendship for

Israel in other ways. Following the actions of the Japanese terrorists in the Lod Airport Massacre, the society presented an ambulance to the airport as a gesture of sympathy. Although those in this society do not consider themselves Jews, they revere the Jewish scriptures as well as the Christian, believing that "without Israel we would have neither redemption nor salvation."

Among the many other peoples believed by themselves or others to be from the lost tribes are the Armenians,* Mohammedan Berbers of West Africa, the six million Christian Ibo of Nigeria, and the tribesmen of Afghanistan. This last group follows a number of ancient biblical customs. Native chronicles refer to them as "Beni Israel." Ironically, such a belief has not stopped the Afghans from discriminating against the Jews living in their country.

Some Jewish communities are exotic reminders of the vast reach of the Diaspora. Such are the mountain Jews who live in remote villages and rocky ledges in the Caucasus or in the areas surrounding the western shore of the Caspian Sea. These Jews claim origins going back to the destruction of the First Temple. In India there exists a group numbering ten thousand who call themselves "Bene-Israel" (Sons of Israel). Living in the Bombay area, wearing Indian clothes, and speaking the country's vernacular language, they claim descent from Jews who fled from Judea before the Maccabean revolt in 175 B.C.E. and journeyed by sea to India.

Borrowing from the caste system of its "host" country, the Jewish community is broken into two classes, one that is labeled white and regards itself as the real Bene-Israel. The other, the black group, is considered inferior.

Another group in India, the Jews of Cochin, also

---

* "The tradition of a Jewish origin in both the religious and racial composition of Armenia had long existed; the Lost Ten Tribes were supposed to have found residence there."—*The Jewish Influence on Christian Reform Movements.*

follows the caste system. Even though there are only about a thousand such Jews, they have three castes: the superior, which is called white; the middle, which is called brown; and the lower, which is called black.

Jews have even lived in the Sahara as cave dwellers. According to the *Pictorial History of the Jewish People*, their settlements could be found in the stony ranges that form part of the Atlas Mountains in North Africa. Some of them inhabited caves in mountain summits; most lived "in a series of crater holes or stone labyrinths that are common in this volcanic region." Now resettled in Israel, they believe they are descended from captives brought from Judea to the Atlas Mountains by Titus after the destruction of the Second Temple.

Probably most fascinating of all are the Falashas or Black Jews of Ethiopia.* Their origins are obscure. They themselves believe they are descended from Jews who came to Ethiopia three thousand years ago from Jerusalem and were, in turn, descendants of the Queen of Sheba and King Solomon. Although they are black, they think of themselves entirely as Jews. They call themselves "Beta-Israel" (House of Israel), and even the name Falasha, which means "emigrant" in Ethiopic, is symbolic of their outside origins. Estimates about the size of this group have ranged from as high as half a million by an eighteenth-century British explorer, to missionary reports of the nineteenth century estimating their number at 200,000, to recent estimates of 20,000.

And then there are the stories of converts to Judaism. In Russia during the fifteenth century many nobles and Christian priests became Jews in a religious movement that swept the country. The movement was

---

* Not to be confused with the Falashas are the small groups of blacks in America who have been attracted to Judaism, with a number of them undergoing proper conversion. A black Jew serves on the staff of the Lubavitcher rabbi and another, an ordained rabbi, is listed as lecturer by the Jewish Welfare Board.

called the "Jewish Heresy." And there is the case of the Khazars, a powerful Turkish tribe living in southern Russia. This warlike tribe, when told to adopt a religion around the year 740, is purported to have investigated Judaism, Christianity, and Islam before becoming Jews. The Jewish Kingdom of the Khazars lasted until approximately the middle of the thirteenth century.*

Finally, there are the cases in which non-Jews have acted so much like Jews that it makes you wonder who they really are. Lincoln Steffens, the original investigative reporter in American journalism, became intrigued with Judaism in his early days on a New York newspaper. He frequented the Jewish area of New York, had a *mezuza* nailed to his office door, went from synagogue to synagogue on the high holidays, and even fasted on Yom Kippur.

A similar example involves one of the greatest artists of all times. Rembrandt was christened and raised as a Protestant, but he was so friendly with Jews that some people thought he was Jewish. He bought a house and lived in the Jewish quarter of Amsterdam, used Jews as models for many of his paintings, had numerous Jewish friends, painted many portraits of Jews (thirty-seven out of his two hundred portraits of males are of Jews), and painted many scenes from the Jewish scriptures.** When Rembrandt fell on hard times in his later years and became bankrupt, he was given both spiritual and material help by a rabbi.

The feeling that everybody has a Jewish Connection—certainly an ironic feeling in view of the small number of Jews in the world—is caused even by nonhumans. I respectfully call your attention to a column by Ann Landers that appeared in newspapers across the country during September of 1973. Ann Landers

---

* One of the Byzantine emperors was known as Leo the Khazar because his mother came from this tribe.

** Among Rembrandt's paintings of Jewish subject matter was "Woman Cutting Her Nails," showing part of a woman's preparation for the *mikvah*, the religious ritual bath.

(who is, of course, Jewish) printed a letter from one of her readers about an English Setter named Leviticus who kept kosher! The dog had lived in a Jewish household for his first four months before coming to the letter writer. "Not only did the dog refuse to eat meat that wasn't kosher," the writer explained, "but we had to put a Yiddish newspaper under the bowl. We tried both the *Chicago Sun-Times* and the *Wall Street Journal*, but Leviticus couldn't be fooled." The letter was signed "Right Hand Up."

Ann Landers responded by citing a newspaper item published in the Toronto *Star* about a kosher cat. The cat, owned by Rabbi Lewis Farrell, seemed to know the Jewish dietary laws because, according to the newspaper item, "he refused to drink milk when meat was served." Ann Landers went on to relate that "frequently, the kosher cat demonstrated his dedication to the dietary law for guests—to their utter amazement."

Of course, there's a simple explanation for the kosher cat and dog. It's the same thing that was responsible for Rembrandt's Jewish life style, the Jewish Pope, the stories about American Indians as Jews, Hitler's grandfather, Columbus's mother, and the lost Jews said to be roaming through nearly everyone's ancestry. As Jimmy Durante used to say, "Everybody wants to get into the act!" Perhaps that says a lot about the Jewish Connection.

VII

The Book of the
People of the Book

*The Bible as the
major ingredient in the
Jewish Connection*

FACT: The Bible has been translated into over one thousand languages.

FACT: The first book of importance published in America was the Book of Psalms, which is now so rare it has brought $151,000 at an auction.

FACT: The Red Sea is never mentioned in the Bible.

FACT: One Bible group has distributed 900 million Bibles.

FACT: Such expressions as "sour grapes," "fly in the ointment," and "stumbling block" come from the Bible.

FACT: One Hebrew word is now used almost universally. *amen*

FACT: The Congress of the United States once officially endorsed the printing of a Bible—and urged Americans to buy it.

WE ALL WINCE WHEN we're subjected to a speech or piece of writing that is studded with clichés. We tend to forget that these tired expressions were once bright, witty, apt, or succinct ways of saying something and that they became clichés precisely because they communicated an idea so quickly. Once one person said them other people began using them, and so they spread until all their original brilliance was worn away.

As any word buff knows, many clichés have come to us from Shakespeare and the Bible.* In other words, there is a strong Jewish Connection in our everyday speech!

What better way, for instance, is there to describe the sensation of eating a peanut-butter sandwich than to say, "This stuff sticks to *the roof of my mouth*." This cliché occurs twice in the Jewish scriptures. In Job 29:10 is the statement: "The voice of the nobles was hushed, and their tongue cleaved to the *roof of their mouth*." And in Psalms 137:6: "Let my tongue cleave to the *roof of my mouth*, If I remember thee not; If I set not Jerusalem above my chiefest joy."

There are dozens of other biblical phrases in everyday use. Here are just a few examples:

From Job: "But ye should say, why persecute him seeing *the root of the matter* is found in me?" (19:28).

From Ecclesiastes: "Dead flies cause the ointment ..." (10:1). Hence, *fly in the ointment*.

From Jeremiah, a double-barreled passage: "The

---

* Shakespeare, though, drew so heavily upon the scriptures that Emerson said of him, "Shakespeare leans upon the Bible."

fathers have eaten a *sour grape*, and the children's *teeth are set on edge*" (31:29).

From Isaiah: "Hark, thy watchmen! They lift up the voice, Together do they sing; For they shall see, *eye to eye*, The Lord returning to Zion" (52:8).

When a man tells his woman that for her he will go "to the ends of the earth," he is just repeating what the Book of Psalms said long ago: "All the ends of the earth have seen the salvation of our God" (98:3). And when he tells her she is "the apple of his eye" he is really echoing the turn of phrase found in Deuteronomy: "He kept him as the apple of his eye" (32:10).

New parents are invariably advised not to "spare the rod and spoil the child." That saying comes not from Dr. Spock, but from Proverbs: "He that spareth his rod hateth his son; but he that loveth him chasteneth him betimes" (13:24). "Out of the mouth of babes" is another expression found in Psalms (8:3).

One can find all sorts of ready-made advice in the Book of Ecclesiastes: "a living dog is better than a dead lion" (9.4) and "eat, drink, and be merry" (8:15).

Individual words, as well as phrases, have their Jewish Connections:

"Scapegoat" was first used in Leviticus 16:10 to describe the goat used in the Yom Kippur service during the days of the Temple, when the High Priest would symbolically place the sins of the congregation upon the head of a goat and then send it into the wilderness to certain death. The goat, carrying away the people's wrongs, was a scapegoat.

"Jubilee" was the name used in the Torah to describe the one year in fifty when the Land of Israel was to lie fallow, debts forgotten, and indentured servants freed—so that both fields and people could have a new beginning. The references to Jubilee can be found in Leviticus 25:11-34, 39-54 and in 27:17-24.

"Shibboleth," which is defined in the dictionary as "any test word or password," is derived from the story told in Judges 12:1-6. The word was used by the Gileadites to identify the escaping Ephraimites, who could not pronounce the "sh" sound.

A "Jezebel" is, according to Webster, "any woman regarded as shameless, wicked, etc." The word derives from the wicked woman who married Ahab, king of Israel; she is mentioned in I Kings 16,19 and II Kings 9:7-10, 30-37.

"Satan" has come to mean the Devil in Christian theology, but in Hebrew the word means "enemy" or "adversary." It is used, among other places, in Job, but ironically, not in the five books of Moses.

You could conduct an entire, if somewhat erratic, conversation with quotes of Jewish origin:

"Why aren't you working?" asks your mother-in-law. "You want to live off *the fat of the land?*" (Genesis 45:18)

"Not quite, Mother," you reply. "I'm relaxing after passing my last exam by *the skin of my teeth.*" (Job 19:20)

"Well, you should take my advice about your career instead of acting *holier than thou.*" (Isaiah 65:5)

"Mother, please. I try to take your advice. After all, you've been giving it to me since I married Esmerelda. But I am just one of those people who have to think about things for a while. *The race is not to the swift.*" (Ecclesiastes 9:11)

"Just listen to me. Analyze yourself and then *set your house in order.*" (II Kings 20:1)

"That's what I keep telling your daughter. Look, I just can't do things off *the top of the head.*" (Deuteronomy 28:35 and 33:16)

"I don't know about you. You've got to be more aggressive in this world. You probably think *the meek shall inherit the earth.*" (Psalms 37:11)

"Not since I married into your family. Look, Mother, I have ideas for my future. I'm going to be a success, you'll see. I'm not going to let anything be a *stumbling block.*" (Isaiah 8:14)

"I'm glad to hear you say that. You're a good boy.

I always knew that, no matter what your father-in-law always used to say—you know, *can the leopard change his spots?*" (Jeremiah 13:23)

"Don't you have some shopping to do? This conversation is getting to be *the bitter end.*" (Proverbs 5:4)

"All right, I'll leave you alone. But if you don't find a job soon, I'll never be at peace. I just know I'll never live to a *good old age.*" (Judges 8:32)

"Amen!" (appears fourteen times in the Jewish scriptures).*

Ironically, the Christians have done the most to spread the words of the Hebrew Bible, for the vast majority of Bibles printed by Christians include the Hebrew Bible (referred to by Christians as the Old Testament), either by itself or bound with the Christian scriptures (called the New Testament). And, since the Hebrew Bible is much longer, the Jews have gotten more than equal time in all Bible printing. Even the first edition of the King James Bible, published in 1611, has a title-page illustration showing the crests of the twelve tribes of Israel, Moses with the Ten Commandments, Aaron dressed as the High Priest, and the name of God in Hebrew.

In the annals of the written word, there has been no success story like that of the Bible. Between 1800 and 1950, one and a half billion copies of the Bible were sold, and year after year, millions more are purchased. The Bible has been the top best-seller of all books published, topping even that perennial group of sales leaders—cookbooks. The American Bible Society alone has distributed 900 million Bibles and parts of Bibles since its founding in 1816. As P. Marion Simms, the Bible historian, has pointed out, "The vast majority of all the books that have ever been published has been Bibles."

---

* "Amen," Hebrew for "so be it," is used not only by Jews, but by Christians and Moslems as well; hence it has become nearly universal. The word is first used in Numbers 5:22.

Note that the first book selected to be printed in movable type by Johann Gutenberg was the Bible.

Note, too, that the first book of importance printed in North America in English was the Book of Psalms.* Known as the *Bay Psalm Book* and translated straight from the original Hebrew, this work, published in 1640 in an edition of 1,700 copies, is now comparable in value to the Gutenberg Bible. With only four copies known to exist, a *Bay Psalm Book* auctioned in New York in 1948 fetched $151,000.

Not only has the Bible been the first book to be printed in many countries, but in several cases the Bible was the first book to be printed in a language. As of today, the Bible has been translated into over 1,000 languages**—including, since the early settlers tried to convert the native populace, various American Indian dialects, such as Chippewa, Algonquin, Cree, and Micmac. In fact, the translation of the Bible into Mohawk in 1663 by John Eliot was the first Bible to be printed in America (the 600-page volume devoted 464 leaves to the Jewish canon, only 126 to the Christian).

In addition, there have been such oddities as the "Thumb Bible,"† and the specialized Bibles, such as those done in Braille. One of the most interesting of the specialized editions was the Soldiers' Bible. Oliver Cromwell, the Puritan leader, wanted his troops to be "religious men" and so had printed in 1643 a 16-page pamphlet called *The Souldiers Pocket Bible*, which he required his soldiers to carry. Later, in the United States, the American Tract Society printed 20,000 copies of a similar adaptation, 24 pages in length, updated with current American spelling and punctuation, and issued it in 1861 during the Civil

---

* Interestingly, the first book printed in America in Hebrew (1809) was also an edition of Psalms.

** Even among modern books, the Bible is the world's most translated work, as shown by the most recent study conducted by UNESCO. The second most translated work was that of another Jewish mind, Karl Marx.

† It measured only 1 by 1½ inches and was used for various versions, one, most appropriately, for children.

War. Its contents comprised 125 verse paragraphs from different parts of the Bible, 121 of which were from the Hebrew scriptures. Although total distribution is not known, the society printed another 74,000 in 1862 and was still publishing the Soldiers' Bible in the Spanish-American War and World War I. When a "Bible famine" developed in the South during the Civil War, Union prisoners in Richmond were able to sell their Bibles for as much as $15 a copy to get money for food.

The American attachment to the Bible is reflected in the fact that the Congress of the United States once recommended, sanctioned, and officially endorsed the printing of a Bible—and the congressional resolution appeared in its first printing in 1782. This Bible, the first in English published in the United States, was the work of Robert Aiken, a Philadelphia printer; its 1,400 pages contained both the Jewish and Christian scriptures. The official endorsement read: "Resolved That the United States in Congress assembled, highly approve the pious and laudable undertaking of Mr. Aiken, as sub-servient to the interest of religion, as well as an instance of the progress of arts in this country, and being satisfied from the above report of his care and accuracy in the execution of the work, they recommend this edition of the Bible to the inhabitants of the United States, and hereby authorize him to publish this recommendation in the manner he shall think proper." This is the only resolution of its kind ever passed by Congress—but it did not help Aiken's Bible compete with imports that were selling for less.

Jews look to the Bible to provide validity for much in their history. Moslems and Christians, too, regard the scriptures as the primary source of their cultures. In view of the dependence of the world's three great religions on the Hebrew texts, it is fortunate that the ancient writings have been so carefully preserved.

The Jews have taken great pains to insure the validity of the biblical text. The Torah scrolls in which the five books of Moses are preserved—and it is from these scrolls that portions are read in the synagogue services—must be handwritten with scrupulous attention to details by pious, learned Jews.

To guard against changes, every aspect of the work of the scribes and their rendering of new Torah scrolls is rigidly prescribed. Each Torah is written on fifty-seven parchments sewn together, with a set number of columns on each sheet, letters to the line, words to the section. A Torah scroll found to have an error— even though it might be only one wrong letter or part of a letter—is considered unfit for use. Such a scroll is immediately removed from the presence of worshipers and put aside to be corrected.*

While the synagogue reader is reading aloud from the Torah scroll, the congregation is dutybound to follow closely. At the slightest mispronunciation or error, the congregation is to call out the correction to the reader. The reader is not to continue until he has made the correction himself, out loud. This practice is still followed in most synagogues.

In such a way, Judaism sought to prevent alterations to the Torah. A rabbinic injunction underscores this by warning against adding to or taking from the laws of the Torah. A credo of the Jewish religion is that every letter in the Torah has a purpose and to add to or delete even one letter tampers with its essence.

Thus, the validity of the Torah text has been preserved through the centuries by the simple but effective method of sanctification. Bearing out the wisdom of this approach are the oldest scrolls now in existence—the Dead Sea Scrolls. A two-thousand-year-old scroll of the Book of Isaiah found among the Dead

---

* The ink used by many scribes is made from an ancient recipe that utilizes copper wash, which is white in its natural state but turns black when mixed with water.

Sea Scrolls contains virtually the same wording as the Book of Isaiah Jews use today.*

As for the historical validity of the Bible, one example demonstrates what might be called "The Law with 3,300 years of Proof."

The Bible, in Leviticus 11:1-8, makes the distinction between kosher and non-kosher meats, stating that the only animals that may be eaten are those that chew their cud and have cloven hoofs. Animals having neither or only one of these characteristics cannot be used as food. The Bible then goes on to state that there are four animals in the world that have only one of the two kosher marks: the camel, the hare, and the badger—all of which chew their cud but do not have cloven hoofs—and the pig, which has cloven hoofs, but does not chew the cud.

Rabbi Menachem M. Schneerson, who studied at the Sorbonne and as the Lubavitcher Rebbe is today leader of one of the largest segments of Hasidic Jews, once pointed out that this statement has been amazingly borne out by the passage of time: "In the nearly 3,300 years since the Torah was given at Sinai—despite the vast increase in scientific knowledge and despite man's explorations into the furthest corners of the world—none other than these four have ever been found to have only one of the characteristics of a kosher animal."

The Israelis have made the pursuit of corroborating evidence of biblical statements a national pastime. Findings in archeological digs have invariably proved the Hebrew scriptures to be accurate. In fact, Israel's army has used biblical passages for information about the trails and terrain used in wars thousands of years ago. During the Six Day War, Israeli troops used an

---

* *From the Beginning*, a book on the Israel Museum where the seven Dead Sea Scrolls are on display, describes the differences between the Dead Sea manuscript of Isaiah and today's text as being only "some minor differences in wording." And yet, not only are the Dead Sea Scrolls two thousand years old, but, as *From the Beginning* states, this scroll was "actually in use for about one hundred and fifty years before being hidden in the cave."

out-of-the-way trail from Jerusalem to the Jordan River to surprise Jordanian troops. Israeli commanders, never having set foot before on the Arab-occupied territory, had discovered the route by consulting the Jewish Bible.

Historian Will Durant has underscored the veracity of the Hebrew Bible. "In its outlines and barring supernatural incidents," he writes in *The Story of Civilization*, Volume 1, "the story of the Jews as unfolded in the Old Testament has stood the test of criticism and archeology: every year adds corroboration from documents, monuments or excavations." Citing the fact that the discovery of potsherds in 1942 confirmed parts of the Book of Kings, he declines to place the burden of proof about the Bible's accuracy on its believers: "We must accept the Biblical account provisionally until it is disproved."

The paradox is that despite this passion for accuracy, the Bible has been mistranslated and misinterpreted for centuries.

If you were asked what forbidden fruit Adam and Eve ate in the Garden of Eden, would you answer "apple"? Most people would. Yet in the Bible the apple is not mentioned. In fact, the type of fruit is not named; we are told simply that it was a fruit of the Tree of Knowledge.

Rabbis have speculated that the fruit on that Tree of Knowledge was a fig. You will recall that when Adam and Eve discovered the fact of their nakedness they hurriedly clothed themselves in fig leaves. The logical assumption is that they used the leaves of a tree near at hand, and what tree was closer than the Tree of Knowledge? The Talmud asserts another symbolic linkage between the fig leaves and the fruit of the tree: "Wherewith they had sinned they also made amendment."

If you were asked what sea was miraculously parted for the Children of Israel in their flight from Egypt, would you answer "the Red Sea"? Most people would.

But that is not what the Bible says in its original form. The Hebrew name for that sea is *Yam Soof*, which means "Sea of Reeds." At no time in the Bible is the Hebrew word for "red" used in referring to the body of water that has come to be called the Red Sea. This must be one of the most glaring errors in history. Either an early translator of the Bible misinterpreted "reed" as "red" (although only in English are the two words close in spelling), or else the body of water that in the Bible parted for the Children of Israel was in fact different, possibly northward in the marshy area dotted with reeds in which the Suez Canel was built.

One of the greatest works of Renaissance sculpture is Michelangelo's "Moses." This monumental figure, posed with tablets in hand as the great Lawgiver, has an equally monumental flaw: Moses has two small horns on his head, of the kind you might find on a young deer. Why? This quaint notion comes from another mistranslation.

When Moses was depicted in the Bible as coming down from Mount Sinai with the Ten Commandments, he was said to have "rays of light" shining from his head. When the Bible was first translated from Hebrew into Greek by Aquila Ponticus in the second century, the word *karan* (ray of light) was mistakenly interpreted as *keren* (horns).

Such mistranslations, with their widespread implications, demonstrate the immense power of the Hebrew Bible. Its language shapes our language; its words shape our world.

Indeed, the Bible, with its message of monotheism, is the great contribution of the Jews to the world. It is through the Bible that mankind has discarded its beliefs in idol worship, paganism, and human sacrifice, with their burdens of ignorance and fear. It is through the Bible that Jew, Christian, and Moslem share a common heritage, the worship of a Supreme Being. Oddly enough, it was Mohammed who first called the Jews the "People of the Book." But generally overlooked is the fact that Mohammed was not referring only to Jews when he said it. He was talking about members of all those religions that, like Judaism, had been influenced by the Bible. So we are all People of the Book, because—quite simply—the Book, a product of Judaism, has become the property of all people.

When Christians and Mohammedans accepted the Hebrew Bible as a base on which to build their faiths, they made the Bible the supreme Jewish Connection. In the Bible a vast segment of the world's population can find a common point of origin. In the turmoil of our times, this fact is—to paraphrase a Jewish prophet —surely more than just a "drop in the bucket" (Isaiah 40:15).

VIII

The Jews in
Promised Land Number Two
(America, What Else?)

*The acid test
of the Jewish Connection*

FACT: The first person on Columbus's voyage to set foot in America was a Jew.

FACT: Abraham Lincoln had a Jewish chiropodist who carried out secret peace negotiations with the Confederacy.

FACT: Hollywood's first sex symbol was Jewish.

FACT: Hebrew was considered so important in early America that three major universities used it on their seals.

FACT: Benjamin Franklin, John Adams, and Thomas Jefferson wanted the seal of the United States to depict the Israelites escaping from Egypt.

FACT: Henry Kissinger is not the first Jewish Secretary of State in American history.

CONSIDER THE OBJECTS and scenes that symbolize America. The Liberty Bell, Valley Forge, the Alamo, Appomattox. The battle cry "Remember the Maine!" Teddy Roosevelt's Rough Riders. The famous picture of the marines raising the flag atop Iwo Jima. The Statue of Liberty, the world-wide symbol of the United States.

These symbols and other essential parts of the story of America are surprisingly associated with Jews. Though small in number, the Jewish people have been involved in the very essence of American history.

The Liberty Bell, sounded to announce the signing of the Declaration of Independence in 1776, is one of the best-known embodiments of the revolutionary spirit. The inscription on the bell has been cited as America's motto: "Proclaim liberty throughout all the land unto all the inhabitants thereof." Strange but true, this statement comes from the Jewish Bible. Leviticus 25:10 uses it in reference to the ancient Israelites' celebration of the jubilee, the fifty-year anniversary when the land was allowed to lie fallow, debts were forgiven, slaves were freed, and everyone began anew. The passage is a critical part of Jewish history, because it is one of the regulations God gave to Moses on Mount Sinai for Jewish life in the Promised Land. Why did the early Americans use such a phrase as the rallying cry of the Revolution? As will be seen, it was but one of many ways in which early America made its own Jewish Connection.

Valley Forge is a name rooted in all our memories as the place where the patriots made great sacrifices for the ideals of the American Revolution. But not usually noted is the fact that among the huddled soldiers in ragtag uniforms trying to keep warm during the harsh winter of 1777-78 was a Jew serving in a vital role. He was Dr. Philip Moses Russel, one of George Washington's surgeon mates who tended the troops so well that later Washington would commend him for "assiduous and faithful attention to the sick and wounded."

Russel's participation is a reminder that at the time of the American Revolution two thousand Jews were living in the colonies—and more than one hundred Jews fought in the Revolutionary War on the side of the patriots. One fighting unit had so many Jews it was called "the Jews' Company." At least forty Jews held important posts in the army, including four lieutenant colonels, three majors, and six captains.

Davy Crockett and other fabled American heroes were killed at the Alamo in 1836. Less well known among those who fought and died there was a Jew—Abraham Wolf. And the Jewish Connection did not end there. Santa Anna, the Mexican warrior whose troops overran the Alamo, was later captured by an expeditionary force that included Leon Dyer (1807-1883), a Jew who had risen to the rank of major in the Texas army. (Dyer, by the way, also has the distinction of having been one of the founders, with his brothers, of the first meatpacking plant in the United States.)

Appomattox is a small town in central Virginia where, on April 9, 1865, Confederate General Robert E. Lee surrendered to Union General Ulysses S. Grant. Present at the ceremony that day was Benjamin B. Levy, one of six Jews awarded the Congressional Medal of Honor in the Civil War, the first war in which the United States awarded it. Oddly, a Jew had also been present when the Confederate government was established in Montgomery, Alabama, on February 14, 1861. Thomas Cooper DeLeon was a writer who fought with the South during the war and later recorded his observations in *Four Years in Rebel Capitals*.

The presence of Jews at both the beginning and

the end of the Confederacy indicates the extensive involvement of Jews in America's most devastating war. Of the 200,000 Jews living in America at the time, 6,000 fought for the Union and 1,300 for the Confederacy. In addition, nine generals in the Civil War were Jewish; the first Quartermaster General of the Confederate army was a Jew, Abraham C. Myers. While one Jew was trying to secure British and French recognition of the Confederacy, another—whose name, at his request, has never been divulged—secretly loaned the United States $5 million, which was used as a bond in a legal maneuver that stopped Britain from sending the Confederacy ironclad ships that would have broken the Union blockade of the South. And another Jew, the financier August Belmont, was, according to Lincoln's biographer Carl Sandburg, influential in shaking the belief of European bankers in the future of the Confederacy.

Without doubt the most important person in the cabinet of the Confederacy was Judah P. Benjamin (1811-1884), who holds the distinction (not Henry Kissinger) of being the first Jewish Secretary of State in America. Elected a U.S. Senator from Louisiana in 1853 and again in 1859, Benjamin stuck with the South when the Civil War broke out. Confederate President Jefferson Davis appointed Benjamin first Attorney General, then Secretary of War, and finally Secretary of State. Davis relied so heavily on Benjamin's advice that he was called "the brains of the Confederacy."

Remember the *Maine*? The sinking of the U.S. battleship on February 15, 1898, sparked the Spanish-American War. Fifteen of the sailors who lost their lives when the ship went down were Jewish. Several months earlier, the captain of the *Maine* had been a Jew, Adolph Marix, who had been given his appointment to the Naval Academy by Abraham Lincoln. He headed the board of inquiry that investigated the *Maine* tragedy, and later rose to the rank of vice admiral. The first volunteer accepted by the War Department in the Spanish-American War was Colonel Joseph M. Heller, a Jewish doctor who left a successful medical practice to become Acting Assistant Surgeon in the Army; and the first to fall in the attack at Manila was a Jew, Sergeant Maurice Joost of the First California Vounteers.

The Rough Riders so distinguished themselves in the Spanish-American War that their regimental commander, Theodore Roosevelt, was propelled into the national limelight. Among the Rough Riders were numerous Jews. Teddy Roosevelt praised them after the war, saying, "One of the best colonels among the regular regiment who fought beside me was a Jew. One of the commanders of the ship which blockaded the coast so well was a Jew. In my own regiment, I promoted five men from the ranks for valor and good conduct in battle. It happened by pure accident (for I knew nothing of the faith of any one of them) and these included two Protestants, two Catholics, and one Jew." In addition, the first of the Rough Riders to be killed in action was a sixteen-year-old Jew, Jacob Wilbusky.

Perhaps the most famous modern image of American courage in battle is that of U.S. Marines raising the Stars and Stripes atop Mount Suribachi on Iwo Jima. The famous photograph was taken under combat conditions by the Associated Press photographer Joe Rosenthal, a Jew who was awarded the Pulitzer Prize for his remarkable achievement.

The Statue of Liberty would not have been completed if it had not been for Jews. France donated the statue to America, but its pieces sat in a warehouse for several years before there was enough money to build a pedestal and assemble the monument. One of many fund-raising projects was an auction at which a poem, "The New Colossus" by the Jew Emma Lazarus, was purchased for the surprisingly high figure of $1,500. Its words, welcoming those "huddled masses yearning to breathe free," helped fire public interest in the project to such an extent that they were inscribed on the statue when it was completed.

Another who helped even more was the publisher Joseph Pulitzer, whose father was Jewish. An immigrant himself, Pulitzer carried on a vigorous campaign in his New York newspaper to spur donations. A postage stamp later issued to honor Pulitzer acknowledges his role by showing the Statue of Liberty in the background.

The monumental figure in New York harbor welcomed the thousands of newcomers who gave America the reputation of being a "melting pot." This vivid metaphor for the mixture of diverse people joining in common purpose in a new land was first presented by a Jew. Israel Zangwill (1864-1926), an important Jewish playwright, novelist, and Zionist, titled his 1908 play about immigrant life in America *The Melting Pot*, thereby creating a term used ever since to describe America's special role in the world.

The names of two of the most important social programs designed to reshape America were the brain children of Jews. Judge Samuel Rosenman (1896-1973), one of Franklin Delano Roosevelt's closest advisers and most important speechwriters, coined the term "New Deal." (He also first used the phrase "the Brain Trust" to label the experts FDR assembled to advise on extricating America from the Depression.) As for Lyndon Johnson's "Great Society," this was a term first developed by speechwriter Richard Goodwin (né Richard Ginsberg, born in the Jewish section of Boston in 1931).

Even Uncle Sam has Jewish blood in his veins! The name Sam is short for Samuel, the name of one of Israel's greatest prophets.

This brief examination of the nation's major historical symbols shows only the tip of the Jewish Connection in America. The rest of the iceberg reveals that Jews have helped shape the United States from its beginning.

Today, more Jews live in the United States than in any other country. America's Jewish population is more than twice that of Israel (nearly 6,000,000 in the U.S. versus 2,806,000 in Israel). In fact, more Jews now live in America than have ever lived in any one country in world history—including the Land of Israel of thousands of years ago.

New York City, with its Jewish populace of more than 2,000,000, has history's largest grouping of Jews in one city, a greater number than now live in Jerusalem, Tel Aviv, Moscow, London, Paris, and Buenos Aires—the six cities highest in Jewish population outside the United States—combined.

The first wave of Jewish immigrants came with the earliest settlers. These were the Sephardic Jews of Spanish and Portuguese descent, remnants of Jewry's Golden Age in Spain, who came in the mid-1600s and 1700s to escape the Inquisitions in their native lands. They considered themselves the aristocracy of the Jewish people.

In the mid-1800s came the second wave, the German Jews, who fled a poverty-stricken homeland that was taking out its economic frustrations on the Jews by segregating them into ghettos, imposing special taxes on them, restricting Jewish trade and travel, even regulating Jewish marriages. This segment of Jewry, successful entrepreneurs in a more hospitable era of European life, would give birth to the "Our Crowd" financiers and innovative businessmen.

In the late 1800s and early 1900s came a third distinct wave, the East European Jews fleeing the ruthless pogroms and anti-Semitism of the Czars. These Jews were among the most religious in the world, and huge numbers of them poured into America. Between 1881 and 1910, the Russian and Polish Jews who came to America were counted at 1,562,800. Even for a people experienced in expulsion and exile, this constituted the largest movement of Jewry since the beginning of the Diaspora.

Only the imposition of restrictive immigration

policies in the United States—such as the Immigration Acts of 1917, 1921, and 1924—stemmed the flow. In fact, America's policy became so restrictive to the Jews that, contrary to common belief, only 16 percent of displaced persons admitted following World War II were Jewish.

And yet, in one of those ironic sidelights, America is now being pollinated with newcomers from two of the largest Jewish populations outside the U.S. A sizable number of Jews emigrating from the Soviet Union now live in America, and many Israelis come to the United States to study or work on a temporary basis or, in some cases, to live permanently.

Thus, while the State of Israel, the land of Jewish origins and longings, represents the Jewish spirit, America has come to represent, in a special way unparalleled in history, the Jewish body.

There is something special about the Jewry that has emerged from the "melting pot." American Jews may well be, in the Darwinian sense, among the best of Diaspora Jewry, for only the most perceptive could foresee both the coming dangers at home and the greater opportunities so far away; only the strongest could survive the mayhem that created the various tidal waves of Jewish immigration; only the fittest could overcome culture shock and language change to adapt to the New World.

Several studies of turn-of-the-century immigration reveal the extraordinary nature of the Jews who came to America. According to a report printed at the end of the 1800s, the Eleventh Census of the United States showed the Russian and Polish Jews to have the lowest mortality rate of any ethnic group in New York during the five years ended May 31, 1890.

In 1906, Dr. Edmund J. James, president of the University of Illinois, and four associates* corroborated this finding in a study encompassing Phila-

---

* Oscar R. Flynn, Dr. J. R. Paulding, Mrs. Simon N. Patton, and Walter Scott Andrews.

delphia, Chicago, and New York. Their report cited a supporting passage on the longevity of the Jews from *The Races of Europe* by W. Z. Ripley:

> Suppose two groups of one hundred infants each, one Jewish, one of the average American parentage (Massachusetts), to be born on the same day. In spite of all the disparity of social conditions in favor of the latter, the chances, determined by statistical means, are that one-half of the Americans will die within forty-seven years; while the first half of the Jews will not succumb to disease or accident before the expiration of seventy-one years.

The project further noted that the low mortality of Jews in "the New York ghetto, considered the most densely populated spot on earth," was "the more remarkable" because the living conditions there—"poverty, overwork, ill-ventilated sweat-shops, overcrowding in the tenements, lack of fresh air and sunshine"—would normally contribute to the spread of infection. "We are forced to conclude that they [the Jews] do possess some relative immunity or a greater power of resistance to the noxious effects of contagious diseases."

Dr. James also noted that the Jewish immigrant was "comparatively untainted by alcoholism and foul blood diseases [syphilis]," and went on, "Although the Russian Jew comes from a country where typhus and smallpox are endemic, and cholera often ranges epidemically, he has never brought these diseases with him."

The Jewish immigrant also had an important social heritage. Dr. James reported that "beyond any other nationality, the Jew in America cares for his own and needy. . . . There are practically no Jewish street beggars. . . . And there is a further fact of the utmost significance and consequence, there are practically no American-born Jewish poor."

In yet another study, carried out by the U.S. Immigration Commission in 1910, Jewish immigrants were found to have a literacy rate of 74 percent, significantly higher than the 60 percent overall figure.

The experience of the Jew in America presents a unique opportunity to test the theory of the Jewish Connection. The United States, with the separation of church and state built into its laws, is the most hospitable land of the Diaspora, offering the Jewish people one of their longest periods of religious and civil freedom. If the Jewish Connection is valid as a hypothesis, then the largest concentration of Jews, enriched by diverse groups of immigrants, allowed to participate in a nation to their fullest potential, should show a Jewry responding with contributions unparalleled in Jewish history. The evidence, much of it located in the recesses of American history, reveals that indeed America owes much of her essence to her pervasive Jewish Connection.

The story of this influence starts with Columbus's discovery of the New World. Numerous Jews were involved in the expedition as financiers, as developers of its navigational tools, and as members of the crew. Yet, perhaps most significant—and most overlooked—of all is the fact that a Jew was the first of Columbus's crew to set foot in America.

Luis de Torres was a brilliant court interpreter, a master of many tongues, and Columbus's trusted friend. His fluency in Hebrew was important in Columbus's thinking because of the possibility that, if he did not find a new route to India, any natives he encountered could be descendents of the Lost Ten Tribes of Israel, and Hebrew might serve as a common language. When the explorers reached the New World, de Torres was first sent ashore to determine if the natives were friendly, and Hebrew was undoubtedly among the languages he used in his attempt to communicate with them.

De Torres found that the natives spoke in a language he had never heard, and so he communicated with them in sign language. They seemed friendly, though, and when de Torres returned to the ship he still thought they could well be a lost tribe of Israel.

De Torres also encountered something unusual on his first trip ashore: he saw the natives smoking tobacco. He became the first white man known to smoke a peace pipe and later introduced the use of tobacco to Europe.

De Torres was also the first white man to settle in the land that Columbus had discovered. He was so impressed with its lushness and beauty that he persuaded Columbus to let him settle there. An Indian chieftain gave him some land and King Ferdinand provided him with a pension. He built a house, grew tobacco, traded with the Indians, and lived out his life peacefully in the New World.

The implications of de Torres' life story are enormous. They mean that a Jew was a landowner and farmer in the New World long before other groups, races, creeds, or nations settled there. A Jew was the original pioneer, years before the Pilgrims hit Plymouth Rock. Even today's Thanksgiving celebration owes something to de Torres. He noticed a strange bird in the New World, and in a letter to friends back home he described it, using the Hebrew word for peacock as mentioned in the Bible—*tukki*. According to one explanation, this word sounded like "*turkey*" and this pronunciation came to be used to name the bird so much associated with American celebrations.

There is no indication that any Jew or secret Jew was on the *Mayflower*, but there is some evidence that a Jew was on the next ship to America—the *Fortune*, which came to Plymouth in 1621. The accepted histories of American Jewish history list Jacob Barsimson, a native of Holland who landed in New Amsterdam on August 22, 1654, as the first Jewish settler in what is now the United States. But there is a possibility that Moses Simonson, a passenger on the *Fortune*, was Jewish. As touched upon in the book *Jewish Pioneers and Patriots*, a lively debate among his descendants appeared in such newspapers as the Philadelphia *Ledger* and the Boston *Post* from December, 1920, to January, 1921. One of his relatives, Moyses P. Simmons, emphatically denied having a Jewish ancestor. "With no disrespect to the Jewish People," he was sure his forebear was a "Symonds, Simonds, Symans," of Devonshire, Dorset, Gloucester and various other English places—in other words, a Protestant. Another, however, said that he was "satisfied that my ancestor Moses Simonson was a Jew." Interestingly, this view was voiced by a descendant who is listed as being both a Ph.D. and a Reverend.

The settling of Jews in America is the happy outcome of three of the saddest periods in the Diaspora. Ironically, the ruthlessly anti-Semitic policies of Spain, Portugal, and England seemed to propel the Jews to the new land and pave the way for their acceptance there.

The close link between the Spanish expulsion of the Jews and the founding of America was noted by Columbus in his personal log: "After the monarchs had expelled the Jews from all their kingdoms and their lands . . . they commissioned me in the same month to undertake this voyage to India." The last day for the 200,000 Spanish Jews to leave Spain was August 2, 1492—the same day on which Columbus completed the loading of his ships and ordered his men aboard. Paradoxically, at the very time Spain was denying religious freedom to Jews, she was helping open a New World that would provide Jews with more religious freedom than they had ever had.

The Spanish expulsion worked another wonder. Many of the expelled Jews wound up in Amsterdam, where the beneficent attitude of the Dutch allowed them to become important members of the mercantile world. Here they built banking houses, factories, and new industries. A century and a half later, when Holland moved into a key position in the colonization of

America, Jewish involvement in the Dutch business world resulted in the Jews' being allowed to settle in America.

The first group of Jews arrived in New Amsterdam during the first week of September, 1654, after a perilous nine-month sea journey covering thousands of miles. They were descended from Jews who had fled Portugal a century earlier because of the fiendish Portuguese Inquisition (which had been far worse than the Spanish Inquisition), and who had gone to Dutch-controlled Brazil, where they could openly practice their religion. Now they were once again fleeing Portuguese anti-Semitism, for Portugal had overrun Brazil and, after a nine-year siege of the city of Recife, had given the six hundred Jews there the classic nonchoice: convert or depart.

Despite tremendous property losses, all chose to leave for the Netherlands. Sixteen ships filled with Jews and most of the Protestant Dutch in Brazil departed, but one of the ships was captured by a Spanish pirate ship and released only after being rescued by a French privateer, the *St. Charles*. Its captain agreed to take the Jews to the nearest Dutch port, New Amsterdam, for a price of 2,500 guilders, but the already destitute Jews had only 900 in cash among them. The captain took what they had and said they could raise the rest by selling their possessions when they arrived in the Dutch colony.

So it was that twenty-three Jews (four married couples, two women, and thirteen children) arrived in America without money or possessions. But the biggest problem they faced was the Dutch Director-General Peter Stuyvesant, who wrote to his bosses back in Amsterdam that the Jews wanted to remain, but he termed them "very repugnant" and a "deceitful race." Besides, he pointed out, "owing to their present indigence they might become a charge in the coming winter."

Again, though, a tragic event in Jewish history placed Jews in the right place at the right time. The

Dutch West India Company officials instructed Stuyvesant to let the Jews stay because Jewish stockholders (descendants of Spanish exiles) were important in the firm and other Jews (descendants of the Portuguese exiles) had helped the Dutch settle Brazil.

Stuyvesant continued to try to limit the rights of Jews in New Netherlands, but at each turn the Jews wrote in protest both to the Dutch West India Company officials and to their co-religionists in Amsterdam asking them to help them plead their case. Stuyvesant was forced to stand aside as Jews won the rights to observe their own Sabbath, to purchase land to build a cemetery, to be free of special taxes, to stand guard, to trade on the Delaware, and to purchase real estate. This march of freedoms secured by those Jews may well have set the precedent for minority rights in America.

The authorities, however, still denied Jews in the New World rights that were forbidden to Jews in Amsterdam. They could not have synagogues or worship together publicly (they could do so in private, however), nor could they "establish themselves as mechanics," or "have open retail shops" (Jews, who would later play an important role in developing the department store for America, were not allowed to own shops in New York City until 1686).

Another directive from Amsterdam could have had earthshaking consequences: "They [Jews] must without doubt endeavor to build their houses close together in a convenient place on one or the other side of New Amsterdam, at their choice—as they have done here." In other words, they were to live in a ghetto. The Jews, however, ignored the directive and, as it was not enforced, a dangerous first was avoided: no ghetto was established in New Amsterdam. Today America can boast there has never been an official expulsion of Jews or official ghetto for Jews. No major European country can say the same.

The thwarting of Stuyvesant's anti-Semitism has a major significance for Jewish—and non-Jewish— history. If the first Jews in New Amsterdam had been persecuted, other Jews might not have found America to be so hospitable. Not only would they have been forced out of what was becoming the commercial center of the New World, but the precedent of a hostile climate for Jews would have been established there. Later Jews might not have viewed America as friendly and could have cast their lots with other countries. After all, the centers of Jewish life were still in Europe and the Middle East.

In retrospect, then, another ironic aspect of the Jewish Connection emerges. If it had not been for the Spanish and Portuguese inquisitions and expulsions, Jews would not have traveled so early and in such numbers to America—and would not have found themselves so well situated for the future. One fact clearly illuminates this point: In 1955, three hundred years after the first Jews arrived destitute in New Amsterdam, 20 percent of the millionaires in America were Jewish.

Another uncanny aspect of the Jewish experience in America also involves the happy outcome of a tragic event—the English expulsion.

The English, who were the most important group to colonize America, had a strong tradition of anti-Jewish policies. In 1290, when England gave the Jews the "choice" of converting or leaving the country, not one gave up his religion. It was back to the ships for the Jews.

For the next four hundred years the English people knew Jews only through biblical stories, religious plays, and second-hand accounts from other countries. So when the Puritans came to colonize America they brought with them an idealized picture of the Jewish people and religion drawn from their beloved Bible.

Thus, while Shakespeare depicted the Jews as ruthless moneylenders in the character of Shylock, the Puritan populace thought of them as the bearers of a proud heritage, first receivers of the word of God. Consequently, when the Jews arrived in the English colonies, they found a culture already fertilized by their religion and ideals.

Here are some aspects of the Jewish-Puritan Connection:

• The Puritans so revered the Hebrew scriptures that they were viewed as "Jewish fellow travelers."

• In 1649, a motion was made in the House of Commons to observe the Lord's Day on Saturday instead of Sunday. There was even a movement afoot to begin the celebration of the Sunday Sabbath the night before as Jews do, and this practice was later actually instituted in America.

• The Puritans refrained from doing any work on their Sabbath.

• In church, Puritan men and women sat apart, as do Orthodox Jews in their services.

• In England, the banners of the Puritan military regiments were inscribed with the Lion of Judah, and the Puritans would ride into battle singing Psalms.

• Thomas Harrison, Cromwell's aide, once proposed that the Mosaic Code be incorporated into English law. Later, in America, John Cotton, considered "the foremost architect of New England theology," spoke out for the adoption of the Mosaic Code as the basis of the laws of Massachusetts.

The Puritan Pilgrims fashioned their Massachusetts Bay Colony as a Bible Commonwealth—a theocracy like ancient Israel. When the Puritans sailed to the New World in search of religious freedom, they saw themselves as the Children of Israel fleeing Egypt. The Atlantic Ocean became the Red Sea, the New World became the Promised Land, and the Massachusetts Bay Colony became the New Jerusalem.

Once they arrived in the New World, the Puritans used the Bible as the foundation upon which to build their new lives. As Kate Caffrey points out in *The*

Mayflower, "The Bible was the blueprint for the Good Society, the building of Zion on earth. Its ideas pervaded all aspects of life; small everyday details referred to it." Thanksgiving, for instance, evolved from the biblical Feast of Tabernacles or Succoth, which the Children of Israel had first celebrated in the desert after fleeing Egypt.

Hebrew was an important language to the Puritans. When Harvard was founded, Latin, Greek, and Hebrew were taught there, and Hebrew was given the most attention. All students were required to spend one day each week for three years on it, and those preparing for the ministry had to learn to read the Jewish scriptures in the original Hebrew.

As other colleges were founded in America, they followed Harvard's lead. Yale, Columbia, Brown, Princeton, Johns Hopkins, and the University of Pennsylvania also started out teaching courses in Hebrew— all the more remarkable because no university in England at the time offered it.*

A vestige of early America's interest in Hebrew can be found in the university seals of Yale, Columbia, and Dartmouth. Beneath a banner containing the Latin "Lux et Veritas," the Yale seal shows an open book with the Hebrew "Urim Vtumim," which were the words on the breastplate of the High Priest in the days of the Temple. The Columbia seal has the Hebrew name for God at the top center, with the Hebrew name for one of the angels on a banner toward the middle. Dartmouth uses the Hebrew words meaning "God Almighty" in a triangle in the upper center of its seal.

So prevalent was the study of Hebrew that a new textbook, *The Hebrew Sun Dial*, was introduced to make it easier. This popular work professed to teach the elements of Hebrew in just twenty-four hours. In

_____

* Hebrew had, however, been taught in many continental European countries since the fifteenth century.

addition, a Hebrew correspondence course was taught by a Yale professor.

The Puritan interest in the Jewish scriptures and Hebrew led to a widespread interest in the Jewish people. Cotton Mather, the leading clergyman of his day (1663-1728), recorded in a diary his every meeting with a Jew, and wrote repeatedly that, whenever he heard a Jew was in town, he arranged to get together with him. Mather dreamed of converting a Jew, for he believed that a place in heaven was assured for one who could make a Jewish convert, and he even wrote a book of arguments by which such a conversion might be achieved. And yet, for all his effort, his diaries never indicate success in such an endeavor.

Mather devoted a significant part of his life to studying the subject of the Jews. From 1693 to 1700, in what he termed "one of the greatest works that I ever undertook in my life," Mather researched and compiled a massive six-volume history of the Jewish people—which was never completed and has yet to be published in any form! The only place you can see his *Biblia Americana* is in the Archives of the Massachusetts Historical Society.*

Early Americans, with their concentration on the Hebrew scriptures, naturally gave biblical names to many of their towns—and that practice has continued. The important Hebrew word *Shalom* (peace), transliterated as "Salem," was first used in Massachusetts, and eventually came to be the name for twenty-five other towns in America. Other biblical names still in use in America include Jericho, Jordan, Hebron, Canaan, Bethlehem, Goshen, Sinai, Beersheba, even Sodom (in New York, of course). Important men in Jewish history also figure in American place names:

---

* Oddly, the first Jewish history to be printed in America appeared almost one hundred years later in a venerable piece of Americana—the very first *Old Farmers' Almanac*. Published in Boston in 1791, this issue contains an article entitled, "A Brief Account of the Persecution of the Jews."

Moses, New Mexico; Noah, Tennessee; David, Kentucky; Abraham, Utah; Samson, Alabama; Gideon, Missouri; Joseph, Idaho.

A suburb north of the nation's capital in Maryland is called Bethesda, the name originally given to a section in the northern part of Jerusalem, the capital of the Land of Israel. And then there is the now famous apartment complex in Washington associated with one of America's major political scandals—Watergate. A part of the Old City of Jerusalem around the Temple was called the Watergate.

The fact that the American Revolution was equated with the Israelites' quest for freedom from their Egyptian taskmasters can be seen in the official seal proposed for the new nation in 1776 by Benjamin Franklin, Thomas Jefferson, and John Adams. Their preliminary design pictured Moses and the Children of Israel safely across the Red Sea, with Pharaoh and his army being overwhelmed by the closing waters. In the top center of the suggested seal was the pillar of fire mentioned in the Bible as the protector of the Israelites.

The Bible tells us that after Joseph helped Egypt survive a devastating famine, "a new Pharaoh arose who knew not Joseph" and threw the Children of Israel into slavery. Jewish commentators have long debated whether this "new Pharaoh" was a successor to the one who had raised Joseph to Viceroy of Egypt, or was the same Pharaoh undergoing a heartless change in attitude. The question itself underlines the treatment Jews have received at the whims of the changing monarchs of this world.

Jews have often had non-Jewish friends in high places, but while kings, emperors, popes, and czars have shown them support, such allegiance has never been consistent in the annals of any nation. An individual ruler or series of rulers might be friendly, but eventually one who was cruel and discriminatory would come to power—or a leader who was kind on one occasion would on the next be destructive.

Only America has been different—and vastly so. For, throughout history, the presidents of the United States have been uniformly warm to the Jews.

Benjamin Franklin may have initiated this trend when he signed a petition for funds to lift the mortgage of one of the first synagogues to be built in Philadelphia—and he himself contributed five pounds. Other early American leaders, including Thomas Jefferson, James Madison, and James Monroe, acknowledged their personal debt to Haym Salomon, a wealthy Jew who helped finance the American Revolution.* Salomon helped the economically struggling future presidents when the Treasury ran short by advancing them money with which to live during the days of the Continental Congress.

America's commitment to Jewish aspirations was voiced from its very founding. George Washington, replying to letters of support from three of America's Jewish congregations following his first inauguration,** wrote what has become the nation's credo of religious freedom: that in a move "unparalleled in the history of nations," not just tolerance but fundamental political principles would secure "inherent natural rights" of religious freedom for Jews and other "inhabitants of every denomination."

(Incidentally, Jews had preceded Washington's ancestors to America. Washington's great-grandfather, John Washington, came to Virginia in 1657, three years after the first Jewish community was formed in New Amsterdam.)

John Adams, the second President, wrote: "I will

---

* Historians differ as to whether Salomon personally loaned over $600,000 to fund the rebel army, or arranged for loans. He was captured twice by the British, his property was confiscated, and he died penniless. Even though Salomon's widow was destitute, the only official gratitude shown him has been the kind governments find easy to give: putting him on a 10-cent postage stamp.

** A rabbi was among the fourteen clergymen in attendance.

insist that the Hebrews have done more to civilize men than any other nation." Adams also expressed his support for "the restoration of the Jews to their own land," and since his time American presidents have shown understanding of the need for a Jewish homeland. Zionism has, in fact, been endorsed by every president since Wilson. As early as 1924, America expressed this sentiment officially by becoming a party to the Palestine Mandate. Harry Truman, over strong State Department objections, had the United States recognize Israel just eleven minutes after her declaration of independence.

In 1840, when the civilized world became aroused over news that thirteen Jews had been imprisoned and tortured in Damascus on a discredited ritual-murder charge, American Jews for the first time appealed to the United States government by sending a letter to President Martin Van Buren—only to find out that Van Buren had five days before intervened in the situation. Eventually, after appeals from America, England, and Austria, the thirteen Jews were released.

The only anti-Semitic edict ever officially issued in the United States occurred during the Civil War. As the Union armies pushed into the South, traders and peddlers swarmed in their wake to do a swift business. So many unauthorized personnel were underfoot that General Ulysses S. Grant became irritated. He issued an order—now known as Order No. 11—specifically barring Jewish peddlers and tradesmen from the liberated areas and evicting the ones who were there. It is not apparent why the Jews were singled out when they were only part of the problem (there were many non-Jewish traders in early America, as the phrase "Yankee peddler" shows).

Abraham Lincoln, who was soon swamped with angry messages from American Jews, could not fathom Grant's reasoning. Within weeks he struck down the order, remarkable action at a time when the country was at war and cooperation between the commander-in-chief and one of his top generals was critical.

There is further irony in Grant's attitude toward the Jews, since later, as president, he acted with unusual favor toward them. He appointed a Jew to be governor of the vast Washington Territory then being settled, and he almost became the first president to appoint a Jew to the cabinet. He asked Joseph Seligman, a leading financier of the day, who had helped float bonds for the Union during the Civil War, to become his Secretary of the Treasury. Seligman, a Jewish immigrant who had made a vast fortune, had a large business to oversee and he regretfully declined.

President William H. Taft, after much public clamor, broke off trade relations with Russia for discriminating against Jews, a very significant precedent for the present-day Jackson Amendment, which would give the USSR most-favored-nation status in commercial transactions only if Russian emigration barriers for Jews and other minority groups are eased.

Theodore Roosevelt became the first president to appoint a Jew to the cabinet* when he made Oscar Straus head of the newly created Department of Commerce and Labor. Roosevelt also submitted a petition—signed by 12,500 Americans, including senators, governors, three archbishops and seven bishops—to the Czar to protest the pogroms then raging in Jewish settlements throughout Russia and called on the Russians to desist from religious persecution.

It was Franklin Delano Roosevelt who really swung open the door to high government positions for Jews. One of his appointments, though, had a special irony. After he nominated Felix Frankfurter to the U.S. Supreme Court, a contingent of Jews met with Roosevelt to urge him to rescind the move, for fear that the Senate confirmation debates would engender an anti-Semitic reaction. In a neat reversal of business-

---

* The appointment of Jews to the U.S. cabinet is now of great significance because it places a Jew in line of succession to the presidency.

as-usual, the President had to explain to the delegation that Jews should not be subject to discrimination in appointments to important jobs because of their religion.

Roosevelt also relied heavily on statesman and financier Bernard Baruch, whose talents were utilized by chief executives from Wilson to Eisenhower, and who became known as "the advisor to presidents."

The warm presidential attitude toward Jews has had far-reaching effect. The constitutionally guaranteed right to religious freedom has been cited as the reason why Jews have prospered in America, but laws have a way of being distorted with loopholes and misinterpretations. In fact, the constitution of the Soviet Union is very similar to America's, with comparable freedoms and guarantees. What makes Russian society so vastly different is the way in which its leaders interpret the constitution and instruct their people. The leader sets the tone for a country, and the voice of a nation is often but the echo of a leader's statements and thoughts.

The freedom Jews enjoy in America today can be largely attributed to the fact that U.S. leaders have been singularly free of official or even unofficial anti-Semitism. Illustrating this is the number of presidents who have had close relationships with Jews.

Oscar Straus used to send a case of matzohs every year to President Grover Cleveland.

Harry Truman started out in the haberdashery business with Eddie Jacobson, and their lifelong friendship would later prove important in the creation of the State of Israel: Jacobson helped set up meetings between important Jewish leaders and Truman.

FDR was close to a number of Jews, especially Felix Frankfurter, whom he consulted on most of the New Deal legislation.

When Lyndon Baines Johnson suddenly found himself President on the afternoon of November 23, 1963, he telephoned Texas lawyer Irving Goldberg and asked his old friend how to go about being sworn in.

Goldberg referred him to Judge Sarah Hughes, who administered the oath of office on the presidential plane.

In fact, Johnson's political career was launched with the help of a Jew. Abe Fortas advised LBJ in his first race for the Senate, when Johnson squeaked through by less than a hundred votes, and thanks to Fortas survived a legal challenge to the election results. Johnson later appointed Fortas to the Supreme Court.*

Nowhere is the relationship of American presidents with Jews more revealing than in episodes involving George Washington and Abraham Lincoln. Let's first look at Washington's Jewish Connection.

As everyone by now knows, George Washington slept all over early America—at least if all those signs that say "George Washington slept here" are right. This mobility was a necessity for a general in a revolution, but once Washington became President he was supposed to reside in either his own home, Mount Vernon, or presidential quarters while the Executive's Mansion was being built (construction of the White House started in 1792).

In the fall of 1793, Washington was about to leave Mount Vernon for Philadelphia, where the Third Congress was to convene, when he heard of a yellow fever outbreak there. (At its height, the epidemic killed one hundred people daily.) He asked his Attorney General to find him accommodations in Germantown, near but outside the endangered city.

Attorney General Edmund Randolph complied as well as he could. Since the epidemic had forced many Philadelphians to flee to Germantown, accommodations were scarce. (Thomas Jefferson, for instance, had to sleep in a bed in the corner of the dining room at the King of Prussia Tavern.) Washington was lucky to get three rooms in the house of a Reverend Frederick Herman.

---

* Johnson nominated Fortas to become Chief Justice, but the nomination ran into resistance over Fortas's business, not religious, affiliations. Shortly afterward, Fortas resigned from the Supreme Court.

After he arrived late on Friday, November 1, Washington lost little time in looking around for a less cramped residence from which to conduct his presidential business. He soon discovered that a Jew who had served under him in the Battle of Long Island owned an elegant two-and-a-half-story mansion nearby. Colonel Isaac Franks had quite distinguished himself in the Revolution. Having enlisted at the age of seventeen, he had been wounded several times and imprisoned by the British, and at the Battle of Long Island had been known as Washington's right-hand man. Washington had said of him that "he was a soldier who served his country well and was concerned more with the welfare of his country than the glory of his person."

This relationship now came to Washington's rescue. He arranged to rent his "right-hand man's" house for himself and his servants and used it as his official residence* until December 1, when the epidemic finally abated in Philadelphia.

Franks sent his ex-tenant a bill for $131.54—which seems a modest sum for a month's rent, but Washington did not see it that way and protested the amount. Franks reduced his bill to $75.56, indicating that besides rent it represented payment for a missing flatiron, four broken plates, one large fork that had been lost, and for "the damage done to a large Japanned waiter made use of in the service of the President." In addition, Franks noted that he had expended $2.50 "for cleaning my house and putting it in the same condition the President received it in."

---

* The Colonel Franks home was the site for some important decisions that continue to have an impact on the nation. It was here that Washington struggled with the question of at what distance from shore American sovereignty protected ships from pirates. Jefferson argued that precedent set the authority over territorial waters at the most at the limit of sight, about twenty miles, and at the least the range of a cannon ball, about three miles. Washington, who did not want to contend with the British over this (they wanted the shorter range to make French raiders more vulnerable), decided in favor of the three-mile limit. He specifically desired his decision to be a temporary one, but it persisted as American law. Territorial water limits are still being debated.

There is no record that Washington protested further.

Despite this slight disagreement, the two continued to be friends, and during the last four years of his life Franks received a military pension and held several civil posts. He also became the first Jew to have a portrait done by Gilbert Stuart.

As for Abraham Lincoln, the tale of his close relationship with a Jew borders on the zany.

Isachar Zacharie was an English-born Jew who studied chiropody under a prominent English scientist. He built a successful practice in America, treating such prominent citizens as Henry Clay and John C. Calhoun. Wherever he went—and he traveled as far as California—he collected testimonials about his work. He soon established himself, says one account, as "perhaps the best chiropodist in America."

The ambitious foot doctor wanted to make contact with President Lincoln, whom he probably considered to have the biggest feet in America—symbolically and, at Lincoln's height, possibly literally. Zacharie hit on the idea that just as each army regiment had a chaplain it should have a chiropodist as well.

When two New York newspapers published articles on his suggestion for foot care for foot soldiers, Zacharie sent clippings to E. M. Stanton, the Secretary of War. Stanton was cool to the idea, but he met Zacharie, and allowed him to treat his feet. Soon Zacharie's patients also included the Secretary of State, and Generals McClellan, Banks, and Burnside. Zacharie was working his way up to Lincoln foot by foot.

Finally, Zacharie became the first chiropodist to treat Lincoln's foot problems. In a handwritten note, dated September 22, 1862, Lincoln testified to the effectiveness of the therapy: "Dr. Zacharie has operated on my feet with great success, and considerable addition to my comfort." The statement created quite a stir, and the New York *Herald* commented: "Dr. Zacharie trimmed the feet of President Lincoln and all his Cabinet. He is a wit, gourmet and eccentric, with a splendid Roman nose, fashionable whiskers and an eloquent tongue, a dazzling diamond breast-pin, great skill in his profession, ingratiating address, a perfect knowledge of his business and a plentiful supply of social moral courage."

Zacharie continued to treat Lincoln throughout his days in the White House, and they became friends. According to *Jewish Participants in the Civil War* by Harry Simonhoff, "In a short time no one enjoyed the President's intimacy to a greater degree. He [Zacharie] had entree to the White House at all times."

Zacharie eventually dropped his idea for an army corps of chiropodists, which had been widely spoofed by the press. But he had other ideas that captured Lincoln's interest.

Zacharie volunteered to travel to New Orleans in early 1863 as a special agent of the President to evaluate the Union rule of the newly captured city and make suggestions for ways of handling the reconstruction of the South at war's end. Lincoln agreed, and Zacharie spent six months undercover in the South. He returned to a warm greeting by the President.

This experience gave Zacharie the germ of another idea. His contacts with Union sympathizers in the Confederacy led him to believe he could serve as a peacemaker between the North and the South. He asked for a pass to proceed to Richmond, where he would hold secret talks with Confederate officials. Secretary of State Seward objected and for six weeks Lincoln pondered the idea. Finally Lincoln agreed, and Zacharie went to Richmond via Harpers Ferry.

What happened next is unclear. Zacharie did meet with the Confederacy's Secretaries of State, War, and Navy, and the Provost Marshal General of Richmond. Zacharie claimed his mission opened the negotiations for peace and on October 21, 1863, the New York *Herald* commented on the meeting in an editorial and outlined the peace plan supposedly presented by Zacharie.

According to the newspaper, it was proposed that the Federal government would transport the Confederate President, cabinet, and army to Mexico, which Jefferson Davis's 150,000 troops would conquer. Davis would be President of a new country where slavery would be allowed, the southern states would return to the Union, and peace would be restored.

It is highly doubtful that Abraham Lincoln—or anyone—would advocate such a plan. The editorial that spelled out this outrageous plot must be considered the bizarre finish of a bizarre tale. Following this secret mission for Lincoln, Zacharie soon went back to his chiropody and faded from public view. But he had played a part in an important American tradition—that of close friendships between Jews and the nation's leaders.*

There have, of course, been occasional anti-Semitic outbursts in America. Jews have been and continue to be excluded from some industries, social clubs, and commercial enterprises. But, in terms of the official posture of a nation, America has been remarkably receptive to the Jews.

In response to this atmosphere, Jews have flowered in the United States, making unparalleled contributions to the shape and substance of the nation. Here are just a few of the more interesting, yet often overlooked, Jewish Connections in America.

The next time you relax on Labor Day, think of Samuel Gompers, an English-born Jew who was one of the founders and for almost forty years president

---

* One of the more fascinating accounts of a president who was helped by a Jew concerns Thomas Jefferson—and the results can be seen on the back of the nickel. Monticello, Jefferson's stately home, was purchased in 1836 by Uriah P. Levy, who bought the mansion to rescue it from neglect and decay. Levy, a Commodore in the U.S. Navy, later instructed his family to donate Monticello to the Federal government for preservation as a public memorial.

of the American Federation of Labor (A.F. of L.). In 1894 he finally succeeded in his efforts to get Congress to make the first Monday in September a legal holiday to honor the working man.

When you enjoy another hour of sunlight during daylight-saving time, think of Marcus M. Marks. A clothing merchant who retired at forty-five to devote himself to public service, Marks was president of the Borough of Manhattan from 1914 to 1916. In 1915 he became the first person to suggest that the United States adopt the idea of daylight saving, which was in use in England during World War I to conserve fuel. Congress voted approval of the plan in 1917.

When you watch the Triple Crown of horse racing, remember that the Belmont Stakes—and the track where it's run, Belmont Park—are named for a German-born Jew. His real name was August Schonberg, but it was as August Belmont that he became a leading American financier and so active in politics that in 1860 he became chairman of the Democratic National Committee. In changing his name to Belmont, he kept its meaning. "Schonberg" means "beautiful mountain" in German. "Belmont" is simply the French version of his name.

The next time you put on a pair of America's most American clothing—bluejeans—say a kind word for a man whose name has become one of the world's best known—Levi Strauss. As a twenty-year-old Jewish immigrant from Bavaria, Strauss designed the rugged pants for California gold miners in 1850. The miners liked them so much that they called them, with the familiarity born of affection, by their inventor's first name—Levi. Today, Levi Strauss and Company is the world's largest pants manufacturer, and Levis are fashionable on two continents.

When you turn on your radio or television, think of David Sarnoff, the pioneer of network broadcasting. In 1915, he drafted a plan to market "radio music boxes" to bring entertainment to American homes, and this idea led to the first mass production of radios. In 1926, he founded the National Broadcasting Company, the first radio network. Later, under his direction, Radio Corporation of America took the lead in developing black-and-white and later color TV. In 1944 the Television Broadcasters' Association conferred on Sarnoff its highest citation and title, "The Father of American Television."

Many of America's best-loved songs were written by Jews. "God Bless America," which became America's second national anthem during World War II, is the creation of Irving Berlin. "Oklahoma," the tribute to America's Midwest, was written by Oscar Hammerstein II. "Swanee," the song that recalls the early days of the South, was written in just fifteen minutes by George Gershwin and popularized by another Jew, Al Jolson. Gershwin also wrote the first jazz piano concerto, "Concerto in F," and introduced it in Carnegie Hall in 1925.

Jews were also among the pioneers who launched America's expansion. The first white child born in Georgia was Jewish. A Jew founded Montgomery, Alabama. Two Jewish brothers were involved in the founding of Louisville, Kentucky, and Wheeling, West Virginia. Green Bay, Wisconsin, was originally a trading post started in 1794 by Jacob Franks, a Jew. Barnard Gratz, a wealthy Jewish merchant of colonial times who speculated in land in Illinois, once owned much of what is now Chicago. Two Virginia Jews— Jacob I. Cohen and Isaiah Isaacs—employed Daniel Boone to survey the western lands. Records of their dealings with Boone, which still exist, are peppered with Yiddish phrases.

In recognition of Jewish pioneers, an estimated ninety places in America have been named after them. These include Aaronsburg, Pennsylvania; Altman, Georgia; Altheimer, Arkansas; Levy, New Mexico; Mayer, Arizona; Newman, California; and Solomon,

Kansas. Kaplan County in Louisiana and Kaufman and Castro Counties in Texas were also named after Jews.

As Calvin Coolidge remarked, "the business of America is business."

The Jews have been tending to America's business— and very well at that—for centuries.

When you study early America's vital industries, you will find Jews at the center of many. The sperm-oil industry, important because of the better lighting provided by burning whale oil, was introduced into America by Aaron Lopez* and his father-in-law, Jacob Rodriguez Rivera, Marrano Jews who upon arriving in America openly practiced their religion. The first indigo manufacturing plant in America was founded by the Jew Moses Lindo, who was born in Portugal, educated in England, where he learned the dye business, and in 1756 came to Charleston, South Carolina. The largest fur trader in the colonies was the New York firm of Levy, Lyons and Company, headed by Hayman Levy, who was also the first boss of John Jacob Astor.

On the dark side of the picture, Jews have been excluded from some of the major business of America —the automotive, steel, and chemical industries, as well as insurance, banking, and engineering. However, individual Jews have been able to break through the barriers. In the field of copper production, for example, which was vital to early America, in 1812 the Jewish Hendricks Brothers firm built the first rolling mill in the United States at Soho, New Jersey. Among the companies their business supplied were Paul Revere and Son, and materials they produced went into both the battleship *Constitution* and Robert Fulton's steamship.

---

* Lopez maintained an admirable practice in his business: to promote friendly relationships with Christians and to maintain his own faith, he had a standing rule that no ship was ever to leave his dock in Newport, Rhode Island, on the Jewish or Christian Sabbath.

But the real story of the Jewish Connection with business in America is told not in such long-ago terms, but in today's world.

When you buy or sell stock, consider that a Jew was among the twenty-one founders of the New York Stock Exchange.

When you fuel up your car, thank the Jews for the convenience of the drive-in gas station. Louis Blaustein and his son Jacob were among the first to dispense gasoline this way and to develop a type of gas pump that told the customer just how much he was getting for his money. From this innovative beginning the Blausteins went on to build one of America's major oil corporations.* And leave it to a couple of Jews to choose the most patriotic name of all—the American Oil Company. Later the Blausteins developed the first anti-knock gasoline, called Amoco, and this was the fuel used by Charles Lindbergh on his historic *Spirit of St. Louis* flight from New York to Paris.

When you shop in a department store, you benefit from the merchandising ideas of many Jews. Consider Adam Gimbel. At the age of twenty-five, after struggling for seven years as a peddler in the South, Gimbel opened a small shop in Indiana in 1842, and almost immediately introduced new storekeeping ideas. He advertised the opening of his store in a handbill—the first time this approach had ever been used. He offered to return the purchase price to any dissatisfied customer—the first refund policy. He gave all shoppers the same service, regardless of their race or status—yet another novel idea. And finally, because so many of his customers had to travel great distances to make their frequent visits, Gimbel introduced the most groundbreaking idea of all—stocking his store with a large variety of goods under one roof for their convenience. Thus was born one of the first department stores.

---

* When Jacob Blaustein died in 1971, he was one of the ten richest men in America.

Another Jewish merchandising genius was David Lubin. Born in Poland in 1849 of Orthodox parents, Lubin wound up at the age of twenty-five in Sacramento, where, above a basement saloon, he opened a small shop and named it "One Price Store." Lubin initiated the idea of selling products at fixed prices that were clearly marked on each item. The success of his store enabled Lubin to create not only the largest retail store in Sacramento, but to open a branch in San Francisco. Thus was founded one of the earliest chain stores in America. Lubin, however, went on to be among the first to use yet another concept to bring his merchandise to the people—he decided to sell through the mail. This idea was promoted by another Jew, Julius Rosenwald, who oversaw the expansion of the largest mail-order house of all—Sears, Roebuck and Company.

The concept of ready-to-wear children's clothes was also developed by an American Jew. Before 1889, all children's clothing was home-made. When Louis Borgnicht, a poor young immigrant peddler, discovered that no one made children's aprons (in those days all little girls wore aprons), he and his wife made a few samples in children's sizes. They sold quickly. Borgnicht made children's dresses and found that the demand was even greater. He decided to devote himself full time to making clothing for children, thereby creating a totally new industry that others entered in large numbers. Borgnicht came to be called "King of the Children's Dress Trade."

When you go to the movies, sit back and enjoy the foresight of the Jews. Until Jewish businessmen entered the field, the motion-picture industry was viewed as a frivolous entertainment at best, hardly worth the investment of real dollars. Samuel Goldfish, a successful glove salesman in New York, became intrigued by the brief snippets of moving pictures being shown in New York nickelodeons and formed the idea that an entire play could be made into a movie. He invested $5,000 and talked several others into investing, including a director by the name of Cecil B. De Mille. With this money, the group in 1913 filmed *The Squaw Man*, the first feature-length movie produced in Hollywood. Goldfish later changed his name to Goldwyn, became a co-founder of MGM (Metro-Goldwyn-Mayer), and the rest—as they say in Hollywood—is history.

Other movie firsts achieved by Jews are:

• The first theater to be used solely for the showing of motion pictures was built by Adolph Zukor, who founded the Paramount Picture Corporation.

• The first full-length sound picture, *The Jazz Singer*, was produced by the Jewish Warner Brothers.

• The star of the first "talkie"—in fact, the first three talkies—was Al Jolson, the son of a cantor. He followed *The Jazz Singer* with *The Singing Fool* and *Mammy*.

• The first sex symbol in movie history, Theda Bara, was Jewish. (It is interesting to note that two other sex symbols in movie history—Marilyn Monroe and Elizabeth Taylor—converted to Judaism.)

Some other notable Jewish names in the founding of the motion-picture industry are Louis B. Mayer, Lewis Selznick, William Fox, Jesse Lasky, Marcus Loew, and Irving Thalberg; and there has been a seemingly endless list of Jewish stars, from the Marx Brothers to Dustin Hoffman. Among the all-time top-grossing films are the Jewish-oriented *Ten Commandments* at $43 million and *Fiddler on the Roof* (which was also the longest-running Broadway play in history) at $35.5 million.

Other aspects of the Jewish Connection in America are all around. The best-selling adventures of rabbi-detective David Small and other successful books featuring a Jewish subject matter; Barbra Streisand and other luminaries of the entertainment field; the humor of the "Borscht Belt" comedians; respected leaders in so many fields—the Jewish influence seems without end.

Yet, in some fields, Jews have made their way slowly. In politics, only in the mid-nineteenth century were Jews allowed to hold public office in, for instance, Maryland. America, with the largest Jewish population in the world, has yet to elect a Jew to the presidency—in contrast to heavily Catholic France, which has had three Jewish prime ministers. Nor have Jews been elected to Congress and governorships in numbers related to their percentage of the population.

Things show signs of changing in this regard. The 94th Congress had twenty-four Jews (three senators and twenty-one representatives), the largest contingent ever. And a recent survey asking Americans to name the men and women they most admired showed Jews at the tops of both lists—Henry Kissinger and Golda Meir.

Since recognition is vital to survival in national life, the results of another public opinion poll are revealing. In 1973, Secretary of State Kissinger was found to have the highest recognition rate of any person not a president in the history of America. Only the President, then Richard M. Nixon, was recognized by more people—81 percent compared with Kissinger's 78 percent. The poll showed the Secretary of State far ahead of any of the presidential hopefuls at the time, including Senator Edward Kennedy.

For Jews, America has been not only the land of the free but the land of the acid test. The American Jewish experience would prove just how much the Jews could contribute if they were not burdened with the onerous taxes, pogroms, separation into ghettos, special laws, and exclusionist policies Europe had heaped upon them for centuries.

For Jews, America has been a kind of Promised Land in the Diaspora, but at the same time it has given non-Jews an unprecedented opportunity to benefit fully from the talents of the Jew—an opportunity Europe, in its narrow-mindedness, never allowed itself. Is it just a coincidence that while America has flowered these past three hundred years Europe has withered? Has world history repeated itself, as when Spain expelled its Jews and soon began to lose its preeminence in the world?

These questions underline a final irony in the Jewish Connection.

The curious thing about the Jews is not so much the fact of their survival but the ways in which their survival comes about. The Jew possesses a resilience bordering on the eerie, and a threat to Jewish existence is often turned back upon those who posed it.

Consider once again Peter Stuyvesant, who attempted to expel the first group of Jewish immigrants to America. Not only did he not succeed in his lifetime, but centuries later the Jews had the last laugh on him. In *The Grandees*, Stephen Birmingham tells that in 1969 the old Church of Saint Mark's in the Bowery, where Peter Stuyvesant and eight generations of Stuyvesants are buried, was saved from real-estate developers by being declared a historic site by New York City's Landmarks Preservation Commission. The chairman of the commission, who made the announcement, was a New York architect, Harmon Hendricks Goldstone—a direct descendant of one of the twenty-three Jews Stuyvesant tried to expel in 1654.

IX

Who Else Would Make House Calls?

*The unusual involvement of
the Jews in medicine*

FACT: Until a Jewish doctor showed differently, Americans believed the tomato was poisonous.

FACT: During the Civil War, both the Union and the Confederacy appointed Jewish doctors to head their medical departments.

FACT: The doctor hailed as America's father of pediatrics was a Jew.

FACT: The March of Dimes to combat polio was the idea of a Jewish comedian.

FACT: The first successful operation for appendicitis was performed by a Jewish surgeon.

FACT: A Polish Jew who pioneered a new field of medical research gave us a word now common in our language—vitamin.

FACT: The Talmud, written nearly two thousand years ago, contains references to oral contraceptives and artificial insemination.

ROCK MUSIC STARS MAY get more money . . . motion picture stars may be more famous . . . political leaders may get more press coverage . . . but no group is given more of our respect and reliance than physicians.

Why has medicine consistently ranked as the elite of the professions? Why do doctors receive so much esteem?

The answer is obvious. The one most equipped to help us in our struggle against mortality fulfills our most basic need. He who keeps us healthy will always have a special place in our hearts.

Is it just a coincidence, then, that of all the trades, occupations, services, and businesses, Jews are most associated with the medical profession? Even jokes underline the power of this Jewish Connection. Doesn't every Jewish mother of popular mythology long to be among the select who can beam, "My son, the doctor"? Don't we josh about the curative power of that unique Jewish medicine—a bowl of hot chicken soup?

Yet even this Jewish Connection has its ironic over-tones. For centuries Jews were either excluded from medicine as a career or were denied the right to practice it among Christians. Such barriers can be found as recently as this century, when many medical schools were closed to Jewish applicants and others imposed strict quotas on the number of Jews they would accept.

An example of this kind of discrimination can be found in the life of Monty Hall (yes, the emcee of the long-running TV game show "Let's Make a Deal" is Jewish). His autobiography, *Emcee Monty Hall*, tells about his college days in Canada, when he tried to launch a career in medicine. Although he had done very well in undergraduate school and stood among the top ten of three hundred pre-med students applying to medical school, he was not one of the seventy accepted. The reason, writes Hall: "There was a quota system at the time, though no one would talk about it. Winnipeg had a large ethnic population, and many Jewish students applied to med school. The school accepted three or four students from each minority, including women, and gave the rest of the places to [male] Anglo-Saxon Protestants."

Disappointed but determined, Hall took the advice given to promising med school rejects: he took another year of science. He earned good grades and was elected president of the Science Student Body—the highest honor for a science student. He applied again to medical school, and was rejected a second time.

Hall went back to school for yet another year. This time he was elected president of the entire university student body. At the end of the term, he applied to medical school once more—and once more was turned down.

In one of the greatest stories of determination since Robert Bruce, Hall decided to stay in school one more year. This time he also took steps to fight the admissions policy of the medical school with a group of interested lawyers and businessmen.

But, during that year, Hall secured a part-time job on a Winnipeg radio station and was caught up in the excitement of the entertainment field. At the end of the year he did not bother to apply again to medical school. However, the pressure he had exerted began to have results: "That year, of seventy-eight or eighty who were accepted for Medical School at the University of Manitoba, I believe twenty-six were Jewish, and many others were members of other minority groups." Monty Hall had made a good deal for his fellow Jews.

Despite such discrimination in the past (and Hall's experience in Canada had many counterparts in the

United States earlier this century), Jews today represent 9 percent of the doctors in America—three times the percentage of Jews in the nation's total population. In addition, the largest proportion of Jews winning Nobel Prizes has been in the area of medicine.

What could better show the history of the Jewish-medical Connection than the fact that during the Civil War both the Confederacy and the Union turned to Jews to head their medical departments? The first Surgeon General of the Confederacy was Dr. David de Leon of South Carolina (he had previously been commended by the U.S. Congress and known as "the fighting doctor" for his heroism against Santa Anna's troops). In 1865, Dr. Jonathan Horowitz was appointed chief of the U.S. Bureau of Medicine and Surgery—the Union counterpart of de Leon's position.

Why this involvement of Jews in medicine? Perhaps the best answer lies in the Bible and Talmud, which were far ahead of their time with practices subsequently shown to be medically beneficial. Consider the following:

• An oral contraceptive is frequently mentioned in Jewish writings dating back nearly two thousand years. The Talmud and other rabbinic literature refer to "a cup of sterility" or a "potion of roots."* The contraceptive drink known to ancient rabbis could, in different dosages, also bring about increased fertility—a remarkable similarity to modern drugs that can both stimulate and stop ovulation.

• The first reference to artificial insemination in world literature is in the Talmud, which was written seventeen hundred years before science established that conception was possible without intercourse.

• Moses Maimonides (1135-1204) was considered both the greatest rabbinic thinker and the foremost

---

* See the Talmudic tractate *Yevamot* 65 b. The references to oral contraceptives in rabbinic literature are discussed by Immanuel Jakobovits, now Chief Rabbi of England, in his book *Journal of a Rabbi*.

physician of the Middle Ages. The author of such commentaries on the Bible and Talmud as the *Mishnah Torah* and *Guide for the Perplexed*, Maimonides was linked for centuries with Moses, the leader of the Children of Israel. Indeed, one of the sayings of Jewry is "from Moses to Moses there was none like Moses."

Maimonides, who was born in Spain but spent most of his life in Egypt, wrote not only religious works but medical treatises on such subjects as asthma, hemorrhoids, poisons, and sexual intercourse. Some were printed in Latin and studied in the universities of Europe for five centuries after his death. He was by far the most renowned doctor of his day, and served the Sultan Saladin as his personal physician. His reputation as a healer was so widespread that in far-off England, King Richard the Lionhearted heard about him and asked him to become the court doctor, but Maimonides declined. He is still so highly esteemed that in 1975 the Hebrew University of Jerusalem purchased his twelfth-century study of the Mishnah for $461,000—at that time the highest price ever recorded for a single manuscript at auction.

Another good reason for the strong Jewish Connection in medicine is Judaism's emphasis on this world. Although the Talmud and the oral tradition of Judaism discuss reward and punishment in an afterlife, the five books of Moses include not a single mention of hell or heaven. In effect, the Hebrew Bible is an instruction manual on how to conduct oneself in this life.

Life! It is clearly precious in the Bible. A Jew is instructed to carry out 613 commandments, yet he may violate all but three to save a life.* Although an ascetic approach was practiced by some Jews in the latter

---

* The three laws that cannot be violated to save a life are those forbidding idolatry (which strikes at the very basis of Judaism), adultery (which violates the family structure), and murder (which in itself is a negation of life).

days of the Second Temple, Judaism, unlike other religions in both the East and the West, has not fostered monasteries and does not advocate a removal from society. Marriage and the raising of a family have always been honored in the Jewish religion. In fact, the first commandment to be found in the Bible is the command "to be fruitful."

While the laws of the Torah are given with no medical explanations, many of them can be seen as promoting personal and public hygiene. Indeed, as one book on medicine has noted, Moses emerges as the first great teacher of preventive medicine. Dr. James J. Walsh, in a foreword to *Jewish Contributions to Medicine in America*, writes, "Jews were noted for their work in hygiene and preventive medicine as well as in pathology. They were always intensely practical, and not at all likely to be run-away with by theories and superstitions."

Among the laws of the Bible that have been shown to be medically beneficial are circumcision and dietary restrictions. Circumcision has been shown to prevent phimosis (an abnormal condition in which the foreskin becomes so tight it cannot be drawn back), balanitis (inflammation), and cancer. "Virtually no cases of cancer of the penis have been reported in individuals circumcised at birth," says *The Biblical World*, edited by Charles Pfeiffer, in a comprehensive entry on medicine. "In ethnic groups where circumcision is not practiced the incidence of cancer of the penis is significant." The benefits of circumcision extend to women, too: "Physicians noted the low incidence of cancer of the cervix in Jewish women, especially in the population of hospitals treating almost solely Jewish patients. In racial settings where circumcision is not performed, the incidence of cancer of the cervix is significant." In addition, smegma, the secretion found under the foreskin of the uncircumcised male, has been found to have "cancerogenic activity . . . not present in the circumcised male."

The dietary laws have served the Jews as a safeguard against trichinosis, a disease caused by eating infected pork. The laws against eating fish without scales and seafood such as oysters have also been found to be medically valid. Dr. Ralph Major, in a *History of Medicine*, says these regulations are significant because "all poisonous fish have no scales." The prohibition against eating oysters must have spared Jews from epidemics because, he notes, oysters "on many occasions in modern times have caused epidemics of typhoid fever and other infectious diseases."

Indeed, history has borne this out with ironic results. Since Jewish communities were less affected by the plagues that periodically swept through Europe, many times the charge was made that Jews must be poisoning wells to create the disease. Mobs would attack the Jewish communities that seemed unnaturally free of the illness. The Jews invariably found it harder to escape the epidemic of pogroms that followed.*

The many Jewish laws prohibiting the consumption of meat from injured or diseased animals, outlining the careful inspection of ritually slaughtered animals, calling for the draining of all blood from meat before serving (infectious germs travel in an animal's circulatory system), washing the hands before a meal, even, as in Deuteronomy, stringent laws about disposing of human excreta—all are amazingly similar to a modern hygienic system. *The Biblical World* quotes Edgar Erskin Hume, who in *The Military Sanitation of Moses in the Light of Modern Knowledge* characterizes Moses as "the greatest sanitary engineer that the world has ever seen" and says the doctrines of the Bible "could be summed up by the objects of sanitation today: pure food, pure water, pure air, pure bodies, and pure dwellings."

The doctor, like the rabbi, was revered by the Jewish community, for both dealt with the essentials of existence: the rabbi attended to spiritual needs, the

---

* The Black Death alone, which Jews were accused of starting by poisoning wells, resulted in pogroms that destroyed 510 Jewish communities in Europe.

doctor took care of bodily needs. And their functions were seen as interdependent, as the Talmud itself shows. Just as many of its pages are filled with religious discussions, it also contains many passages on matters of health, revealing an advanced state of medical awareness among the ancient rabbis. In addition to its early references to oral contraceptives and artificial insemination, the Talmud also mentions anesthesia for surgical operations (it's called "sleeping drug"), amputations, false teeth, artificial limbs, and caesarian operations.

There are two periods in history—the Middle Ages and modern times—when the Jewish involvement in medicine came to full flower. Significantly, these two periods of time are separated by the long agony of the ghetto that restricted the Jew from the world at large.

It has been estimated that in the Middle Ages over one-half of the rabbis and other Jewish intellectuals were physicians by occupation. There was, for instance, Amatus Lusitanus. This Portuguese Jew lived in the sixteenth century and was for most of his life a Marrano. Because of his renown as a doctor and scientist, he became the physician to the family of Pope Julius III and treated the Pope himself. But even as the Pope entrusted his health to a Jew he was working against the Jewish heritage. In 1553, Pope Julius III ordered the Inquisition to burn every copy of the Talmud to be found in Italy.

The Jews were able to become preeminent as physicians in the early Middle Ages for several reasons. First, they were familiar with the medical texts being developed in the East by their Arab neighbors. They knew the language of the Arabs, could read their books, and maintained contact with their Jewish brethren in the East while living in Europe. Even more important, the Jews were receptive to the latest medical ideas. They were not bound by the superstition and reliance on incantations and holy relics of the general European populace. While the Jews' practical approach to life encouraged scientific exploration, others in Europe remained hidebound by religious dogma and opposed medicine as the work of atheists thwarting God's will. Not until European universities began developing medical studies in the thirteenth century did Christian health skills begin to rival those of Jewish doctors. When that occurred and the Jewish physicians were not so badly needed, Christian Europe began excluding Jews from medical schools and allowing Jewish doctors to treat only Jewish patients.

A few examples: The Council of Béziers in 1246 ordered the excommunication of any person who consulted a Jewish physician. The Council of Vienna in 1267 decreed Jewish doctors could not treat or offer medical advice to Christians. Church decrees issued in 1272, 1284, 1293, 1326, 1337, and 1434 prohibited Jewish physicians from seeing, treating, even prescribing medicine for Christian patients. In 1306 Jewish physicians were expelled from Montpellier, where Jews had been permitted to attend medical school for 200 years.

How, then, did Jews become so famous as medical practitioners in medieval Europe? Why did kings and clergymen use the services of Jewish doctors? How is it that a long line of Jews ministered to the medical needs of popes—right in the Vatican?

Because, quite frankly, the higher the person's rank, the better position he was in to ignore the laws against Jewish doctors. Popes Paul III, Alexander VI, Julius II, Leo X were all treated by Jews. Pope Gelasius II had a Jewish physician he called "his friend" and recommended to a bishop. Pope Boniface VIII used a Jewish doctor, Isaac ben Mordecai, to treat an eye ailment. Just as "there are no atheists in a foxhole," it seems there were no anti-Semites when a fever struck.

Ironically, some of the popes who used Jewish doctors—Boniface IX, Eugenius IV, Nicholas V, Calixtus III—legislated decrees against Jews.

Monasteries and nunneries also consulted Jewish

doctors in opposition to Church law. Wrote Arnold of Vilanova in a complaint to the King of Sicily in the fourteenth century, "We recall having learned from the preachings of the clergy that any believer is [subject to] excommunication and commits a mortal sin who calls in a Jew for the cure of his bodily ailments. We see, however, that the custom is for no other physician to enter cloisters than a Jew; this is the case not only of cloisters for men, but for women as well." According to one chronicler of the Middle Ages, until Christian universities began teaching rational medicine in the thirteenth century "there was scarcely a court or bishopric in Europe which did not boast its Jewish doctor."

Among the secular rulers served by Jewish doctors were the Christian kings of Spain until Ferdinand and Isabella, various sultans of Turkey* and Egypt, various kings of Portugal, Sicily, France, England, and even some of the Holy Roman Emperors (such as the one with the obvious medical problem: Louis the Bald).

Another Jewish-medical Connection has resulted in the popularity of a plant most of us take for granted: the tomato. In early America, tomatoes were considered poisonous and were used only as a garden ornament (they were called, strangely enough, "love apples"). It was a Portuguese Jew known as Dr. Siccary, a pioneer physician in Virginia, who in 1733 explained they were edible and healthful. Dr. Siccary, however, seems to have gotten somewhat carried away by his enthusiasm. He also said that "a person who should eat a sufficient abundance of these apples would never die."

It is during modern times that Jews have made perhaps their greatest medical contributions. What

---

* Suleiman the Magnificent, Sultan of the Ottoman empire from 1520-1566, liked his Jewish doctor so much that he exempted him and his family from all taxes.

better way to understand the impact of this Jewish Connection than by living with it—from birth on? Consider the following scenario:

The big day has finally arrived and you are born.*

Because you're a strapping little tyke, you give a lusty yell. After the nurses show you to your mother, you're taken to the hospital's nursery, where you await the first visit from your pediatrician.

Many people probably think we have always had pediatricians, but it's not so. In fact, the honor of being the father of pediatrics in America and establishing the country's first medical clinic for children belongs to Dr. Abraham Jacobi (1830-1919). Among his many recognized achievements** in the specialty of treating children, he was the first pediatrics professor. The lectures he gave at the College of Physicians and Surgeons in New York are cited as "the starting point of clinical and scientific pediatrics in this country." By 1870, owing to his efforts, pediatrics and especially the feeding of infants were for the first time approached as a science.†

Under the direction of your pediatrician, you are soon being fed whole milk. Dr. Jacobi, who was one of the first to recognize the need to boil milk, had a lot to do with the healthfulness of your diet. But he wasn't the only Jew so involved. His work inspired Nathan Straus, a highly successful New York businessman and philanthropist, to establish pasteurized-milk depots for the children of the poor, as well as tuberculosis-prevention centers to stem a then-ram-

---

* *Mazel tov!*

** Dr. Jacobi also attracted attention outside the pediatric field. In his second year in practice, he invented the laryngoscope to examine the difficult-to-reach larynx.

† The importance of Dr. Jacobi's work in behalf of child care can be seen in one startling fact reported in the *World Book Encyclopedia*: until 1870, more than a third of all children in the world died in their first several years of life. The *Encyclopaedia Britannica* notes that owing to the lack of pediatric knowledge prior to the twentieth century "twenty percent to forty percent of all infants born alive died during the first year of life."

pant disease caused largely by milk from diseased cows.

Straus had attended a convention in Europe where Louis Pasteur demonstrated the importance of heating milk to rid it of germs. Impressed, Straus launched the movement in America to pasteurize milk* and in 1892 set up the first pasteurized-milk stations. It took twenty years, but thanks to Straus's efforts, state governments throughout America eventually established the local apparatus to inspect milk. Today pasteurization is taken for granted.

A few months later your mother feels a need to give you cute-but-active-little-thing something to make sure you grow big and strong. So, with the advice of your pediatrician, you are taking vitamins. That's very interesting, because a Polish Jew originated the word "vitamin."

Casimir Funk, born in 1884, worked in England at the Lister Institute before coming to the United States in 1915. While working on a project to cure beriberi, he discovered that a compound derived from yeast proved potent against it. Since he believed the anti-beriberi factor belonged to a class of chemical compounds called amines, he termed it "vitamine," which is Latin for "life amine." Furthermore Funk, sensing that many diseases resulted from deficiencies in the diet, proposed that beriberi, scurvy, pellagra, and rickets resulted from a lack of "vitamines."

Funk was incorrect only in that not all "vitamines" were amines. Later, in 1920, the British scientist Jack Cecil Drummond instituted the custom of labeling certain soluble substances by the term coined by Funk, but dropping the "e" to indicate that amines were not part of them. Thus were born the names of the first vitamins discovered—vitaman A, vitamin B, and vitamin C. Funk, the original author of the term,

---

* Straus also founded a Pasteur Institute in Palestine and there set up health centers and food stations for needy Arabs and Jews. His activities led President Taft, in a somewhat muddled yet well-meaning speech, to say, "Nathan Straus is a great Jew and the greatest Christian of us all."

became research consultant in 1936 for the U.S. Vitamin Corporation.*

Soon you are ready to be immunized against some of the diseases that have afflicted children throughout history. One of the vaccines you receive will protect you against poliomyelitis. Known since ancient times, polio had presented scientists with an especially difficult battle. In 1952, 57,879 cases of polio causing 3,300 deaths were reported in the United States—the highest figures ever recorded.

A year earlier a Jew, Jonas E. Salk, son of a New York garment worker, had begun research on polio prevention at the University of Pittsburgh. In 1954, his new vaccine was tested on 1,800,000 children—one of the largest field experiments in United States medical history. By 1955 the Salk vaccine was ready for use throughout the country. In 1961 another Jew, Albert Sabin of the University of Cincinnati, developed an oral polio vaccine also declared safe and effective for widespread use. The result of the research efforts of these two Jewish doctors: in 1974, twenty years after the Salk vaccine was first tested, only seven cases of polio were reported in the United States.

The massive research monies that made these vaccines possible were collected through an idea of another Jew. The entertainer Eddie Cantor was a close friend of President Franklin Delano Roosevelt, who was afflicted with polio. As told by Eddie Cantor in his autobiography, *Take My Life*, he and FDR were talking one day about ways to raise contributions for polio research, when Roosevelt asked him if he could organize a campaign to raise a dollar a year from a million people. Cantor responded that he thought a million contributions would slide to only

---

* One can only bemoan the loss to our language when Funk decided not to follow the usual scientific practice of naming his discovery after himself. What an interesting world we would have if we took One-A-Day Funks instead of vitamins.

several hundred thousand a year if FDR wasn't re-elected.

"Why not let everyone in on this for ten cents?" Cantor suggested. "I think I can get you ten million dimes faster than a million dollars."

When Roosevelt asked how the dimes would be solicited and where they would be sent, Cantor replied, "Just give me the use of your name and address, Mr. President. You have a lovely address here! I'll bet you the American people flood the White House. You may lick infantile paralysis with this march of dimes."

The President slapped Cantor's knee in jubilation. "Eddie Cantor, you've just given us our slogan, 'The March of Dimes.'"

The campaign was launched and within seventy-two hours, the White House was inundated with mail containing dimes. A series of radio broadcasts featuring Cantor and other stars followed, and the March of Dimes became a part of the American research scene. Today, with polio having been conquered, the March of Dimes is funding research into birth defects.

As your proud parents look on, you continue to grow. Of course, you may still contract some disease or infection, but there are drugs to take care of most of them. For instance, there are the antibiotics, termed "miracle" or "wonder" drugs. The first of these to be discovered was penicillin, but the second—and the first wonder drug to be discovered in America—resulted from the efforts of a Jewish microbiologist.

Selman Abraham Waksman, who had been a Yeshiva student during his youth in Russia, carried out exhaustive research in his laboratory at Rutgers University, and in 1945 discovered the antibiotic streptomycin, which is successful against infections that resist penicillin and sulfa drugs. Streptomycin was also the first drug successful in the treatment of tuberculosis. Other ailments you might contract that streptomycin would help combat: typhoid fever, pneumonia, dysentery, whooping cough, influenza, infections of the urinary tract, wound infections such as gas gangrene, and even gonorrhea. For his achievement, Dr. Waksman was awarded the Nobel Prize for medicine in 1952.*

You're in elementary school now, and one day you don't feel just right so you go down the hall to the nurse's office. As your temperature is being taken, you can thank a nice Jewish lady for founding America's system of public school nursing.

Although raised in luxury, Lillian D. Wald (1867-1940) took a nurse's training course in a New York City hospital. There she was exposed to the plight of the poor, and after graduating she taught classes to show the disadvantaged how to care for themselves. She went to live on New York's Lower East Side, began a program of nursing visits to the poor, and finally founded the first nonsectarian visiting nurse program in the United States. Her base of operations was the Nurses' Settlement, later known as the Henry Street Settlement, which she founded on the Lower East Side. Here she helped launch another idea that spread throughout America. She converted the backyard into a small park to give the local children a place to play off the crowded streets. Thus was born the idea for city playgrounds.

As you grow, you get colds, just like everybody else. Fortunately there are cold remedies, and a drugstore is just a phone call or a short drive away—thanks to Dr. David de Leon, the head of the Confederacy's medical department, who, according to the book *Poor Cousins*, had the idea for the American drugstore.

Maybe your symptoms persist and you think you don't have a cold, after all. Your mother takes you to

---

* Back in 1941, a Rutgers University official had recommended that Waksman be dismissed as an economy move. At that time Waksman was earning $4,620 annually. After his discovery of streptomycin, Rutgers received royalties from drug companies for every gram of streptomycin sold.

a specialist, who, most likely, will start you off with "scratch tests" to determine if you have an allergy. This procedure was developed by a Jew, O. M. Schloss, in 1912. Another important medical discovery, the "Schick test" to identify diphtheria, also was the work of a Jew—Dr. Béla Schick, an immunologist and clinical professor of diseases of children.

During one of your visits to the doctor's office, you find yourself reading the diplomas and certificates on his wall. Is he a member of the American Medical Association? An American Jewish physician, Dr. Isaac Hays, was one of that organization's founders.

Born in Philadelphia in 1796, Hays, an ophthalmologist, proposed the creation of the National Medical Association, which became the AMA, in a resolution to the New York Medical Society in 1846. He became the group's first treasurer, and in 1847 wrote a code of ethics that served as the basis of the principles of the AMA, as well as of state and county medical societies in the United States. He also played a leading role in the field of American medical journalism.

You're in your teens now. You've had a few illnesses, but nothing too serious, and your growth is continuing nicely. After all, as a result of arduous research we now understand a lot more about nutrition than we once did. For instance, pellagra, a disease especially afflicting the South up to the beginning of this century, was thought to be contagious. Joseph Goldberger, a Hungarian-born Jew who entered the U.S. Public Health Service in 1899, made a thorough study of the disease and concluded that it was not spread from one person to another, but caused by poor nutritional practices. Among Southern whites, he found the cause to be malnutrition; in the case of Southern blacks, it was the large quantities of sugar, syrup, cornbread, coffee, and sweet potatoes in their diet. Goldberger concluded from his research that the lack of milk and meat, the main sources of vitamin B, caused the disease; he could produce it in prisoners simply by limiting their diets.

Goldberger spent the rest of his life researching various diseases, often using himself as a guinea pig, with near-fatal results.* At his death in 1929, he had, according to the *World Book Encyclopedia*, "added to the knowledge of yellow fever, typhoid, typhus, Rocky Mountain spotted fever, straw-mite itch, measles, diphtheria and influenza." Goldberger's major legacy, though, as stated by *The Pictorial History of the Jewish People*, was in the area of nutrition: "More then any one else in the world Goldberger laid the basis for the science of nutrition which calls for a balanced diet for the preservation of health."

Let's suppose that one day you have an attack of appendicitis. This once was invariably fatal, but don't worry—now an operation can save your life. While you're recuperating, you might say "thank you" to the Jew who was the first doctor in the world to diagnose appendicitis and to operate successfully on it—Dr. Simon Baruch (1840-1921). Until he accomplished this in 1888, appendicitis had either been treated medically—not always a sound, or successful, approach—or by opening and cleansing the abdominal cavity. Dr. Baruch had the revolutionary idea of taking out the diseased appendix before it ruptured. Dr. John A. Wyeth, a renowned surgeon, told the New York Academy of Medicine in 1894, "The profession and humanity owe more to Dr. Baruch than to any other one man for the development of surgery of appendicitis."

Dr. Baruch made numerous other contributions to medicine, such as discoveries in connection with malaria, the diseases of childhood, and the importance of cleanliness in preventive medicine. His involvement in promoting washing and bathing as a means to health included the opening of America's first pub-

---

* Among his unorthodox methods: he injected the blood of a person suffering from pellagra into his own veins, and later ate a mixture of the products from the body of a pellagrin to demonstrate that the disease was not infectious. While conducting experiments on himself to study malaria and typhus, he nearly died.

lic bath, and he was called "the Apostle of Bathing."
Another of his notable achievements: his son was
Bernard Baruch, the famed financier and advisor to
presidents.

You're now in college or maybe working when
you see a Red Cross poster on the bulletin board
asking for blood donors. Being a good citizen, you
volunteer. As you lie on the table and the nurse
probes for your vein, think about the importance of
the American Red Cross in our public health system
—and then think about the debt we all owe to a Jew
who was present at its inception.

As everyone knows, Clara Barton was the founder
of the American Red Cross, but her "right-hand man"
—and therefore the number one man in the early days
of the organization—was Adolphus Simeon Solomons, a New York–born Jewish publisher. Solomons
(1826-1910) was in 1851 the special dispatch bearer
to Berlin for Daniel Webster, then Secretary of State.
In 1859, he became printing contractor to the United
States government and in 1871 was elected to the
House of Representatives from the District of Columbia. Active in Washington's civic and philanthropic
affairs, Solomons joined with Clara Barton in trying
to get America to form a branch of the International
Red Cross, which had been organized in Geneva in
1863. (America had been cool to the idea because of
European support for the South during the Civil War,
and this attitude continued for eighteen years because
of congressional fear of foreign entanglements.)

On May 21, 1881, the first meeting called to consider the formation of an American Red Cross and to
urge America to ratify the Geneva Convention was
held in Solomons' home. Here the decision was made
to organize the American Association of the Red
Cross. Solomons was elected vice president.

President Chester A. Arthur signed the Red Cross
Treaty in 1882, and when the International Red Cross
Congress was convened in Geneva in 1884, Clara
Barton was appointed along with Solomons and one

other person to represent America. Solomons was later elected the first American vice president of the International Red Cross, and his name was placed second to that of Clara Barton on the certificate of incorporation.

Solomons was also one of twelve people who petitioned Congress in 1903 asking for a reorganization of the association as the American Red Cross. In 1905, Congress responded by granting a new charter that reorganized it as the American National Red Cross we know today.

A further Jewish Connection with the formation of the Red Cross in America lies in the fact that the first uniforms for Red Cross nurses were designed by a Jew. Henry A. Dix, a Russian immigrant who had built up a large business manufacturing uniforms for waitresses, maids, and saleswomen, was selected for the job during World War I. The design he came up with became internationally known as a symbol of the Red Cross.

Later, Dix was asked by the U.S. government to provide uniforms for army and navy nurses. When he died in 1938 at the age of eighty-eight, he no longer owned his garment company: sixteen years earlier he had simply given it to his employees.

Now you're old enough to fall in love, and you decide to get married. You and your beloved go to get your marriage license and find that you must take a blood test to be certain you do not have syphilis. This is a health measure for you, your spouse-to-be, and any children you may have, because this disease is transmitted, with fatal results, to offspring.

The medical procedure to detect syphilis is called the Wassermann test after its developer, the German Jew August von Wassermann. A physician and bacteriologist, Wasserman (1866-1925) achieved worldwide fame in 1907 when he first announced his discovery, which indicates both past infections and present activity of syphilis by identifying syphilitic antibodies in the blood serum. The test is so reliable that the Medical Research Council of England said of it: "There is no process of biochemical diagnosis that gives more trustworthy information or is liable to a smaller margin of error than the Wassermann test when it is performed with completeness and with proper skill and care."

If you find that you have syphilis, another Jew is ready to help. Paul Ehrlich (1854-1915), a German biochemist, created modern chemotherapy with his discovery of a cure for syphilis—called Salvarsan or "606" because Ehrlich discovered it on his 606th experiment. For his work, Ehrlich won the Nobel Prize in 1908.

But let's hope you pass your Wassermann test, and you and your beloved are married. The great day arrives when your baby is born and, having given a lusty yell, is taken to the nursery to await the first visit from the pediatrician. You give thanks, of course, to the founder of pediatrics, Dr. Abraham Jacobi. . . .

Which brings us to the moral of this chapter. You can get through life without the Jews, but not well.

X

You Always Hurt
the One You Love

*A different look at
the persecution of the Jews*

FACT: "Hip! Hip! Hooray" is based on an anti-Semitic phrase.

FACT: The Portuguese expulsion caused only eight Jews to leave the country—but was the most brutal on record.

FACT: The century and a half since the emancipation of the Jews has been the worst period of persecution in Jewish history. More Jews have been killed since emancipation than were alive when it began in the 1800s.

FACT: Jews in Russia had to pay a special tax to wear a *yarmulkah*.

FACT: In eighteenth-century Prussia, Jews were forced to buy white porcelain monkeys from the royal factory as a condition for marriage—or burial.

ONE CAN NO MORE talk about Jews without mentioning persecution than one can tell the story of the three little pigs and leave out the wolf. But, in another of those twists in Jewish history, persecution has occasionally helped make the Jewish Connection.

First, let us look at ways in which anti-Semitism has affected the lives of some noted Jews. Because of anti-Semitism, Albert Einstein did not win the Nobel Prize for his general theory of relativity. Philipp von Lenard, a German anti-Semite who sat on the Nobel Prize committee, argued each year for seven years against Einstein's selection. Not until 1921 did Einstein receive the Nobel Prize and then it was for a less monumental discovery.

Then there was the college degree that took forty-one years. In 1831, James Joseph Sylvester became the first Jew allowed to enter Cambridge University, but because of anti-Jewish restrictions not until 1872 was he allowed to take his degree. By then he was established as one of England's leading mathematicians.

There is even the case of a Rothschild who was blocked by an anti-Semitic barrier. Lionel de Rothschild campaigned to become a member of the English Parliament and was elected, but because he refused to take the Christian oath of office then required, he was not seated. Rothschild campaigned again, won again, and was again refused the right to serve. Still he persisted. Over the course of eleven years, he pressed for his right to be sworn in as a Jew and seated in the House of Commons.

Rothschild's battle was ironic in terms of the times. Jews enjoyed considerable emancipation over a large part of Europe, the Rothschilds had more prestige than the families of most of the members seated in Parliament, and Jewish-born Benjamin Disraeli was one of the most important figures in British life. Finally Lord Lucan, who had been responsible for the unsuccessful Charge of the Light Brigade, recommended that each House of Parliament authorize its own oath to be taken by its members. This broke the bottleneck, and the suggestion was passed into law.

On July 26, 1858, Lionel de Rothschild presented himself again before the House of Commons, and this time took the oath on the Hebrew Bible with his head covered according to Jewish ritual. Strangely enough, the official record indicates that, having won his eleven-year battle, Rothschild never uttered a word in the time he served!

Anti-Semitism has, of course, inflicted pains a great deal harsher than impediments to elected office and delays in winning awards. While the actual word "anti-Semitism" was not coined until the late nineteenth century, literature disparaging the Jews has a long history. In the ninth century Agobard, the Bishop of Lyons, wrote the first known anti-Semitic pamphlet, "Concerning the Insolence of the Jews."

It has taken the century we are so proud to call modern to produce the most savage outburst of anti-Semitism of all time—the Holocaust. The world is supposedly progressing toward a greater civilization, but for the Jew society is actually regressing. The last hundred years have been the worst century of persecution in the history of the Jews. And this intensification of anti-Semitism has actually come in the wake of the emancipation of the Jews, when the ghettos were supposedly abandoned and the Jews welcomed into the world at large. It has been estimated that more Jews have been murdered since emancipation than were even alive when it began at the dawn of the nineteenth century.

Through the centuries, two major reasons for persecution were the repeated claims that the Jews killed

Christ and that Jews used the blood of Christian children in making unleavened bread for Passover. Jewish law, however, is diametrically opposed to the very principles involved in these two accusations. Crucifixion was a form of execution used against many of the people Rome subjugated, including the Jews. But Jewish law directed that the death penalty could be inflicted in only one of four ways—stoning, burning, beheading, and strangulation.

As for the infamous blood libel that hounded Jews through the ages, one need only remember that Jews are stringently restricted from the use of blood. The Jewish dietary laws call for the draining of all blood from any animal before it is eaten, and Jews are instructed to discard an egg if it shows even a drop of red. And yet the blood libel was so widespread that an English ballad about a young English boy said to have been crucified by Jews for his blood was made into twenty-one different versions, some of which were sung in the United States.*

When the brutal persecution of the Jews is reexamined in the light of the nook-and-cranny theory of history, some special ironies emerge. For instance, the expulsion of the Jews from Portugal in 1497 is unanimously considered one of the major tragedies in Jewish history. Yet, because of its extreme ferocity, it resulted in the expulsion of just eight Jews!

Here is how that happened.

In 1497, the King of Portugal decreed that Portugal's 20,000 Jews would be expelled by the end of October unless they accepted Christianity. During the months leading up to the deadline, authorities decided not to wait for volunteers, but to conduct a mass forced conversion. On March 19, 1497, all children of ages four through fourteen were ordered to be present for baptism on the following Sunday—which happened to be the first day of Passover. On

---

* The false accusation that Jews used the blood of Christian children had a most ironic precedent. The pagan Romans charged early Christians with killing Roman children to use their blood in the mass.

that day, children were taken bodily from their homes and forcibly converted.

During the final week before the target date for expulsion, the brutality of the forced conversions was intensified. Many Jews were forced into a palace with no food or water; the only alternative to starvation was conversion. Other Jews were put into a dungeon, which was then nearly walled up, and for a week were reminded of their "choice." By the end of October, only eight Jews were left. All the rest had either converted or died. This handful of Jews was then expelled to carry out the king's decree.

For three hundred years Jews had to contend with the Inquisition, which uprooted the lives of some of the most important Jewish communities in the history of the Diaspora. Neither age nor sex nor position in life, nor even the passage of time, could save one from its ruthless policies. One Portuguese family was first implicated in 1656. After escaping and assuming another name, all were discovered and sentenced to life imprisonment—twenty-four years after the case first started. One woman was first seized by the Inquisition when she was twenty-two, was tried five more times over the next eighteen years, and again brought to trial when she was eighty. That time, the inquiry lasted five years and she was tortured three times. She finally died from the mistreatment.

The Inquisition was not limited to Spain and Portugal. It had informers in France, England, Holland, Italy, Turkey, Africa, India, and the New World. And it lasted longer than is popularly known—its last incident occurred in the nineteenth century, when a schoolteacher was burned at the stake on July 26, 1826.*

---

* When the first full edition of the Hebrew prayer book was printed in America, the editor dropped a long-standing prayer inserted during the height of the Inquisition to commemorate those burned at the stake. Explained the editor, "Martyrdom having ceased and the liberality of mankind assuring us it will no more be revived, it was thought best to omit the prayer." The year was 1826—the same year the Inquisition burned the schoolteacher.

Not all persecution of the Jews has taken such brutal form. At various times in history, Jews have been ordered to wear special hats (usually laughable ones, like the funnel-shaped hat seen in medieval paintings), robes, aprons, and badges to distinguish them from the general population. The need for such identifying symbols is in itself an interesting comment on the extent to which Jews must have been integrated.

Generally accepted as the first to institute the wearing of outward signs was the Arab leader Khalifa Mutawakkel, who in 850 ordered non-Moslems to wear a yellow patch on their sleeves as well as a yellow head covering. The first act of this sort in the Christian world was in 1215 at the Lateran Council, when Pope Innocent III ruled that any Jewish male above the age of thirteen and any Jewish female above the age of eleven must wear a mark, usually a patch, in the front and back of an outer garment.

In some Moslem countries, Jews could not carry swords or ride horses. In the city of Frankfurt in the sixteenth century, Jews had to tell the magistrates when they were receiving out-of-town guests, and Jewish homes had to display a distinctive emblem (usually one selected by authorities for its grotesqueness). In Prague in the seventeenth century, Ferdinand II ordered Jews to listen to a church sermon every Sunday or pay a fine for being truant. (Any Jew found falling asleep during the sermon was also fined.) And in Palermo and Crete Jews were ordered to act as executioners.

What Jews could or could not do to make a living fell under a bewildering array of laws. In one country, Jews could not be shopkeepers; in another, they were allowed to be craftsmen, but not so in a third. They could deal in wood and leather in one place, but not in another. They would be encouraged to start a factory in one country and strictly prohibited elsewhere. They could sell alcohol in one area and be prohibited from doing so in a neighboring region.

Prussia's revised General Privileges of 1750 was a hodgepodge of dos and don'ts. Jews, could deal in foreign or home leather that was prepared but undyed, but they could not trade in raw or dyed leather. They could do business in raw calf and sheepskin, but not in raw cow or horse hides. They could be involved with manufactured woolen and cotton items, but not with raw wool or woolen threads.

Sometimes the authorities outwitted themselves. One country during the mid-seventeenth century required Christian merchants not to have more than a 7 percent profit, while restricting Jewish businessmen to 3 percent. Instead of hurting Jews and helping Christians as was intended, the law did just the opposite. Customers bought more from the Jews because their prices were lower, and the Jewish merchants prospered—which only brought on more hatred from the authorities.

The harassment of the Jews often took the form of petty actions. There is, for instance, what could well be the worst case of faulty mail delivery in history. On the Friday afternoon of November 22, 1619, the Jews of Prague sent a batch of letters to fellow Jews in Vienna. The time was a year and a half after the beginning of the Thirty Years' War and, possibly for military reasons, the mailbag was seized. The letters were not returned but stored in the government's archives—until three hundred years later, when they were finally rescued.

Somehow the Jews found a way to cope with all of the rules, regulations, orders, and harassments. For instance, there was an edict that the Jews in the ghetto of Rome could build only one building for a house of worship. Anyone who knows anything about the Jews knows that they cannot long endure with just one synagogue (or organization, or committee). So the Jews of the Roman ghetto built the one allowed structure, but designed it to house five separate synagogues, with five different entrances.

The form of persecution that is most often overlooked is economic. While the world has been well aware of physical attacks on Jews and Jewish communities, a host of generally unnoticed laws and practices have exploited Jewish money and labor. Ironically, the effect of these policies has often been to extend the reach of the Jewish Connection.

The economic rape of the Jews started with the use of Jewish slave labor in Egypt as told in the Bible, but the practice did not end there. It is thought that the Colosseum in Rome was built in the year 80 by slaves brought from the Land of Israel, remnants of the Jewish population conquered in the siege of Jerusalem ten years previous.

Another famous structure believed to have been built by the use of Jews is France's best-known museum. The Louvre was not erected with Jewish labor but, according to several historians, with the help of Jewish money. One of its builders, Philip Augustus, is said to have secured money for the venture from a source of funds tapped by many European rulers—the Jews.

The use of Jews as moneylenders during the Middle Ages was in many ways just an elaborate system for rulers to lend money out to their subjects at interest rates that would be charged by the Jews; then, through taxes on the Jews, the rulers would vacuum the money into their own pockets. Albert Guérard in his book *France, a Modern History* notes about Philip Augustus that "like most rulers in medieval Europe, he allowed the Jews to gather wealth and then virtuously squeezed it into his own treasury."

Important events in history are also connected with the money of Jews. While Columbus's first expedition was funded by loans secured by Marranos, his second voyage was paid for largely by money and property taken from the Jews who had recently been expelled from Spain. According to *The Jews in the Making of America*, even the valuables left by Jews to relatives who had converted and stayed in Spain were taken and sold to meet the expenses of the expedition—

and Jewish religious articles were also liquidated for it. "Mantels which had been used to cover the scrolls of the law were seized and sold to provide money. According to a Royal Order of May 23, 1493, it was from this fund that 10,000 maravedis were paid to Columbus upon his return as the reward for him who would sight land first."

Throughout history, discrimination against Jews has been caused not so much by hatred for the Jewish people as a lust for Jewish wealth or a fear of Jewish competition. Notice that, despite the Nazis' supposed abhorrence of any contact between Jews and Aryans, they used Jewish hair, skin, skulls, bones, and ashes for various purposes, ranging from clothing for Nazi soldiers* to soap, lampshades, and paperweights. In addition to taking cash, dental gold, jewelry, and watches from Jewish victims, the Nazis also confiscated and used such personal items as eyeglasses, shoes, shavers, scissors, wallets, purses, blankets, scarves, canes, ear mufflers, baby carriages, combs, handbags, pipes, suitcases—even, incredibly, underwear.

But this was nothing new. A favorite practice throughout the ages was to capture Jews either during war or in kidnapping raids, and then hold them for ransom by either the family or the Jewish community. As early as the first centuries of the Christian era, a body of Jewish law grew up around the handling of ransom requests. Later, ransoms were asked of Jews imprisoned on accusations of ritual murder and the blood libel, and sometimes prominent Jews were seized by a ruler to extort a payment.

One such case involved the noted Rabbi Meir of Rothenburg, who was imprisoned by the Hapsburg Emperor Rudolf during the latter part of the thirteenth century. Meir refused to let his friends buy his release for 20,000 marks in silver—an enormous sum.

---

* The hair of Jewish concentration-camp inmates was cut off and processed into felt and spun into yarn. Women's hair was made into innersoles for U-boat crews and felt stockings for railway men.

He remained a captive for seven years, until his death in 1293. The Hapsburgs eventually did make some money off the rabbi, though—fourteen years after his death, a religious Jew ransomed his bones.*

The Jews were subjected to another interesting economic ploy—the arbitrary cancellation by a king, emperor, or pope of any debts or interest on loans owed to Jews. In Germany, such an edict was known as a *Totbrief*; in Spain, the name was *Moratoria*.

Just some of the major examples: Louis VII of France in 1146 exempted the Crusaders of all debts to Jews. Philip Augustus relieved Christians in 1180 of monies they owed to Jews, provided that one-fifth of that amount would be paid to the crown. Louis VIII in 1223 annulled all debts that had been outstanding for five years or more and canceled interest on debts of less than five years. In 1299, King Albert of Germany deprived Jews of interest and directed that it be paid to the monastery of Eberbach. In the fourteenth century alone, such edicts were issued eight times—in 1312, 1315, 1316, 1323, 1326, 1332, 1385, and 1390.

These economic measures against the Jews were important because they eventually spilled over into other forms of persecution. The expulsion of Jews from a country was always accompanied by the complete cancellation of debts to them. A tax on Jewish communities during the Middle Ages was invariably motivated by either a desire to gain the Jews' valuables or the wish to wipe out debts.

A document that has come to us from the pen of a non-Jew tells how the Jews of Strasbourg were herded into their cemetery on St. Valentine's Day in 1348, and more than two thousand of them were burned alive because of a superstitious belief that they had caused the Black Death. Only those who accepted

---

* The ransoming of a dead body was not out of the ordinary. Numerous cases are on record of Jewish bodies being dug up from cemeteries and held until the family paid for its return.

baptism were spared. Notes the writer, "And everything that was owed to the Jews was canceled, and the Jews had to surrender all pledges and notes that they had taken for debts. The money was indeed the thing that killed the Jews. If they had been poor and if the feudal lords had not been in debt to them they would not have been burnt."

Sometimes, though, a ruler found the Jews more economically advantageous alive than dead. Monk William of Newburgh wrote that England's King Richard the Lionhearted, on being told about the York riots in 1190, became outraged over the massacre of the Jews "both for the insult to his royal majesty and for the great loss to the treasury."

U.S. Chief Justice Marshall knew what he was saying when he declared, "The power to tax is the power to destroy." Governments throughout history have used taxes in destructive ways against the Jews.

Ironically, taxes have been with the Jews since the beginning of the Jewish nation.

The Bible tells us that the Children of Israel had to pay a tax while in the desert. Later, during the time of the Second Temple, Jewish communities outside the Land of Israel paid Jews in Jerusalem a special tax for the maintenance and operation of the Temple. When the Second Temple was destroyed, the Romans converted this voluntary tax into the Fiscus Judaicus or "Jewish Tax" and cruelly diverted the money to the upkeep of Jupiter Capitolinus, the temple to the Roman god—a practice that continued through the fourth century. The emperors of the Holy Roman Empire in Germany renewed the levy, giving it the name *Opferpfennig* and putting the funds into their own treasuries.

Taxation of the Jews during the Middle Ages was so onerous that, according to one estimate, in England prior to the expulsion of the Jews in 1290, Jews contributed one-thirteenth of the royal receipts. During the fifteenth century, Jews paid taxes equaling one-fifth of the revenues of the larger cities in the German empire. Jews also had to contribute to various wars and were burdened with a number of double taxes.

Benjamin Franklin pointed out the inevitability of both death and taxes; during the Middle Ages, Jews had to pay a tax on death itself. It was a special tax levied on cemetery use. But in addition, to get to the cemetery, the family had to pay "escort money." Shades of the Mafia! There was also the "Jewish body tax," which travelers were forced to pay local authorities for a military escort as they passed through a city.

European Jews also paid a "protection" tax. Since they were considered the personal property of the king—who could and did sell them, pawn them, give them as gifts—they had to provide compensation for being under his wing. It sounds just like the shakedown of the corner grocer by a local hoodlum.

Jews also paid a special "coronation tax" to every emperor, king, and prince when he ascended his throne, and a special "imperial" tax—as in the case of the Jews in Frankfurt-am-Main, who were ordered to supply all the parchment needed by the emperor's chancellery, all the bedding required by the court, and all the pots and pans for the palace kitchen, and to pay extra sums to imperial officials. And then, of course, the Jews had their regular taxes to pay, just like everybody else.

Here is just a sampling of some of the other taxes imposed on Jews:

• The Golden Penny tax, an assessment of one florin imposed throughout the German empire during the second half of the fourteenth century on every Jew above the age of twelve who possessed over 20 florins.

• The *Laibzoll*, a special tax Jews in Germany had to pay from the sixth century through the eighteenth every time they crossed a frontier or entered a city.

• In the early nineteenth century in the Austro-Hungarian Empire, Jews had to pay a tax on the candles they used for Sabbaths and holidays.

• In the middle of the eighteenth century in Prussia, Jews were forced to buy—at exorbitant rates—such porcelain products as white monkeys to help finance the porcelain industry. Frederick the Great had bought the Berlin Porcelain Works in 1763, and purchase of its goods was a condition for Jewish marriages, funerals, and even for the right to own houses. The tax led to the accumulation of so much porcelain by the Jews that its resale drove down the price of the wares being produced in the royal factory. In 1787 this tax was replaced by a cash payment of 40,000 thaler, exacted from the Jewish community at large.

• The czars placed a tax on every kosher animal slaughtered, every pound of kosher meat, and every religious article of clothing worn by Jews. To wear a skullcap, Russian Jews had to pay five silver rubles per *yarmulkah* per year.

In the middle of the twelfth century, a form of physical abuse was changed to a tax. Charlemagne had instituted the custom of giving each Jew at Eastertime a smack on the ear hard enough to knock him down. An obviously civilizing world changed this custom into a tax, which Jews had to pay to the canons of St. Serin of Toulouse.

Jewish students at the University of Padua during the Middle Ages were exempted from the requirement calling upon Jews to wear a red hat; they could wear a black headdress like the other students. However, in exchange, the Jewish students were to maintain an open house on graduation day and stock enough food and drink to serve anybody who wanted to come by.

Often the authorities were not satisfied with the payments they received. Joseph of Siena, a trader dealing in old clothes and remnants at the beginning of the seventeenth century, left memoirs which record that the grand duke came to his city in 1625 and appointed two men to collect a levy to pay for his entertainment. The two emissaries came to Joseph and "demanded a pair of sheets, a bed canopy, a blanket, and a pillow—twice as much as they imposed upon anyone else." Joseph says that he "gave them everything they asked" but one of the emissaries did not like the merchandise. Says Joseph, obviously pained at the indignity of it all, the emissary "thrice threw what I gave into the middle of the street with great contumely and derision, telling me that it was not enough, and that they desired better stuff."

The irony in all this is that even when the Jews tax themselves they pay more than anyone else. Citizens of the modern State of Israel are the highest-taxed people in the world. During 1976, their average tax rate soared to 70 percent of their income. The second-closest nation, Norway, had an average levy of 46 percent.

Of course, the high tax rate in Israel is primarily due to its security needs, with 38 percent of the national budget in 1975 going for defense. At least these Jewish taxes are going toward insuring a Jewish state and not toward supporting a royal porcelain factory.

Fortunately, Jews have learned to laugh about their taxes. Several years ago, when the Israeli government built a modern, multistory home for the nation's tax agency, Israelis immediately dubbed the building "the Second Wailing Wall."

The age-old campaign against the Jews survives today in an expression that shows extreme jubilation: "Hip! Hip! Hooray!"

One of the derivations of this word can be found in *Brewer's Dictionary of Phrase and Fable*, in which "Hip" or "Hep" is said to be the first letters in the Latin expression *Hierosolyma Est Perdita*, "Jerusalem is destroyed."

"Hip! Hip!" was shouted at the Jews by German knights during the Middle Ages. It was the slogan used by the Crusaders on their march to Jerusalem. It was also used in the title of the Hep Movement, which first erupted in Würzburg, Germany, in 1819 and spread throughout the country. Its leaders lusted for revenge against Jews and provided a stimulus for German nationalism that eventually culminated in the Holocaust. Their battle cry was "Hep! Hep! Hep! Death and destruction to all the Jews!"

"Hooray," according to the same reference book, "derives from Slavonic *Hu-raj* (to paradise)." In other words, "Hip! Hip! Hooray!" says *Brewer's*, means "Jerusalem is lost to the infidel and we are on the road to paradise."

"Hep" has also, according to another source, been traced to the German word meaning "Give," so that when the Jew baiters descended on a Jewish community during the course of a pogrom they yelled out "Hep! Hep!" for the Jews to give up their monies and valuables.

The use of the phrase "Hip! Hip! Hooray!"—so steeped in the suffering of Jews of not-so-long-ago— as a shout of joy is an irony that is very much a part of the Jewish Connection. Even more paradoxical is the fact that, in trying to abuse the Jews, the persecutors helped preserve them.

How? Consider the ghetto. Although life there was grim (one ghetto was called "the Inferno"), it had its advantages for Jewish survival. The ghetto created a close-knit Jewish community. It allowed a form of autonomy, since the authorities, once having confined the Jews to one quarter, were often willing to let them govern themselves. In fact, Jews at times asked to have ghettos. A section of their own would be easier to safeguard against assaults, and a close community could safeguard against any diminution in the ranks of the faithful. One historian has noted that the ghetto made certain that a people without a homeland had land of their own. Another, Lucy Dawidowicz, placed the ghetto in perspective this way:

The medieval ghetto had originated as a strategy for Jewish existence and survival [she writes in *The War Against the Jews*]. During the Crusades Jews petitioned for separate quarters within whose walls they might better defend themselves. . . . Later when the church advocated the ghetto as a means of separating Christians from Jews, the voluntary Jewish quarter was transformed into an obligatory ghetto, walled, its two gates guarded by Christian gatekeepers who locked the inhabitants in at night and during Christian festivals . . . but the medieval ghetto was not a prison. Every day Jews left the ghetto to conduct their business outside; every day Gentiles came into the ghetto to conduct their business.

Indeed, the Jewish people could not have survived their history of persecution without some counterbalancing force. The benefits to be found in a ghetto existence during the Middle Ages is one example. But that is a story of Jews helping themselves. Another force for survival lies in the intriguing tale of how aid, even love, for the Jews has come from non-Jews. This other part of the picture might well be called "The Greatest Story Never Told."

XI

The Greatest Story
Never Told

*How non-Jews have helped make the
Jewish Connection*

FACT: The first printing of a complete edition of the Talmud was done by a Christian printer—who was encouraged by a pope.

FACT: A Roman emperor encouraged the Jews to build a Third Temple and under his direction work actually was started.

FACT: A non-Jewish British army officer secretly helped build the Haganah, provided Moshe Dayan with his first formal instruction in warfare, and developed a military strategy still used by Israel's defense forces.

FACT: The first modern history of the Jews was written by a non-Jew.

FACT: The State of Israel was saved by Joseph Stalin.

CONSIDERING THE CENTURIES of persecution the Jews have faced since the destruction of the First Temple 2,500 years ago, the very existence of Jews in today's world is a remarkable achievement. How have the Jews survived? And how have they survived with such vitality?

A large part of the answer lies, of course, in sheer determination—what might be termed staying power. But many times crucial help has come from what seems, on the surface, to be the most ironic, least likely source—non-Jews.

The first chapter of the greatest-story-never-told begins, as do so many pieces of the Jewish Connection, in the Bible.

Moses, having brought the Children of Israel out of Egypt, has problems in controlling this motley crowd of former slaves tasting freedom for the first time in four hundred years. What he needs is an organization to take some of the burden of leadership, especially the responsibility of acting as judge. Who emerges with a plan for Moses? A non-Jew, Jethro, Moses' father-in-law. Moses takes his advice, and a potentially damaging problem in the first stages of Jewish nationhood is averted.

Babylonia's destruction of the First Temple 2,500 years ago and subsequent expulsion of the Jews could have been the death knell for the Jews. This was the first time Jews had been forced into exile, and the experience of other peoples had usually been assimilation and then disappearance. But the Babylonians were soon defeated by the Persians, whose King, Cyrus II, gave permission for Jews to return to the Land of Israel—and encouraged those who journeyed back to rebuild the Temple. As a result, the Second Temple was erected just seventy years later; Jews were able to live and worship in the Land of Israel for another five centuries; and a pattern of international life for the Jews was launched that would last for more than two thousand years—a remnant of Jewry living in the Promised Land, a larger population living outside it, in what was to be called the Diaspora.

The Persian King's important role in Jewish history did not escape the prophet Isaiah, who regarded Cyrus as a divine agent. In fact, Isaiah referred to Cyrus by using the special Hebrew word for those anointed for special service—*Meshiach*, which has come to be translated as "Messiah." This is, though, an indication of how the word Meshiach has been abused, since Isaiah, no matter how much he admired Cyrus, would not have considered a non-Jewish ruler as the longed-for Messiah.

The next world leader to befriend the Jews was Alexander the Great (356-323 B.C.E.), who at an early age became ruler of the then-known world and could have destroyed the Jews, all of whom came under his control. Instead, he left Palestine unmolested and helped found one of the ancient world's great Jewish communities in Alexandria.

The Romans, during their years of world control, were responsible for such major disasters for the Jews as the destruction of the Second Temple, the devastation at Massada, and the loss of Jewish control of the Promised Land that would last until 1948. Why, in all their centuries of power, did the Romans not destroy the Jewish communities outside the Land of Israel? The answer lies in the remarkable kindness of Julius Caesar (100-44 B.C.E.).

More than a hundred years before the destruction of the Second Temple, Caesar set a pattern of support for Jews that was to be followed later by most Roman leaders. Although the Jews experienced periodic changes in fortune, notoriously under Caligula and Nero, Caesar's decrees lasted as the guiding principles of the Roman empire until the time of the Christian emperors—a span of three hundred years.

Caesar's edicts have been termed by one modern historian "the Magna Carta of the Jews." They granted Jews full freedom of worship, rights of assembly for religious worship, permission to collect funds for the local Jewish community, and to send money to Jerusalem for support of the Temple. Because of the Jews' prohibition against working on the Sabbath and their need for kosher food, they were exempt from military service. In addition, Caesar recognized special Jewish courts to deal with cases involving only Jews, so that a Jewish tribunal could handle the problems of the Jewish community.

What Caesar had rendered to the Jews was not forgotten when he was assassinated. The Roman historian Suetonius recorded that Jews mourned Caesar more than any other group and that Jews came nightly to cry and wail at his funeral pyre.

After Caesar's death, his edicts favorable to Jews were upheld by the decree of the Roman Senate and reaffirmed by Roman military commanders throughout the Roman empire. Caesar's grandnephew and adopted son, Augustus, contributed expensive gifts to adorn the Temple in Jerusalem and ordered that a burnt offering be made in the Temple—forever and at his expense—as his way of paying homage to the Jewish God.

Despite Caesar's legacy of tolerance, the Jews in Palestine, like the people of other conquered nations, were considered a subject group, and their eventual revolt was dealt with as a rebellion that threatened the stability of the Roman empire. Titus's army destroyed the Temple not so much in retaliation against the Jews but as a warning to other nations. In traditional Roman fashion, only the Jews in Palestine who had revolted were dealt with harshly, while the Jewish communities in Rome and elsewhere were unmolested.

And when Titus became Emperor in 79, he did not bother Jews living peaceably in the empire.*

Another Roman emperor who left a harsh imprint on the Jewish mind was Hadrian, who crushed the Bar Kochba revolt in 135 with particular ferocity and desecrated the Temple site in Jerusalem by building a shrine to Jupiter. Hadrian was followed by Antoninus Pius, who rescinded many of Hadrian's restrictions against Jewish religious practices. A later Roman emperor, Elagabalus (218-222), had such a warm attitude toward Judaism that he had himself circumcised and would not eat pork. The emperor who succeeded him was Alexander Severus (222-235), who was so friendly to Jews that he was called by his enemies "Syrian archisynagogus," which one historian has said was approximate, for his day, to being called "rabbi."

With the reign of Constantine the Roman emperors became Christian, and Jews started to have real trouble with the authorities. A notable exception to this trend was Julian (361-363), the last pagan Roman emperor. Julian was partial to Jews and antagonistic to Christians. He abolished the special taxes the Jews had been paying. In a famous letter to the Jewish community sent in 362, Julian asked the Jews to offer prayers for "my imperial office" so that "when I have successfully concluded the war with Persia, I may rebuild by my own efforts the sacred city of Jerusalem, which for so many years you have longed to see inhabited, and may bring settlers there, and together with you, may glorify the Most High God therein."

Work on clearing ground and building the Third Temple actually began, as related in *Ecclesiastical History*, written in Greek by Salamanius Hermias Sozomenus about 450. A native Palestinian who claimed to cite eyewitness accounts, he recorded that an earthquake accompanied by fire stopped the work.

---

* Titus's reign as Emperor was extremely brief—only two years—which led Jews of the day to speculate that his untimely death was divine punishment for leading the destruction of the Temple.

Such omens were said to show the Jews were not to be allowed to rebuild the Temple. The historian Will Durant says it was natural-gas explosions that put a temporary halt to the project. The death of Julian in 363 and the return to power of Christian Roman emperors finally ended the idea.

When Christianity became the dominant religion in Europe, an irony of historic proportions took place. On one hand, Judaism was considered not only an outcast religion but an outright foe of Christian dogma. On the other hand, in the minds of the popes and other leading Christian thinkers, the continued existence of Jews served a purpose—reminding Christians of the origins of their faith and showing them what could happen to those who did not accept the Christian way. Thus, although harassment of Jews continued, popes and other authorities were generally careful to preserve the Jewish communities.

While various popes issued bulls and convened councils that set up ghettos, restricted Jewish-Christian contact, and decreed limitations on Jewish occupations, these same or other popes would also come out against the wave of pogroms and persecutions that periodically swept Europe. The occasional appearance of a blood libel, for instance, in which a Christian was said to have been killed by Jews for blood to be used in the baking of matzohs, was condemned by numerous popes.

Pope Gregory I (590-604) introduced the concept that Christianity had an obligation to protect Jews from attack—a principle of tolerance, notes historian Jacob Marcus in *The Jew in the Medieval World*, "which Gregory I had taken over from the later Roman Empire" and which "became basic in the relations between Catholicism and Judaism." Wrote Gregory I in 598: "Even as it is not allowed to the Jews in their assemblies presumptuously to undertake for themselves more than that which is permitted them by law, even so they ought not to suffer any disadvantage in these [privileges] which have been granted them." This sentiment was echoed by a long list of popes in defending Jewry against Christian mob attack.

A series of papal bulls appeared, from the time of Calixtus II (1119-1124) through the fifteenth century, which warned Christians of excommunication or other punishments for forcing Jews to convert, robbing Jews, attacking them, or desecrating Jewish cemeteries. "No Christian shall presume to seize, imprison, wound, torture, mutilate, kill, or inflict violence on them," decreed Pope Gregory X in a typical decree issued in 1272. "In addition, no one shall disturb them in any way during the celebration of their festivals, whether by day or by night."

In that same bull, the Pope declared that, since Jews were not allowed to be witnesses against a Christian, it was only proper that a Jew could be declared guilty only if there were Jewish witnesses to testify against him.* And the infamous blood-libel accusations against Jews were held up to the ecclesiastical light and emphatically denied: "Most falsely do these Christians claim that Jews have secretly and furtively carried away these [Christian] children and killed them, and that the Jews offer sacrifice from the heart and the blood of these children, since their law in this matter precisely and expressly forbids Jews to sacrifice, eat, or drink the blood, or to eat the flesh of animals having claws. . . . Nevertheless very many Jews are often seized and detained unjustly because of this."

Although papal decrees and interventions had limited success in protecting European Jewry—and indeed various popes committed outrages of their own —the Jewish people at least got some support from the Church, which did not advocate the elimination of the Jews as a matter of policy. And, as much as Jews suffered from being followers of the minority

* In England under the charter granted to Chief Rabbi Joseph by Henry I, which defined the Jews as the King's wards, the value of the Jews' oath held against the word of twelve Christians.

religion, the Holocaust came to Europe only when a godless regime swept away whatever moderating influences the Church could exercise.

One way in which the Church helped the Jews survive was in supporting the great cultural achievements of Judaism. For instance, a pope was instrumental in the preservation of Jewish scholarship and the spread of Jewish learning.

Pope Leo X, who reigned from 1513 to 1521, encouraged the printing of the first complete edition of the Talmud. Under his patronage, fifteen volumes of the Babylonian Talmud were printed in Venice beginning in 1519.*

This printing of the Talmud had an impact that is still felt, for its pagination and type layout, with the Talmudic text in the middle and various commentaries along both sides, became the model for all other editions—and is used today.

Pope Leo's actions were especially important in the light of the intermittent Church practice of burning wagonloads of Talmud manuscripts and banning its teaching because of false charges—usually by Jews who had converted—that it criticized Church doctrine. Pope Leo's involvement in the printing of the Talmud was therefore an important step in encouraging religious freedom for Jews, and making available the teachings of the Talmud to world Jewry.

Of course, Pope Leo's efforts did not stop all Talmud burning. In Rome in 1553, great numbers of books of all types of Jewish literature were burned, and later in Poland thousands of volumes of the Talmud were put to the torch. But now the Jews had access to printing presses, and could turn out more copies of the Talmud than could be burned.

---

* Special permission from the Church or the government was required in those days for the printing of a book to insure that the Church or the king was not attacked. Authorities recognized the power of the press from the beginning, so Pope Leo's patronage of a printing of the Talmud was more than symbolic.

Another Christian played an important part in preparing that historic edition of the Talmud. The printer Daniel Bomberg (whose name may sound Jewish, but who was a Christian) had set up his press in Venice in 1516. He devoted great care and attention to printing the Talmud, starting in 1519 wth the tractate on Passover (*Pesachim*) and working steadily on this important project until 1523, when he finished the last tractate, Purification (*Taharot*).

Seemingly fascinated with Jewish literature, Bomberg is said to have done more to spread Jewish learning than any other printer of his time. In the thirty-two years his business operated in Venice, he published an impressive range of Jewish material. He printed not only the first complete edition of the Babylonian Talmud, but later the first complete edition of the Palestinian Talmud as well. He was also first to print the rabbinic Bible, which contained the Hebrew text, a translation into Aramaic, and rabbinic commentaries. This edition, printed in 1517, was the first to present Samuel, Kings, and Chronicles in two books, to separate Nehemiah from Ezra, and to show chapter numbers in Hebrew letters. These innovations had a great influence on future printed Bibles, whether printed in Hebrew or in other languages.

An even more important work was the second edition of the rabbinic Bible printed by Bomberg, brought out in 1524. Since the first edition had been prepared by a Jew who had become a Christian monk, Jewish authorities were hesitant to use it. Rabbi Jacob ben Hayyim, a leading Jewish scholar of the day, persuaded Bomberg to reprint the work in an expanded form with the Masorah* (which had not been in the first edition) and notes showing variant readings. This second rabbinic Bible was considered until this century the standard edition of the entire Hebrew Bible,

---

* The Masorah are the textual notes relating to the "authorized" text of the Hebrew Bible. Originally, the Bible was written in continuous script and had to be divided into words, books, and sections, with the spellings fixed in one accepted form.

being termed in Hebrew *Mikraot Gedolot* (Great Scriptures). It too had a profound effect on Bible translations in Europe, serving not only as the standard Hebrew text, but also as the version from which Luther made his translations and as the basis for the King James Bible.

Over the years, Bomberg printed approximately two hundred books of Jewish interest—including important editions of the Midrashim, tractates of the Mishnah, grammars, prayer books, and treatises on philosophy and ethics. He established a new Hebrew type face and spared no expense in producing books or employing famous Hebrew scholars to help prepare them for publication. One year, he employed two of the leading Hebraic scholars in Europe to work on books he was planning to publish.

Bomberg's importance as a publisher of Hebrew books was eventually supplanted by another firm, operating under the name Bragadini. Its founders, too, were non-Jews.

The spread of Jewish learning was accomplished by so many non-Jews in such diverse circumstances and times that one must marvel about this Jewish-Christian publishing connection. There is the case of the oldest surviving complete copy of a printed, illustrated *Haggadah*. It was written in 1512, not in Hebrew, but in Latin—not in Palestine, but in Germany—and not by a Jew, but by a Franciscan friar. What was the purpose behind this unusual enterprise? The friar wanted to oppose the work of a Jewish convert to Christianity who had been putting out writings attacking the Jews.

For all their interest in reading and in their heritage, no one among the Jews had bothered to compile a modern history of their people. Who eventually came forward to rectify this lapse? You guessed it—a non-Jew.

Jacob Christian Basnage was born in 1653 in Rouen, France, where he became a Protestant pastor. Eventually, because of Catholic persecution, he had to flee to Holland. While living in Rotterdam, he devoted himself to writing a history of the Jews from the days of Josephus to his own day. To compile his seven-volume study, he had to seek information about Jews primarily from Latin sources. But his massive work, published over several years from 1706 to 1711, was very well received in Europe. A Jewish historian of our own century credited Basnage's efforts with laying "the basis for the science of Jewish history: and though his work was far from perfect, it remained the best for a century to come." Only with the work of Jewish historians Jost and Graetz in the nineteenth century did the Jews for the first time have a history written by their own people.

Another history of the Jews by another non-Jew may have had a significant impact on the course of Jewish history itself. Hannah Adams, reputedly the first professional woman writer in America (1755-1832), was the first published American historian of the Jews. A Christian who knew little about the Jews, she was moved to write their history only after she had run into a conflict with another writer on doing a textbook of American history. She turned to Jewish history because she felt it was one field she could write about "without interference." In her preface to her *History of the Jews from the Destruction of Jerusalem to the Present Time,* (published in Boston in 1812), she shows how Christian interest in the Jews for Christian purposes has had the perhaps unintended result of helping Jews. After noting that "the history of the Jews is remarkable" for its "number and cruelty of persecutions" and for "the singular phenomenon of a nation subsisting for ages without its civil and religious polity, and thus surviving its political existence," Hannah Adams writes, "But the Jews appear in a far more interesting and important light when considered as a standing monument of the truth of the Christian religion."

Hannah Adams's book went on to have a beneficial consequence for Jews. In 1820, a German translation was published in Europe, and the section on Jews in America was reprinted a number of times and widely distributed. Before this, European Jewry had been largely ignorant of the experiences of Jews in America. Hannah Adams's sympathetic portrait aroused their interest in this new land called the United States, undoubtedly reinforcing the new but spreading idea that America might be an easier place than Europe in which to be a Jew.

The closeness between Jews and Christians has been based largely on their common roots in the Judeo-Christian heritage, and on the fact, recognized by all people of good will, that both religions are in pursuit of the same basic goal: a world based not on the nobility of class but on the nobility of character. This kind of thinking is epitomized in the development in America in this century of the Hillel Foundation, devised to serve the religious and social needs of Jewish college students.

Dr. Edward Chauncey Baldwin was a professor of literature who had deep sympathy and admiration for the Jews. He pointed out to Jewish colleagues that Catholics and Protestants had Newman and Wesley foundations to promote the growth of good moral and religious character in college students, but the Jews had no similar organization. His observation was soon followed up by the B'nai B'rith, a nationwide Jewish service group, which today supports Hillel Houses on hundreds of college campuses throughout America. Thus, another aid to Jewish survival was supplied by a non-Jew.

The mutual interest in the Hebrew language of the Bible has been another rallying point for the Jewish and Christian faiths. In the sixteenth century, a butcher named Johann Pfefferkorn tried to have the German emperor destroy all rabbinic writings and Hebrew books except the Bible. The books were collected, but before burning them the emperor asked a distinguished Christian scholar and student of Hebrew to investigate the Jewish literature and determine if its destruction would be beneficial to Christianity. Johann Reuchlin (1455-1522) made a careful study and offered his conclusion: he strongly supported the need to preserve the Jewish works. The books were returned to their owners.

The Dominican friars at Cologne ferociously attacked Reuchlin's ruling, fearing the study of Latin, Greek, and Hebrew would undermine the authority of the Church and lead people away from orthodox Christianity. Germany became divided into the Reuchlinists and the anti-Reuchlinists, a schism which historians say was one of the first episodes in the Protestant Reformation—which in itself helped bring toleration and emancipation for Jews.

There is an ironic twist, of course, in the story. Pfefferkorn, who made the original charges against the Jewish writings, was a Jew who had converted under suspect conditions (he was in jail and converted to get out). Standing against the born Jew attacking Judaism was Reuchlin, the born Christian defending it.

Many national leaders have supported Jewish interests at important times in history. Oliver Cromwell, for example, the Puritan leader of England in the middle of the seventeenth century, tried mightily to cancel England's official expulsion of the Jews. He invited Rabbi Manasseh ben Israel, a leading Jewish figure of the time, to travel from Amsterdam and speak before the Privy Council in an attempt to persuade its members to rescind the edict of 1290. The councilmen listened, but voted to continue the policy. No record exists that England under Cromwell ever did officially agree to let the Jews return (in 1962, the Jewish historian Cecil Roth reported that the official record of that time—which he inspected—shows that a later historic meeting, when approval may have been given, was ripped from the book).

With no evidence to the contrary, a legend has persisted that Cromwell quietly allowed some Marranos who had been living in England to practice Judaism openly and then looked the other way while a few more Jews entered England. The trickle eventually turned into a stream of Jews and Cromwell had accomplished what he had set out to do—readmit the Jews to England. It was quite probably in this way—and not through any official act or edict now on record—that Jews came once again to live in England and build up one of today's most thriving Jewish communities.*

Napoleon (1769-1821) was another European leader whose actions helped the Jews. In 1799, during his Middle East campaign, he issued a proclamation urging the restoration of a Jewish homeland in Palestine. A month later, his defeat at Acre cooled his ardor over the idea, but he continued to support other Jewish causes. He convoked the Great Sanhedrin in France, which met from February 9 to March 9, 1807, to discuss Jewish matters—its first meeting since the days of ancient Israel.** The following year, he set up a central Jewish communal administration, working through consistories. Although he was responsible for several restrictive measures against Jews, Napoleon was, for his time, enlightened in his attitude. His extension of civil rights to Jews both in France and in other areas under his control, including Germany and Italy, set the stage for the full-scale emancipation of the Jews in Europe during the nineteenth century, according to *The Standard Jewish Encyclopedia*.

The most momentous event in the two thousand years of the Diaspora has been the creation of the

---

* Chaim Bermant in *The Cousinhood*, a history of the English-Jewish aristocracy published in 1971, states, "The edict of expulsion has never been rescinded and remains on the Statute Book to this day." The question presents itself: why have we never been able to find a record detailing the circumstances restoring the Jews to England?

** The convening of the Sanhedrin reflected what might be termed Napoleon's tolerance of Jews, but intolerance of Judaism. He deliberately opened the meeting on the Sabbath, not all participants were religious, and few rabbis of outstanding scholarship were invited.

State of Israel. This story could not have happened —and surely cannot be told—without reference to several non-Jews who appeared in the Jews' corner at just the right time.

Theodor Herzl, the founder of modern Zionism, understood from the beginning the vital importance of making political contacts to further the cause of what was essentially a politically powerless movement. Enter William Hechler (1845-1931), a British Protestant clergyman born in South Africa of German parents, who was an ardent and early supporter of Zionism (in 1884, he wrote *The Restoration of the Jews to Palestine*). While chaplain of the British Embassy in Vienna, Hechler met Herzl and helped him open those proverbial doors to essential contacts. As tutor to Prince Ludwig, son of the Grand Duke of Boden, Hechler had met the Grand Duke's nephew, the future Kaiser Wilhelm II of Germany, and later was able to introduce Herzl to the German leader. As an indication of the crucial role he played, Herzl mentions Hechler's name on more than one hundred different pages throughout his diaries.*

The non-Jewish name Balfour is associated with the document that first translated Herzl's ideas into a political possibility. Lord Arthur James Balfour (1848-1930), as head of the British government, met with Herzl in 1902-1903. By 1917, Balfour had been sufficiently impressed by Herzl's ideas and by his discussions with Zionist leader Chaim Weizmann to support their goals. As Foreign Secretary, he signed the British government's declaration favoring "the establishment in Palestine of a national home for the Jewish people."

---

* In one entry Herzl comments: "This man Hechler is, at all events, a peculiar and complex person. There is much pedantry, exaggerated humility, pious eye-rolling about him—but he also gives me excellent advice full of unmistakably genuine good will. He is at once clever and mystical, cunning and naïve. In his dealings with me so far, he has supported me almost miraculously."

But, in another ironic example of the ways in which Jewish survival has been served even by those who act from other motives, Balfour, while strongly in favor of a national home for the Jews, was not necessarily a friend of Jews. Kenneth Young, writing in *The Prime Ministers* (edited by Herbert van Thal), reports that Balfour harbored some anti-Semitic views and while favoring immigration to Palestine opposed immigration to England:

> Strangely enough, Balfour was no Semitophile; he once said, after a long talk with Cosima Wagner at Bayreuth, that he "shared many of her anti-Semitic postulates." As Prime Minister he had spoken strongly against alien (in those days almost entirely Jewish) immigration into Britain. And the Aliens Bills, restricting immigration, passed into law in the last year of his premiership. As long ago as 1899 he had remarked in a private letter: "I believe the Hebrews were in an actual majority—and tho' I have no prejudices against the race (quite the contrary) I began to understand the point of view of those who object to alien immigration!"

But Balfour's anti-Semitic thoughts could still prove helpful in the effort to found Israel:

> These attitudes would not, of course, preclude his support for a Jewish national home; on the contrary it was a natural if somewhat cynical corollary. Better the Jews in Palestine than in Britain.

The force of the Jewish Connection also helped persuade Balfour to help the Jews:

> At the same time he was fascinated by the uniqueness of the Jewish race and its history and by such paradoxes as the fact that the founder of Christendom, himself a Jew, had been rejected by his own people. He appreciated the enormous Jewish contribution to science, the arts, and civilization in general.

Thus the sheer force of Jewish activity swept away his doubts and carried him to the forefront of the effort to found a Jewish state:

What he helped to do for the Jews, Balfour pondered late in life, was the most worth-while thing in his political career.

When the Jewish settlers in Palestine of the 1930s needed fighting troops for their drive for independence, they found another non-Jew ready to help. Orde Wingate, a British army officer born in India of Scottish ancestry, played such a key role in the building up of Jewish forces for Israel's eventual army that Yigal Allon, Deputy Prime Minister of Israel, has described his appearance as "an event of historic importance for the Haganah."

Wingate arrived in Palestine in 1936 to serve in the British army as an intelligence officer. Within a short time, he became an enthusiastic Zionist and, with his thorough background in religion (he carried a Bible with him in his campaigns), saw himself and the Jews of Palestine fulfilling the prophecies regarding the return to the Promised Land. He persuaded the British army command in Palestine to allow him to train special Haganah night squads to fight bands of Arab terrorists, and this gave him the opportunity to train Jewish troops. He provided such future Israeli commanders as Moshe Dayan with their first formal instruction in warfare and helped them develop the counter-guerrilla tactics and quick strike capability that are still the basic strategies of Israel's defense forces. Moshe Dayan openly attributes his military policies to Wingate's influence, and the recent book *A History of the Israeli Army* by Zeev Schiff mentions Wingate as "the single most important influence on the military thinking of the Haganah."

In 1939 the British, uneasy over Wingate's close rapport with the Jews, transferred him out of Palestine. During World War II he served with distinction in Burma, where he died in an airplane crash in 1944 at the age of forty-one. But his efforts have lived on in Israel. The Wingate emphasis on quick alterations in strategy to accommodate battle changes and development of an attack force as the best defense are all in evidence in the military thinking of Israeli leaders today. Over the years Israel has named streets, hospitals, an athletic center, and a settlement for orphans south of Haifa (Yemin Orde) after the man who is referred to as "The Friend."

Harry Truman was another non-Jew whose efforts in behalf of the creation of Israel were both timely and remarkable. It has recently become clear that Franklin Delano Roosevelt was not the great friend of Jewish causes he was once thought to be. With Jews already supporting him, Roosevelt showed during the war that he saw no political advantage in pressing for Jewish interests, and later Arab opposition to the creation of Israel would undoubtedly have cooled him to the idea. Walter Laqueur, in *A History of Zionism*, cites the strong doubts of an aide to Roosevelt and later to Truman whether Israel would have been reborn if FDR had continued as President.

It was therefore a stroke of sweet irony that, when the world's attention turned to the debate about a Jewish state in the Mideast, FDR should be succeeded by a man of midwestern America, who may not have appeared to have much in common with Jews, but who helped them immeasurably. For the Jewish people, Truman was the right man to be President at the right time.

Here was a man who throughout much of his life maintained as a close friend Eddie Jacobson, a Jew who had been his business partner in his younger days. At a critical time when Chaim Weizmann was trying to get to see Truman, Jacobson was able to call upon the old friendship to bring together the two leaders for a meeting that paved the way for America's recognition of a Jewish state.

Truman read the Bible twice before he went to grammar school, and when he was sworn in as President kissed the Good Book. He read history voraciously and, long before becoming President, had studied the history of the Mideast. As reported by Merle Miller in *Plain Speaking*, Truman once said, "The whole area is just waiting to be developed. And the Arabs have just never seemed to take any interest in developing it. I have always thought that the Jews would, and of course, they have."

It seems uncannily fortunate that Truman was only filling out FDR's fourth term as President when he made the momentous decisions to support the creation of Israel. It was as though he had been sent to complete what FDR had seemingly become incapable of doing. That mystical view of the special role of Harry Truman was held by many at the time—and possibly acknowledged by Truman himself. Merle Miller recounts that just eleven minutes after Israel became a state, Truman, against great pressure from his State Department, officially recognized it. A year later, the Chief Rabbi of Israel visited Truman and said to him, "God put you in your mother's womb so that you could be the instrument to bring about the rebirth of Israel after two thousand years."

Harry Truman cried when he heard that.

Another non-Jew not only helped create Israel, but saved it. Incredible as it may seem, that man was Joseph Stalin.

The tale of Stalin's role in helping create and then insure the early survival of Israel has been little told; and on those occasions when it has been mentioned, there has been no satisfactory explanation for it. After all, Stalin was, in the words of historian Robert Payne, "a raging anti-Semite."

The first public display of Stalin's special role in behalf of the Jews came on May 14, 1947. After thirty years of anti-Zionist if not outright anti-Semitic actions by the Soviet government,* Andrei Gromyko, the Russian Ambassador to the United Nations, delivered a startling speech to a special session of the General Assembly. In it, the Soviet Union endorsed the Jewish position on Palestine—partition of the land into Jewish and Arab countries. In addition, he spoke of the "exceptional sorrow and suffering" the Jewish people underwent in World War II and said that "the time has come to help these people, not by word, but by deeds." He emphasized the Jewish historical claim to Palestine and the need now to respond to "the aspirations of the Jews to establish their own state."

The Arabs were stunned by the speech; the Jews were jubilant, if bewildered. Throughout the months leading up to the UN vote on partition in November, 1947, Soviet statements grew more emphatic about the need for a Jewish homeland, at times instructing the Arabs to accommodate themselves to this historic necessity. At virtually every step of the debate, the Soviet Union supported the Jewish position—including a rejection of the last-minute move to deprive the Jewish state of the Negev. When the vote was taken, the entire Communist bloc stood in favor of the Jews. Later, when Israel declared her independence on May 14, 1948, the United States would be the first to recognize the new state, but the Soviet Union soon followed, being the first to offer *de jure* recognition, a stronger form of international recognition and one that the United States delayed in giving.

The Soviet Union continued its diplomatic efforts for the struggling Jewish state during its War of Independence. At one point, the Soviets even suggested a UN resolution calling for the withdrawal of foreign (at that time meaning Arab) troops from Palestine. They also opposed a paragraph in the truce

---

* The Soviets were on record with only one pro-Zionist act since the Russian Revolution, a short-lived resolution in 1919.

resolution of April 16, 1948, that would have stopped Jewish immigration to Palestine—an especially ironic stance in light of present Soviet practices. And, on August 18, Soviet delegate Jacob Malik, then President of the Security Council, chided Britain and the United States (not Israel) for indirectly causing the Arab refugee problem.

By 1949, a chill had settled over Soviet support for Israel, and it cooled Soviet-Israeli relations thereafter. By 1953, the break was complete, and the Soviets severed diplomatic relations. But for a period of eighteen months—from May, 1947, through the end of 1948—the Soviet Union had been Israel's staunchest supporter, a stronger ally than even the United States. In early 1948 America had done a sudden about-face and pushed for a trusteeship of Palestine, which the Zionists felt would have dashed hopes for a Jewish state. "There is certainly no question that the Soviet Union played a major role in creating the State of Israel, perhaps a singularly important role in view of the striking vacillation on the part of the American delegation," writes Arnold Krammer in *The Forgotten Friendship: Israel and the Soviet Bloc 1947-53*. The United States also joined with Britain in trying to abide by a UN embargo on arms shipments, leaving the Jews of Palestine with only one major lifeline of weapons—the Communist-controlled country of Czechoslovakia.

Why had Joseph Stalin suddenly parted the Iron Curtain in behalf of the Jews? Why was it done at that crucial time in Jewish history? And why, after those brief eighteen months, did he close the curtain again?

Countless writers have offered answers to these questions, but none has been totally convincing. Even Communists at the time were baffled. Avigdor Dagan, who was active for more than twenty years in Israel's foreign service and served as his country's Ambassador to Poland and Yugoslavia, wrote a book on the relations between Israel and the Soviet Union entitled *Moscow and Jerusalem*. In it he terms Gromyko's speech "a great surprise" and reports that in talks with leading Communists of Czechoslovakia he "gained the impression that the Soviet decision to support the establishment of a Jewish state in Palestine was a surprise for them as well."

Some of the reasons historians and political analysts have cited are: that the Soviets wanted to get Britain out of the Mideast so they supported the Jews in an effort to push the British out . . . that the Russians were angered with the Arabs for being pro-German during the war and sympathetic to the Jews who had suffered at the hands of the Nazis . . . that the Russians wanted to penetrate the Mideast and the Mediterranean and saw a Jewish state as an opening wedge . . . that the Jews were more susceptible to Communist ideology than the reactionary Arabs . . . that a Jewish state would grow increasingly dependent on the Russians and thereby spurn the West . . . and so on.

Dr. Dagan, in listing some of these reasons, notes they "may be partly correct, but none of the authors who have tackled the problem seems to be entirely satisfied with them." Other, less orthodox, explanations have been offered, but these severely strain the limits of credulity—such as the theory that Soviet support for Israel was nothing more than a ploy by the Russians to make the Arabs turn to the Soviets. Even the respected historian Walter Laqueur has proposed an unusual scenario: the Soviets considered the Palestine issue a secondary one, with the decision to support a Jewish state made at lower levels and endorsed by an absentminded Stalin. Dr. Dagan, however, dismisses such an idea. "It is difficult to take seriously the suggestion that this was how things worked in Moscow in Stalin's time or at any later stage."

Further research seems to support Dr. Dagan's skepticism, for there is evidence that Joseph Stalin was very much concerned with the issue of a Jewish state—and that his involvement began as early as 1945.

It was in the spring of that year that David Ben-Gurion first learned about Stalin's views as expressed in a private talk with President Roosevelt and Winston Churchill. According to an unnamed high official of the U.S. government who visited Ben-Gurion in his Tel Aviv home, Stalin had mentioned to Churchill during the Yalta Conference that, as for the Palestine situation, he saw only one solution—"a Jewish state." When Ben-Gurion heard about Stalin's remark, he became convinced for the first time that the Jews would get their own country.

Corroboration of Stalin's early decision to support a Jewish state can be found in the autobiography of Nahum Goldmann, who has been president of the World Jewish Congress and the World Zionist Organization. He recounts that in 1945 he and Chaim Weizmann asked the President of Czechoslovakia, Eduard Benes, who was on his way to a Moscow meeting with Stalin in March, to bring up the Palestine question. When Benes returned, he told them that Stalin had said that "he knew serious wrong had been done to the Jewish people in recent years and he would do everything he could to make up for it." The Czechoslovakian President was told "to assure his Jewish friends that they need not worry about the position of the Soviet Union."

While noting this did not constitute a definite promise of help, Goldmann acknowledges the importance of the surprising Soviet actions in the UN two years later. "I am still not sure that a two-thirds majority for the partition resolution could have been obtained without the assent of the Soviet Union and the other Communist members of the United Nations."

Stalin helped the fledgling State of Israel militarily as well as diplomatically. Such aid was crucial at the time, because Britain and the United States were abiding by a UN embargo on the shipment of weapons to the Mideast. "Stalin helped the infant State of Israel . . . with money and supplies which were channelled through Prague," writes H. Montgomery Hyde in *Stalin: Portrait of a Dictator*.

Even before the Communist coup d'état in February, 1948, the Czechs had been supportive of the Zionists and, because of the need for money in their war-ravaged economy, had been selling weapons to the Haganah. But, once the Communists took over, the aid, according to *The Forgotten Friendship*, was immediately stepped up. Stalin liked having the Czechs rather than Russians as the contact government, since one of his favorite strategies was to shield his role in foreign involvement as a safeguard if anything went wrong.

Between January, 1948, and February, 1949, the Czech government supplied the Jews with 57 million rounds of ammunition, 1 million rounds of antitank ammunition, 24,500 rifles, 10,000 bayonets, 5,000 light machine guns, 880 heavy machine guns, 22 tanks with ammunition, 84 fighter airplanes, and 9,900 bombs.

A pilot training program was set up at a Czech air force fighter base. *The Pledge* includes the following passage on the strange situation: "The impossible was about to happen—a complete air base, staffed largely by Americans, was about to operate behind the Iron Curtain just as the United States and Russia were squaring off over Berlin."

To help repel the impending Arab attack, secret training areas for Israeli troops were established in Czechoslovakia—and a brigade of Czech volunteers was trained to fight with the Israeli army.

The military support for the new Jewish state had to be kept quiet for fear of international repercussions, but the Arabs knew something was going on. On November 29, 1948, in a UN debate, an Arab diplomat charged that Zionists were using weapons "the source of which was known to the U.S.S.R. representative."

In addition, the Soviet Union was also quietly encouraging Jews from Eastern Europe, especially Poland, to emigrate to the western occupation zones of Germany and Austria, with the understanding that they would go to Palestine to participate in the War of Independence.*

In an interview published by the Jerusalem *Post* on May 8, 1973, David Ben-Gurion expressed his gratitude for the Russian military help. Citing the fact that the Arabs had modern weapons with which to fight the 1948 war while the Jews had hardly any arms, Ben-Gurion declared, "The only ones who promised to help were the Russians, who sent us vital arms by way of Czechoslovakia. Without these, we would not have been able to fight back. One day I will tell the story of how the Russians helped us then—not like what they are doing to us today."

Indeed, the military help may have been even more important than the diplomatic. Ben-Gurion was never under any delusions about a UN vote creating Israel. He always felt it would lead to an Arab invasion, and since 1945 he had sought money to buy arms for the real struggle. Abba Eban, in 1947, had told a group of American Jews soliciting funds for military hardware that the UN would probably not even vote for a Jewish state if it were known that Palestinian Jews did not have the arms with which to defend themselves.

But Soviet help ended almost as soon as it began. By 1949, after Israel defeated the armies of Arab nations, the Iron Curtain began to come down on this rare and very brief scene of an atheistic society's aid to a new Jewish nation.

The reasons suggested for the cooling of Soviet ardor for Israel are as numerous and baffling as those advanced for its emergence. The Israelis won the war

---

* Although Russian Jews were prevented from emigrating to Israel, Soviet satellite countries permitted Jewish emigration. During the "thaw years" between 1948 and 1952, Bulgaria, Hungary, Czechoslovakia, Rumania, and Poland permitted almost 300,000 Jews to go to Israel.

too fast and too well . . . the Jews of Russia showed too much interest in Israel . . . the Israelis did not incline toward communism after all . . . Israel had begun turning to the West . . . Stalin realized he had underestimated the disadvantages of opposing so many Arabs and overestimated the advantages of helping so few Jews.

Whatever the reasons, the fact remains that Stalin's only support for a Jewish cause in his entire lifetime came at the one time when such support was absolutely critical—and when the success of that Jewish cause would return Jews to a homeland longed for since the year 70.

One thing is clear, where not much else is. The actions of the anti-Semite Stalin, helping to bring to fruition the efforts of the assimilated Jew Herzl, fit the pattern spelled out by the Law of Irony at work in the Jewish Connection.

XII

So?

Well?

OUR JOURNEY THROUGH the nooks and crannies of the Jewish Connection, and the ironies and surprises we have seen there, should have demonstrated at least one thing. Ours is a world in which something more than ordinary is always going on.

Let's consider one final facet of the Jewish experience that was witnessed by the world at large: the Holocaust. How did it happen? Why to the 6 million Jews? Why to the 14 million non-Jews who also lost their lives in Nazi outrages?

The questions pile up in our minds, seemingly unanswerable. But the archeological excavations of the Jewish Connection have turned up a new piece of evidence that may shed some light.

Hitler and his followers seemed to go out of their way to surround themselves with symbols of evil. The colors they chose—the reds and the blacks—are associated with the devil. The death's head was a favorite visual device—the Nazis' elite corps, the S.S., used the skull and crossbones as insignias on their black uniforms. Hitler named his command headquarters for much of the war the "Wolf's Lair," after the animal so often used to symbolize evil. He even gave a special name to his headquarters for the drive on Stalingrad—"Werewolf."

The Nazis delighted in their fiendishness. Eichmann spoke of jumping joyfully into his grave with the deaths of so many on his hands. Hitler said he was proud to be called a barbarian. Himmler, Goebbels, Goering—all talked of the glories of war and death and destruction, as though defying the warning of Isaiah, "Woe to them who call evil good and good evil."

Who really was this Hitler who shook his fist at life and sought to strangle civilization? And what does he represent in terms of history?

Since names have so often been important—and prophetic—in Jewish life, let's examine the meaning of Hitler's name. In *The Life and Death of Adolf Hitler*, Robert Payne indicates that in the records of the region where the future Fuehrer was born his name is spelled in a variety of ways. Hiedler. Hietler. Hytler. Huetler. Hittler. And once, in 1702, Hitler. Payne's conclusion about the origin of Hitler's name is that it most likely derives "from *Heide,* heath, with its derivative *Heidjer,* heathman, heathen, hence pagan."

Paganism—the very forces of ancient polytheism the Jewish concept of monotheism sought to end!

Heathenism—the irreligious, uncivilized, unenlightened approach to life, which Judaism sought to replace with religious ideals!

Was it just coincidence that Hitler, the greatest enemy the civilized world has ever known, should have a name so closely linked with anti-religious and anti-life concepts?

If Hitler's name has its symbolic roots in paganism, then the people he tried to destroy should be able to look to the roots of their name for prophetic meaning about their role. This is precisely what we find when we look at the name by which the Jewish nation is known. "Israel" is the name that was given to Jacob after he wrestled with the angel and won. It indicates that in his struggles *he will prevail.* What could be more appropriate? The Holocaust led to the Homeland. Hitler, in trying to destroy the Jews, may have helped preserve them as a people.

Is this, then, a world in which the forces of good and evil are fighting for supremacy? Are we witnesses to a struggle between the religious and irreligious approaches to life? Or are we more than observers— are we participants?

The skeptics may argue that there is no divine force at work in the world. But all the efforts of philosophers and religious leaders throughout recorded time have been an attempt to explain life, to bring order out of the seeming chaos around us, to explain, as Carlyle said in commenting on the Book of Job, "the never ending problem—man's destiny and God's way with him here on earth."

The incredible, ironic, bizarre story of the Jews— which under closer scrutiny offers so many indications of meaning and order in our lives—may have a special message that in itself could help explain the ways of God to man.

And that may be the most significant Jewish Connection of all.

Bibliography

More than 300 books and magazine articles, thousands of entries in a variety of encyclopedias, and the resources of six library systems were consulted in the development of *The Jewish Connection*. The sources used are set forth in the following bibliography.

To ensure the validity of facts in this book, the attempt was made to secure at least two—and sometimes three—sources corroborating the same information. While some facts could not be corroborated in more than one source, such facts were used only where no hard evidence existed to the contrary, or where the source of the information was so highly reliable or so privy to the information that an error of fact was most unlikely. Completed chapters or parts of chapters were then submitted to people knowledgable about such material.

In spite of all my efforts to resolve conflicts among sources, I found it necessary at times to decide among different statements on the same historical information. I based my final use of material on those sources my research had indicated to be the most accurate overall.

AUTOBIOGRAPHIES AND DIARIES

Cantor, Eddie. *Take My Life.* Garden City: Doubleday & Co., 1957.
David, Jay (ed.). *Growing Up Jewish.* New York: William Morrow & Co., 1969.
Goldmann, Nahum. *The Autobiography of Nahum Goldmann: Sixty Years of Jewish Life.* Translated by Helen Sebba. New York: Holt, Rinehart & Winston, 1969.

Hall, Monty, and Libby, Bill. *Emcee Monty Hall.* New York: Grosset & Dunlap, 1973.

Herzl, Theodor. *The Complete Diaries of Theodor Herzl.* Edited by Raphael Patai. Translated by Harry Zohn. 5 vols. New York: Thomas Yoseloff, 1960.

Pearson, Drew. *Drew Pearson Diaries, 1949-1959.* Edited by Tyler Abell. New York: Holt, Rinehart & Winston, 1974.

Rubinstein, Arthur. *My Young Years.* New York: Alfred A. Knopf, 1973.

Weizmann, Chaim. *Trial and Error.* New York: Harper & Bros., 1949.

Wright, Orville, and Wright, Wilbur. "The Wright Brothers' Aeroplane." *The Century Magazine*, September 1908, pp. 641 ff.

BIBLE AND RELIGION

Bermant, Chaim. *The Walled Garden: The Saga of Jewish Family Life and Tradition.* New York: Macmillan Co., 1975.

Birnbaum, Philip. *A Book of Jewish Concepts.* New York: Hebrew Publishing Co., 1964.

Brasch, R. *The Judaic Heritage: Its Teachings, Philosophy and Symbols.* New York: David McKay Co., 1969.

Cohen, A. *The Soncino Chumash.* London: The Soncino Press, 1970.

Earle, Alice Morse. *The Sabbath in Puritan New England.* New York: Charles Scribner's Sons, 1891. (Reissued 1968 by Singing Tree Press, Detroit.)

Frank, Harry Thomas; Swain, Charles William; and Canby, Courtlandt. *The Bible Through the Ages.* Cleveland: World Publishing Co., 1967.

Gaskill, Gordon. "Which Mountain Did Moses Climb?" *The Reader's Digest*, June 1973, p. 209.

Goldman, Solomon. *The Book of Books: An Introduction.* New York: Harper & Bros., 1948.

Gontard, Friedrich. *The Chair of Peter.* New York: Holt, Rinehart & Winston, 1964.

Hertz, Joseph H. *The Authorized Daily Prayer Book.* New York: Bloch Publishing Co., 1961.

————. (ed.). *The Pentateuch and Haftorahs.* London: The Soncino Press, 1961.

Jakobovits, Immanuel. *Journal of a Rabbi.* New York: Living Books, 1966.

John, Eric (ed.). *The Popes.* New York: Hawthorn Books, 1964.

Littell, Franklin H. *The Crucifixion of the Jews.* New York: Harper & Row, 1975.

Markowitz, Sidney L. *What You Should Know About Jewish Religion, History, Ethics and Culture.* New York: Citadel, 1955.

Michand, Stephen G. "Haggadahs in History," *Newsweek*, March 24, 1975, p. 64.

Newman, Louis Israel. *Jewish Influence on Christian Reform Movements.* New York: Columbia University Press/Columbia University Oriental Studies, Vol. XX. AMS Press, 1966.

The Soncino Books of the Bible. 14 vols. London: The Soncino Press, 1970.

Torrey, Charles Cutler. *The Jewish Foundation of Islam.* New York: Ktav Publishing House, 1967.

Wollman-Tsamir, P. (ed.). *The Graphic History of the Jewish Heritage.* New York: Shengold Publishers, 1963.

Yerushalmi, Yosef Hayim. *Haggadah and History.* Philadelphia: Jewish Publication Society, 1975.

BIOGRAPHIES

Bortoli, Georges. *The Death of Stalin.* New York: Praeger Publishers, 1975.

Bruce, Robert V. *Bell: Alexander Graham Bell and the Conquest of Solitude.* Boston: Little, Brown & Co., 1973.

Clark, Ronald W. *Einstein: The Life and Times.* New York: World Publishing Co., 1971.

Cohen, Israel. *Theodor Herzl.* New York: Thomas Yoseloff, 1959.

Collier, Richard. *Duce!* New York: Viking Press, 1971.

Cushing, Harvey. *The Life of Sir William Osler.* Vol. 1. New York: Oxford University Press, 1940.

Davis, Mac. *They All Are Jews.* New York: Jordan Publishing Co., 1937.

Elon, Amos. *Herzl.* New York: Holt, Rinehart & Winston, 1975.

Fraser, Antonia. *Cromwell: The Lord Protector.* New York: Alfred A. Knopf, 1973.

Gottgetreu, Eric. "When Napoleon Planned a Jewish State." *The Jewish Digest,* May 1975, p. 66.

Gross, William J. *Herod the Great.* Baltimore: Helicon Press, 1962.

Gunston, David. *Marconi—Father of Radio.* New York: Crowell-Collier Company, 1965.

Hall, Calvin S. "Sigmund Freud—Founder of Psychoanalysis." *Wisdom Magazine,* May 1957, pp. 48–50.

Hoffman, Banesh. *Albert Einstein: Creator and Rebel.* New York: Viking Press, 1972.

Hyde, H. Montgomery. *Stalin: The History of a Dictator.* New York: Farrar, Straus & Giroux, 1972.

Jaffe, Bernard. *Michelson and the Speed of Light.* Garden City: Anchor Books, 1960.

Johnson, Allen (ed.). *Dictionary of American Biography.* New York: Charles Scribner's Sons, 1957.

Josephson, Matthew. *Edison.* New York: McGraw-Hill, 1959.

Landstrom, Bjorn. *Columbus.* New York: Macmillan Co., 1967.

McLellan, David. *Karl Marx: His Life and Thought.* New York: Harper & Row, 1973.

Madariaga, Salvador de. *Christopher Columbus.* New York: Frederick Ungar Publishing Co., 1967.

Manvell, Roger. *Love Goddesses of the Movies.* New York: Crescent Books, 1975.

Marconi, Degna. *My Father, Marconi.* New York: McGraw-Hill, 1962.

Millen, Jonathan (ed.). *Freud: The Man, His World, His Influence.* Boston: Little, Brown & Co., 1972.

Miller, Merle. *Plain Speaking.* New York: G. P. Putnam, 1974.

Mussolini, Rachele. *Mussolini: An Intimate Biography by His Widow.* New York: William Morrow & Co., 1974.

Payne, Robert. *The Life and Death of Adolf Hitler.* New York: Praeger, 1973.

Sandmel, Samuel. *Herod: Profile of a Tyrant.* Philadelphia: J. P. Lippincott Co., 1967.

Scholem, Gershom S. *Sabbatai Sevi: The Mystical Messiah.* Translated by R. J. Zwi Werblowsky. Princeton: Princeton University Press, 1973, Bollingen Series XCIII.

Skinner, Cornelia Otis. *Madame Sarah.* New York: Popular Library, 1966.

Sykes, Christopher. *Orde Wingate.* Cleveland: World Publishing Co., 1959.

Tate, Alfred O. *Edison's Open Door.* New York: E. P. Dutton & Co., 1938.

Untermeyer, Louis. *Makers of the Modern World.* New York: Simon & Schuster, 1955.

Wallace, Robert, et al. *The World of Bernini, 1598–1680.* New York: Time-Life Books, 1970.

THE DIASPORA

Bermant, Chaim. *The Cousinhood.* New York: Macmillan Co., 1972.

Cohen, Israel. *Travels in Jewry.* New York: E. P. Dutton & Co., 1953.

Cowen, Ida. *Jews in Remote Corners of the World.* Englewood Cliffs: Prentice-Hall, 1971.

Federbush, Simon (ed.). *World Jewry Today.* New York: Thomas Yoseloff, 1959.

Hacohen, Devora, and Hacohen, Menahem. *One People: The Story of the Eastern Jews.* New York: Sabra Books, Funk & Wagnalls, 1969.

Postal, Bernard, and Abramson, Samuel H. *The Traveler's Guide to Jewish Landmarks of Europe.* New York: Fleet Press Corp., 1971.

Swartz, Mary I. "Jews in Japan." *Hadassah Magazine,* October 1975, p. 10.

ENCYCLOPEDIAS AND REFERENCE WORKS

Collier's Encyclopedia. New York: Macmillan Educational Corp., 1976.

The Encyclopaedia Britannica. Chicago: Encyclopaedia Britannica, 1969, 1943.

Encyclopaedia Judaica. Jerusalem: Keter Publishing House, 1971.

International Hebrew Heritage Library. New York: International Book Corp., 1969.

The Jewish Encyclopedia. New York and London: Funk & Wagnalls Co., 1901.

The New Catholic Encyclopedia. New York: McGraw-Hill, 1967.

The New Encyclopaedia Britannica (15th ed.). Chicago: Encyclopaedia Britannica, 1974.

The World Book Encyclopedia. Chicago: Field Enterprises Educational Corp., 1975.

Ausubel, Nathan. *The Book of Jewish Knowledge.* New York: Crown Publishers, 1964.

Comay, Joan. *Who's Who in Jewish History.* New York: David McKay Co., 1974.

De Haas, Jacob (ed.). *The Encyclopedia of Jewish Knowledge.* New York: Behrman's Jewish Book House, 1949.

McWhirter, Norris, and McWhirter, Ross. *Dunlop Illustrated Encyclopedia of Facts*. Garden City: Doubleday & Co., 1969.

Pfeiffer, Charles F. (ed.). *The Biblical World: A Dictionary of Biblical Archaeology*. Grand Rapids: Baker Book House, 1966.

Postal, Bernard; Postal, Jesse; and Silver, Rory. *Encyclopedia of Jews in Sports*. New York: Bloch Publishing Co., 1965.

Roth, Cecil (ed.). *The Standard Jewish Encyclopedia*. Garden City: Doubleday & Co., 1959.

Strong, James. *Strong's Exhaustive Concordance of the Bible*. Nashville: Abingdon Press, 1967.

Werblowsky, R. J. Zwi, and Wigoder, Geoffrey. *The Encyclopedia of the Jewish Religion*. New York: Holt, Rinehart & Winston, 1966.

Wurmbrand, Max, and Roth, Cecil. *The Jewish People: 4,000 Years of Survival*. Tel Aviv: Thames & Hudson, 1966.

HISTORY, GENERAL

Boudet, J. (ed.). *Jerusalem: A History*. New York: G. P. Putnam's Sons, 1967.

Caffrey, Kate. *The Mayflower*. New York: Stein & Day, 1974.

Canning, John (ed.). *100 Great Events that Changed the World*. New York: Hawthorn Books, 1965.

Durant, Will. *Our Oriental Heritage (Story of Civilization*, Vol. 1). New York: Simon & Schuster, 1939.

————. *Caesar and Christ: A History of Roman Civilization from Its Beginnings to A. D. 337 (Story of Civilization*, Vol. 3). New York: Simon & Schuster, 1944.

————. *Age of Faith (Story of Civilization*, Vol. 4). New York: Simon & Schuster, 1950.

————. *Reformation (Story of Civilization*, Vol. 6). New York: Simon & Schuster, 1953.

Durant, Will, and Durant, Ariel. *Age of Reason Begins (Story of Civilization*, Vol. 7). New York: Simon & Schuster, 1961.

————. *Age of Louis the Fourteenth (Story of Civilization*, Vol. 8). New York: Simon & Schuster, 1963.

————. *Age of Voltaire (Story of Civilization*, Vol. 9). New York: Simon & Schuster, 1965.

Erlanger, Philippe. *Louis XIV*. New York: Praeger, 1970.

Guérard, Albert. *France: A Modern History*. Ann Arbor: University of Michigan Press, 1969.

Kessler, Henry H., and Rachlis, Eugene. *Peter Stuyvesant and His New York*. New York: Random House, 1959.

Mumford, Lewis. *The Condition of Man*. New York: Harcourt, Brace & Co., 1944.

Van Thal, Herbert (ed.). *The Prime Ministers*. New York: Stein & Day, 1974.

HISTORY, JEWISH

Ausubel, Nathan. *Pictorial History of the Jewish People*. New York: Crown Publishers, 1958.

Dimont, Max, *Jews, God and History*. New York: Simon & Schuster, 1962.

Eisenberg, Azriel. *Jewish Historical Treasures*. New York: Bloch Publishing Co., 1968.

Graetz, Heinrich. *History of the Jews*. 6 vols. Philadelphia: Jewish Publication Society, 1956.

Grayzel, Solomon. *A History of the Jews*. Philadelphia: Jewish Publication Society, 1968.

Israel, Gerard. *The Jews in Russia*. New York: St. Martin's Press, 1975.

Jacobs, Joseph. *Jewish Contributions to Civilization*. Philadelphia: Jewish Publication Society, 1919.

Marcus, Jacob R. *The Jew in the Medieval World*. New York: Harper Torchbooks, 1965.

Osborne, Sidney. *Germany and Her Jews*. London: The Soncino Press, 1939.

Prinz, Joachim. *Popes From the Ghetto*. New York: Horizon Press, 1966.

————. *The Secret Jews*. New York: Random House, 1973.

Raisin, Max. *A History of the Jews in Modern Times*. New York: Hebrew Publishing Co., 1938.

Roth, Cecil. *Essays and Portraits in Anglo-Jewish History*. Philadelphia: Jewish Publication Society, 1962.

————. *A History of the Jews*. New York: Schocken Books, 1964.

————. *History of the Marranos*. Philadelphia: Jewish Publication Society, 1959.

————. *A Jewish Book of Days*. London: Edward Goldston, 1931.

————. *Personalities and Events in Jewish History*. Philadelphia: Jewish Publication Society, 1953.

Rubens, Alfred. *A History of Jewish Costume*. New York: Crown Publishers, 1973.

Stern, Selma. *The Court Jew*. Philadelphia: Jewish Publication Society, 1950.

Waagenaar, Sam. *The Pope's Jews*. La Salle, Illinois: Open Court, 1974.

Wischnitzer, Rachel. *The Architecture of the European Synagogue*. Philadelphia: Jewish Publication Society, 1964.

THE HOLOCAUST

Bloch, Eduard. "My Patient, Hitler." *Collier's* Magazine, March 15, 1941 and March 22, 1941.

Borchsenius, Paul. *And It Was Morning*. London: George Allen & Unwin, 1962.

————. *Behind the Wall*. London: George Allen & Unwin, 1960.

Dawidowicz, Lucy S. *The War Against the Jews, 1933–1945*. New York: Holt, Rinehart & Winston, 1975.

Friedlander, Albert H. *Out of the Whirlwind: A Reader of Holocaust Literature*. Garden City: Doubleday & Co., 1968.

Grumberger, Richard. *The 12-Year Reich*. New York: Holt, Rinehart & Winston, 1971.

Hanisch, Reinhold. "I Was Hitler's Buddy." *The New Republic*, April 5, 12 and 19, 1939.

Hausner, Gideon. *Justice in Jerusalem*. New York: Harper & Row, 1966.

Heydecker, Joe J., and Leeb, Johannes. *The Nuremberg Trial*. Translated and edited by R. A. Downie. Cleveland: World Publishing Co., 1962.

Hunt, Robert, and Hartman, Tom. *Swastika At War*. Garden City: Doubleday & Co., 1975.

Langer, Walter C. *The Mind of Adolf Hitler*. New York: Basic Books, 1972.

Levin, Nora. *The Holocaust*. New York: Thomas Y. Crowell Co., 1968.

Lorant, Stefan. *Sieg Heil!* New York: W. W. Norton & Co., 1974.

Morse, Arthur D. *While Six Million Died*. New York: Random House-Ace Book, 1968.

Shirer, William L. *The Rise and Fall of the Third Reich*. New York: Simon & Schuster, 1960.

Wighton, Charles. *Heydrich: Hitler's Most Evil Henchman*. Philadelphia: Chilton Co., 1962.

Wolman, Benjamin B. (ed.). *The Psychoanalytic Interpretation of History*. New York: Basic Books, 1971.

The Yellow Spot: the outlawing of half a million human beings. New York: Knight Publications, 1936.

ISRAEL

Collins, Larry, and Lapierre, Dominique. *O Jerusalem!* New York: Simon & Schuster, 1972.

Crum, Bartley C. *Behind the Silken Curtain*. New York: Simon & Schuster, 1947.

Dagan, Avigdor. *Moscow and Jerusalem*. New York: Abelard-Schuman, 1970.

"The Dream After 25 Years: Triumph and Trial." *Time* Magazine, April 30, 1973, pp. 26–45.

Eckman, Lester Samuel. *Soviet Policy Towards Jews and Israel, 1917–1974*. New York: Shengold Publishers, 1975.

Elon, Amos. *The Israelis: Founders and Sons*. New York: Holt, Rinehart & Winston, 1971.

Krammer, Arnold. *The Forgotten Friendship*. Urbana: University of Illinois Press, 1974.

Kurzman, Dan. *Genesis, 1948*. New York: World Publishing Co., 1970.

Laqueur, Walter. *A History of Zionism*. New York: Holt, Rinehart & Winston, 1972.

Levin, Meyer. *The Story of Israel*. New York: G. P. Putnam's Sons, 1966.

Postal, Bernard, and Levy, Henry W. *And the Hills Shouted for Joy*. New York: David McKay Co., 1973.

Rath, Ari. "Ben-Gurion Looks Back—and Ahead." *The Jerusalem Post*, May 8, 1973, p. 12.

Ro'i, Yaacov. *From Encroachment to Involvement: A Documentary Study of Soviet Policy in the Middle East, 1945–1973*. Jerusalem: Israel Universities Press, 1974.

Russcol, Herbert, and Banai, Margalit. *The First Million Sabras*. New York: Dodd, Mead & Co., 1970.

Schoenbrun, David. *The New Israelis*. New York: Atheneum, 1973.

Slater, Leonard. *The Pledge*. New York: Simon & Schuster, 1970.

JEWRY, AMERICAN

Birmingham, Stephen. *Our Crowd: The Great Jewish Families of New York*. New York: Harper & Row, 1967.

————. *The Grandees: America's Sephardic Elite*. New York: Harper & Row, 1971.

Carroll, John Alexander, and Ashworth, Mary Wells (completing the biography by Douglas Southall Freeman). *First in Peace*. (*George Washington*, Vol. 7). New York: Charles Scribner's Sons, 1957.

Cohen, George. *The Jews in the Making of America*. Boston: The Stratford Co., 1924.

Flexner, John Thomas, *George Washington: Anguish and Farewell (1793–1799)*. Boston: Little, Brown & Co., 1972.

Friedman, Lee M. *Jewish Pioneers and Patriots*. Philadelphia: Jewish Publication Society, 1942.

Gay, Ruth. *Jews in America*. New York: Basic Books, 1965.

Golden, Harry. *Our Southern Landsman*. New York: G. P. Putnam's Sons, 1974.

Isaacs, Stephen D. *Jews and American Politics*. Garden City: Doubleday & Co., 1974.

James, Edmund J.; Flynn, Oscar R.; Paulding, J. R.; Patton, Mrs. Simon N.; and Andrews, Walter Scott. *The Immigrant Jew in America*. New York: B. F. Buck & Co., 1906.

Kajan, Solomon R. *Jewish Contributions to Medicine in America (1656–1934)*. Boston: Boston Medical Publishing Co., 1934.

Kaufman, I. *American Jews in World War II*. New York: Dial Press, 1947.

Levitan, Tina. *The Firsts of American Jewish History*. Brooklyn: Charuth Press, 1957.

Liptzin, Sol. *The Jew in American Literature*. New York: Bloch Publishing Co., 1966.

Manners, Ande. *Poor Cousins*. New York: Coward, McCann & Geoghegan, 1972.

Markfield, Wallace. "The Yiddishization of American Humor." *Esquire* Magazine, October 1965, p. 114.

Postal, Bernard. "Some Jewish Jottings About Lyndon Baines Johnson." *The Jewish Digest*, March, 1973, p. 1.

Postal, Bernard, and Koppman, Lionel. *A Jewish Tourist's Guide to the U.S.* Philadelphia: Jewish Publication Society, 1954.

St. John, Robert. *Jews, Justice and Judaism*. Garden City: Doubleday & Co., 1969.

Sandburg, Carl. *Abraham Lincoln*. The Sangamon Edition. 6 vols. New York: Charles Scribner's Sons, 1926–1939.

Segal, Charles M. *Fascinating Facts About American Jewish History*. New York: Twayne Publishers, 1955.

Simonhoff, Harry. *Jewish Participants in the Civil War*. New York: Arco Publishing Co., 1963.

Sloan, Irving J. (ed.). *The Jews in America, 1621–1970*. Dobbs Ferry, New York: Oceana Publications, 1971.

Tebbel, John. *George Washington's America*. New York: E. P. Dutton, 1954.

Wischnitzer, Rachel. *Synagogue Architecture in the United States*. Philadelphia: Jewish Publication Society, 1955.

JEWRY, ANCIENT

Grant, Michael. *The Jews in the Roman World.* New York: Charles Scribner's Sons, 1973.

Josephus. *The Jewish War.* Translated by G. A. Williamson. Middlesex, England: Penguin Books, 1972.

Katz, Karl; Kahane, P. P.; and Broshi, Magen. *From the Beginning: Archaeology and Art in the Israel Museum, Jerusalem.* New York: Reynal & Co., 1968.

Keller, Werner. *The Bible as History in Pictures.* New York: William Morrow & Co., 1964.

Leon, Harry J. *The Jews of Ancient Rome.* Philadelphia: Jewish Publication Society, 1960.

Orlinsky, Harry M. *Ancient Israel.* Ithaca, New York: Cornell University Press, 1958.

Schokel, Luis Alonso. *Journey Through the Bible Lands.* Milwaukee: Bruce Publishing Co., 1964.

Vilnay, Zev. *The Holy Land in Old Prints and Maps.* Jerusalem: Rubin Mass, 1965.

LISTS OF INFORMATION

Adler, Bill. *The Illustrated Book of World Records.* New York: Grosset & Dunlap, 1974.

Baron, Joseph L. (ed.). *A Treasury of Jewish Quotations.* New York: Crown Publishers, 1956.

de Bono, Edward (ed.). *Eureka!* New York: Holt, Rinehart & Winston, 1974.

Evans, Ivor H. (reviser). *Brewer's Dictionary of Phrase and Fable, Centenary Edition.* New York: Harper & Row, 1970.

Kane, Joseph Nathan. *Famous First Facts.* New York: H. W. Wilson Co., 1964.

McWhirter, Norris, and McWhirter, Ross. *Guinness Book of World Records.* New York: Bantam Books, 1975.

Mencken, H. L. *The American Language.* New York: Alfred A. Knopf, 1947.

Postal, Bernard, and Abramson, Samuel H. *The Landmarks of a People.* New York: Hill & Wang, 1962.

Robertson, Patrick. *The Book of Firsts.* New York: Clarkson N. Potter, 1974.

Rosten, Leo. *The Joys of Yiddish.* New York: McGraw-Hill, 1968.

True Magazine Editors. *Strange But True.* New York: Fawcett Publications, 1954.

Wallechinsky, David, and Wallace, Irving. *The People's Almanac.* New York: Doubleday & Co., 1975.

MISCELLANEOUS

Addison, Anthony. *What* (A Family Book of Knowledge). London: Berkeley Publishers (Octopus Books), 1974.

————. *When* (A Family Book of Knowledge). London: Berkeley Publishers (Octopus Books), 1974.

————. *Where* (A Family Book of Knowledge). London: Berkeley Publishers (Octopus Books), 1974.

————. *Why* (A Family Book of Knowledge). London: Berkeley Publishers (Octopus Books), 1974.

Asimov, Isaac. *Asimov's Guide to Science*. New York: Basic Books, 1972.

Baron, Joseph L. (ed.). *Stars and Sand: Jewish Notes by Non-Jewish Notables*. Philadelphia: Jewish Publication Society, 1943.

Bevan, Edwyn P., and Singer, Charles (eds.). *The Legacy of Israel*. Oxford: Clarendon Press, 1927.

Brotz, Howard M. *The Black Jews of Harlem*. New York: Schocken Books, 1970.

Ceram, C. W. *The March of Archaeology*. New York: Alfred Knopf, 1958.

Davis, Elizabeth Gould. *The First Sex*. New York: G. P. Putnam's Sons, 1971.

Fraser, John Foster. *The Conquering Jew*. New York and London: Funk & Wagnalls Co., 1915.

Furneaux, Ruper. *The World's Most Intriguing True Mysteries*. New York: Arco Publishing Co., 1969.

Gans, Herbert J. *The Levittowners*. New York: Pantheon Books, 1967.

Garrison, Webb. *How It Started*. Nashville: Abingdon Press, 1972.

Gill, Brendan. *Here at the New Yorker*. New York: Random House, 1975.

Goldberg, B. Z. *The Sacred Fire*. New York: University Books, 1958.

Gunther, John. *Inside Asia*. New York: Harper & Bros., 1939.

————. *Twelve Cities*. New York: Harper & Row, 1969.

Heilbroner, Robert L. *The Worldly Philosophers*. New York: Simon & Schuster, 1967.

Herzl, Theodor. *The Jewish State* (with introduction and biography). New York: American Zionist Emergency Council, 1946.

Korda, Michael. *Power!* New York: Random House, 1975.

Neider, Charles (ed.). *The Complete Essays of Mark Twain*. Garden City: Doubleday & Co., 1963.

Samuelson, Paul A. *Economics*. New York: McGraw-Hill, 1958.

Schwarz, Leo W. (ed.). *The Menorah Treasury*. Philadelphia: Jewish Publication Society, 1964.

Sombart, Werner. *Jews and Modern Capitalism*. New York: B. Franklin Press, 1969.

van den Haag, Ernest. *The Jewish Mystique*. New York: Stein & Day, 1969.

Wilson, Edmund. *To the Finland Station*. Garden City: Doubleday & Co., 1940.

SPECIAL SUBJECTS

American Heritage Editors. *The American Heritage History of Flight*. New York: American Heritage, 1962.

Aron, Michael. "Flying: The Heavens as Airspace." *Harper's Magazine*, September 1975, p. 3.

Boorstin, Daniel J. *Portraits from 'The Americans: the Democratic Experience.'* New York: Random House, 1975.

Bronowski, J. *The Ascent of Man*. Boston: Little, Brown & Co., 1973.

"Did King Solomon Pip Columbus?" *To the Point International Magazine*, July 27, 1974, p. 50.

Ege, Lennart. *Balloons and Airships*. New York: Macmillan Publishing Co., 1974.

Friedenwald, Harry. *Jewish Luminaries in Medical History*. Baltimore:
    Ktav Publishing House, 1946.

————. *The Jews and Medicine—Essays, Vol. 1*. Baltimore: Ktav
    Publishing House, 1967.

Hale, John R. *Age of Exploration*. New York: Time-Life Books, 1966.

Head, Sydney W. *Broadcasting in America: A Survey of Television
    and Radio*. Boston: Houghton, Mifflin Co., 1956.

"Hi, Columbus! Like the Trip?" *Newsweek*, June 9, 1975, p. 46.

Hotaling, Edward. "Columbus: A Jewish Voyage Into the Unknown."
    The Times of Israel Magazine, October 1973, p. 91.

Korey, William. *The Soviet Cage: Anti-Semitism in Russia*. New
    York: Viking Press, 1973.

Landay, Jerry M. *Dome of the Rock*. New York: Newsweek Book
    Division, 1972.

Major, Ralph H. *A History of Medicine*. Springfield, Illinois: Charles
    C Thomas, 1954.

Manchester, William. *The Glory and the Dream*. Boston: Little,
    Brown, 1974.

Salisbury, Harrison E. *The 900 Days*. New York: Harper & Row, 1969.

Semple, Robert B., Jr. "Reuter and His Pigeons Might Not Recognize
    the News Agency Now." *The New York Times*, March 10,
    1976, p. 33.

Tebbell, John. *A History of Book Publishing in the United States,
    Volume I: The Creation of an Industry, 1640–1865*. New York:
    R. R. Bowker, 1972.

————. *A History of Book Publishing in the United States, Volume
    II: The Expansion of an Industry, 1865–1919*. New York:
    R. R. Bowker, 1975.

Wheny, Joseph H. *Automobiles of the World*. Philadelphia: Chilton
    Book Co., 1968.

Yadin, Yigael. *The Message of the Scrolls*. New York: Grosset &
    Dunlap, Universal Library edition, 1962.

Yaffee, Richard. "Columbus' Voyage: Another Exodus?" *The National
    Jewish Monthly*, July–August 1973, p. 5.

Acknowledgments

I CONCEIVED THE idea for *The Jewish Connection* three years ago and since have devoted thousands of hours to its research, organization, and writing. As the book developed, a number of relatives, friends, and specialists gave valuable assistance.

First, I would like to thank my wife, Barbara, who lived this book with me and proved once again that she is my best audience. The enthusiasm of our two older children—Aviva and Stuart—was a great encouragement, as was the birth of our youngest—Seth—during the writing.

My father, Herman Goldberg, provided an early impetus for *The Jewish Connection* by drawing my attention to several incredible facts about Jewish history that he had encountered in his reading. He continued to help locate resource materials and suggest ideas throughout the writing. Other family members who aided appreciably were my mother, Ida Goldberg, my brother, Victor, and my in-laws, Archie and Bette Weiser. Special thanks to my brother-in-law, David Weiser, for constructing a special office to house my books, my typewriter, and myself.

Alan Shecter's enthusiasm for the concept enabled me to persevere, and his suggestions during the developmental stages were especially keen. Dale C. Kessler offered to track down many of the sources I needed, and went from library to library to find hard-to-get volumes. Myra Satisky and Anne Marder not only typed and retyped the manuscript, but offered discerning feedback as well.

Many thanks to the staffs at the Central Library and various branches of Baltimore City's Enoch Pratt Free Library, The Baltimore County Library System, The Bard Library of the Community College of Baltimore, the Baltimore Hebrew College Library, The Johns Hopkins University Milton S. Eisenhower Library, and the Theodore R. McKeldin Library at the University of Maryland.

As the book took shape numerous specialists provided assistance. (Of course, I made the final decision on every statement that appears in the book, and any errors that might exist are mine.) For reading portions of the book, verifying facts, and answering my questions, I thank Dr. Harry Bard, Dr. Malcolm Davies, Rabbi Mendel Feldman, Dr. Sheldon Glass, Rabbi Israel Goldberg, Gwinn Owens, Rabbi Samuel Pliskin, Bernard Postal, and Mark Reches. Dr. Arnold Blumberg, professor of history at Towson State University, read the entire work and used his breathtaking knowledge to clarify many points.

Finally, I wish to express my appreciation for the support I have received from Stein and Day Publishers. Michaela Hamilton and Eve Tulipan were expert editors whose suggestions led to significant improvements in the final product. Particular thanks go to Sol Stein, President of Stein and Day, who more than anyone else helped to transform my original idea into the book it has become.

H.G.

Index

ABOUT THE AUTHOR

M. HIRSH GOLDBERG began to collect unusual facts when he was in elementary school, a hobby which led to his writing a high school newspaper column, "Goldberg's Fabulous Facts." The collecting continued while he went on to earn bachelor's and master's degrees from The Johns Hopkins University, was press secretary to the mayor of Baltimore at the age of twenty-four (at the time, he was the youngest press secretary to the mayor of a major American city), and served as speech writer and public relations advisor for two of Maryland's attorneys general and the Superintendent of Baltimore's public school system.

Cited for excellence in Jewish journalism by the national Boris Smolar Award, Mr. Goldberg writes a weekly column for the *Baltimore Jewish Times*, contributes to the editorial pages of the *Baltimore Sunpapers*, and is author of more than 450 columns and articles, a number of which have been reprinted in the *Congressional Record*, the *Jewish Digest*, and newspapers around the country. Formerly editor of the *Times of Israel and World Jewish Review* magazine, he is now editor of *Mosaic*, the national magazine supplement for Jewish newspapers.

Mr. Goldberg, who was born in Baltimore in 1942, lives with his wife, Barbara, and their three children in Randallstown, a suburb of Baltimore, Maryland.

Here are the Books that Explore
the Jewish Heritage-Past and Present.

Fiction

☐	**Exodus** Leon Uris	11090	$2.25
☐	**The Heart Is Half A Prophet** Ruth Goldstein	10701	$1.95
☐	**Last of the Just** Andre Schwarz-Bart	10469	$1.95
☐	**Mila 18** Leon Uris	10802	$1.95
☐	**The Wall**	2569	$2.25

Non-Fiction

☐	**Questions & Answers About Arabs and Jews** Ira Hirschmann	11199	$1.95
☐	**A Bag of Marbles** Joseph Joffo	6407	$1.75
☐	**The New Bantam-Meggido Hebrew & English Dictionary** Levenston & Sivan	2094	$1.95
☐	**The Essential Talmud** A. Steinsaltz	10199	$2.95
☐	**A Kabbalah for the Modern World** Gonzalez-Wippler	6410	$1.95
☐	**Treasury of Jewish Quotations** Leo Rosten	10877	$2.95
☐	**The War Against The Jews** Dawidowicz	2504	$2.50

Buy them at your local bookstore or use this handy coupon for ordering:

Bantam Book Catalog

Here's your up-to-the-minute listing of every book currently available from Bantam.

This easy-to-use catalog is divided into categories and contains over 1400 titles by your favorite authors.

So don't delay—take advantage of this special opportunity to increase your reading pleasure.

Just send us your name and address and 25¢ (to help defray postage and handling costs).